Was it Only Yesterday?

AUSTRALIA IN THE *TWENTIETH CENTURY* WORLD

Third Edition

SHEENA COUPE ROBERT COUPE MARY ANDREWS

LONGMAN

Addison Wesley Longman Australia Pty Limited
95 Coventry Street
South Melbourne 3205 Australia

Offices in Sydney, Brisbane, Perth, and associated companies throughout the world.

First published 1996
Reprinted 1998

Designed by Anita Adams
Illustrated by Ophelia Leviny and Vasja Koman
Set in 10.5 pt AGaramond
Produced by Addiosn Wesley Longman Australia Pty Limited
Printed in China through Addison Wesley Longman China Limited, Hong Kong
GCC/02
Cover photograph of stamp: Leva Rexona, National Philatelic Collection Australia Post

National Library of Australia
Cataloguing–in–Publication data

Coupe, Sheena.
Was it only yesterday? Australia in the twentieth century world.

3rd ed.
Includes index.
ISBN 0582 80842 1.

1. Australia – History – 20th century. I. Andrews, Mary. II. Coupe, Robert. III. Title.

994.04

The publisher's policy is to use **paper manufactured from sustainable forests**

Contents

Acknowledgements

The publishers are grateful to the following for permission to reproduce copyright material:
Allen and Unwin, p. 31;
Allan M. Nixon for *Somewhere in France, Letters to Home, The War Years of Sgt Roy Whitelaw 1st AIF* © Allan Nixon, p. 42;
Interviews from *Australians at Risk* by Anne Deveson, Cassell, 1978, pp. 213, 214, 216, 217, 227, 229, 230;
Australian Bureau of Statistics, *Year Book, Australia 1995*, Canberra, The Bureau (p. 97), Commonwealth of Australia copyright reproduced by permission, p. 215, (tr);
'The Mabo Judgement–Its Implications' by Henry Reynolds, in *Mabo: Its Meaning for Australia*, Background Report No. 4, Community Aid Abroad, p. 222;
'The Great Depression: Why it Never Happened Again' by Ruth Park, first published in *The National Times*, copyright Kendale Pty Ltd, courtesy of Curtis Brown, Sydney, pp. 76, 79;
'No Place Like Home' by Nikke van der Gaag, pp. 156–7, and 'Singing in Shatila' by Rosemary Sayigh, p. 157, reprinted courtesy of The Guardian Media Group plc, UK, copyright *The New Internationalist*;
From *The Herald* , 22 September, 1951, Reprinted courtesy Herald and Weekly Times, p. 194;
Sir Mark Oliphant for the extract from *The Weekend Australian*, August 12–13, 1995/VJ-Day 50th Anniversary liftout, p. 127;
Pilita Clark, Washington Correspondent, *Sydney Morning Herald*, p. 190;
Sydney Morning Herald, pp. 148, 216, 227;
'The Forgotten Wars' by George C. Church, from *Time*, 9 October 1995, © 1995 Time Inc. Reprinted by permission, p. 166;
Tom Morris for the extract from *The Weekend Australian*, August 12–13, 1995/VJ-Day 50th Anniversary liftout, pp. 126-7

l = left	m = middle
r = right	tl = top left
t = top	bl = bottom left
b = bottom	tm = top middle

For permission to reproduce photographs and illustrative material we would like to thank the following:
Age, pp. 219 (t), 221;
Joan Klatchko/courtesy AIATSIS, pp. 212 (r), 215 (br);
A Moir/*Sydney Morning Herald*, p. 175;
© Andrew Henley/Auscape International (CAH2765), p.6 (b);
Archives Authority of NSW, p. 59 (l);
Austcare, p. 226 (b);
Photograph from the Australian Archives, p. 206;
Australian Associated Press, pp. 132 (t), 137, 150, 152 (t), 155, 159, 164, 178 (b), 179, 187 (t), 202;
Australian Consolidated Press, pp. 79 (l), 109 (t), 118 (tm), 119 (tl, tr),194, 196 (t), 203 (bl),
Australian Information Service, pp. 122 (t, m, b), 185 (l), 188, 203 (br);
Australian War Memorial, pp. 25, 28 (m, b), 30 (t), no G1188 (m), (b), 32, (l), no H17373 (r), 34 (l), 38, 96 (l), 105 (b), 108 (r), 109 (b), 111 (l, r, b), 112 (l, r), 113 no 128108, 114 (t), no 012422 (b), 115 (t) no 007731 (b), 116 no 009783 (tl), no 013053 (bl), 118 no V335 (tl), (tr), no V1101 (br), 119 no V970 (b), 120 (b), 141 no COL/67/198/VN, 145 no CUN/66/504/VN (l), no COM/69/250/VN (r);
Courtesy Battye Library p. 86 no 649P (b);
Beverley Clifford (Sandgate, QLD) ARPS, AFIAP, p. 54;
China International Travel Service, p. 187 (br);
Commonwealth Department of Human Services and Health, p. 214 (r);
Coo-ee Historical Picture Library p. 68 (l, r);
Coo-ee Historical Picture Library and The Australian Olympic Committee, pp.198 (r), 234 (l);
Department of Aboriginal Affairs, pp. 217, 219 (bl), 220;
Department of Health, Housing and Community Services and courtesy Maggie Brady, AIATSIS, p. 215 (l);
Fairfax Photo Library, pp. 77, 83 (b), 86 (t), 90 (l), 117, 199, 204 (r);
Image Library, State Library of New South Wales, pp. 2 (l), 12, 47 (tl, bl), 61 (b), 69, 72 (l), 84 (b), 90 (r), 103 (l);

Jenny Simmons, p. 240;
Reprinted with permission of King Features © 1996 King Features Syndicate, p. 233 (br);
La Trobe Collection, State Library of Victoria, pp. 53 (l), 197 (r), 212 (l);
Les Dixon/*Smith's Weekly* 1949, p. 192 (r);
Leva Rexona, p. 118 (bl);
Library of Congress, USA, photo in the public domain, p. 108 (l);
London Transport Museum, p. 105 (m);
Mark Edwards/Still Pictures, p. 171 (t);
Mirror Australian Telegraph Publications, pp. 83 (t), 88 (b), 146, 196 (b), 198 (l), 200 (t), 205, 214 (l), 218, 219 (t), 226 (r), 229;
Mrs Patricia Anderson, p. 197 (l);
National Gallery of Australia, p. 89 (t);
National Gallery of Victoria and P F Irvine and Co. Solicitors, p. 89 (b);
National Library of Australia, p. 5 no PL 588/2 (t), p. 6 (t), p. 9 no 765/1 (m), (b), p. 36 no 8461 (r), (b), p. 73 (t,b), p. 80(b), p. 201 (b);
National Philatelic Collection Australia Post, pp. 2 (r), 192 (l), 209 (t);
Novosti Press Agency, Moscow, p. 103 (r),
NSW Department of School Education, pp. 10 (b), 41, 50 (l), 51–2;
NSW Government Printing Office, pp. 47 (t), 49, 50 (r), 59 (r), 61 (b), 65 (t);
Peter Cooke/courtesy AIATSIS, p. 219 (br);
The Photolibrary-Sydney, Hulton-Getty, pp. 18 (t, b), 28 (tl), 56 (b), 96 (r), 98, 104 (l, r), 138 (t,b), 176, 179;
Jennifer James/Spooner SRI 0392/© Picture Media, p. 167 (r);
Political Images International/The Commonwealth Secretariat, London, p. 178 (t);
Popperfoto, pp. 75, 97, 102, 151;
Reuters/Ali Jarekji/Archive Photos, (Photo obtained from The Australian Picture Library), p. 158 (t);
Robert Hunt Picture Library, p. 43;
Royal Collection on permanent loan to Parliament House, Canberra/Photo Bruce Moore, p. 4;
Sygma/Austral International, pp. 154, 167 (t);
Tricia Confoy, p. 234 (r);
The Trustees of the Imperial War Museum, London, pp. 21 (Q3990) , 22–3;
UNICEF Australia, p. 171 (l);
US Airforce, p. 107;
US Information Service, p. 160;
US Information Service and Courtesy Jimmy Carter Library, p. 152 (b);
US Information Service: Photo by MMCS (SW) Henderlight, p. 158 (b);
US National Archives photo no. 6-PS-B-49-5285, p. 124.
Victorian Branch of the Textile Clothing and Footwear Union of Victoria, p. 195 (t);
Wild and Wooley, p. 204 (l);
World Vision Australia, p. 185 (r);
Women's Bureau (The Department of Employment, Education, Training and Youth Affairs), p. 235 (r);

Introduction

A soldier tells what it was like on the beaches at Gallipoli. A mother of six speaks of the despair of the Depression. An Aborigine describes his fear for the future in a world where he can't get a job.

Many voices speak in this book. Some real, some fictional, but all authentic. Of course the grand arch of history is here, as it must be, but the authors have taken the view that the voices of the people provide a babel or chorus that places the individual and history in a comprehensible relationship. In this way, the student gets a better understanding of the events, local and global, that have shaped Australia since federation.

This book contains much to identify with, if only by contrast. The student who revels in the mistaken luxury of fast foods may, or may not, find it sobering to contemplate the meagre family diet of the Depression. Such a student may be prompted to ask why things have changed and have they changed for the better—an enquiry that can be extended to musing on wars, international relations, cultural values, education, health, styles of dress and so on; what they are today, what they were yesterday and how it all changes.

To guide and stimulate this enquiry, four kinds of questions are interspersed within each chapter: 'the historian at work', 'check the facts', 'think for yourself', and 'know the chapter'.

Much care has been taken in choosing the illustrations and photos used. The language level, too, has been carefully maintained throughout to facilitate a ready understanding of the issues, especially those where complexity always presents a problem.

A **nation** *is* **born**

New Year's Eve is always noisy. But on 31 December 1900 it was even wilder and noisier than usual. There were about 4 million people in Australia then. All around the country Australians were celebrating not just the start of a new year and a new century, but the birthday of a new nation as well. On 1 January 1901 six colonies were to join together to form a nation—the Commonwealth of Australia.

A birthday celebration

The streets were crowded with excited people intent on making as much noise as they could. They used bells, whistles, gongs, accordions and even pots and pans from the kitchen. For many people the celebrations were also a good excuse for drinking too much.

New Year's Day 1901 was a holiday. The streets of Sydney had been decorated with flags, banners and arches. People dressed up in their best clothes and lined the streets to watch a parade from the Domain to Centennial Park. Stands lined the procession route to provide some seating for the enormous crowd. In the procession were shearers riding horses, soldiers, members of the fire brigade, churchmen, schoolchildren and, of course, lots of politicians. Brass bands played stirring marches. As the parade passed by, the crowd cheered, waved flags and threw flowers.

In Centennial Park 70 000 people had gathered to watch the official ceremony. The new governor general, Lord Hopetoun, read the words and signed the papers that made Australia a country. Guns fired and 10 000 schoolgirls burst into song. Later there was dancing and fireworks.

An official banquet was held that night. Lord Hopetoun, who had been ill, was not well enough to go. But 7000 poor families in Sydney were able to join in the celebrations. Charities had given them coupons that they could use to buy food, so that night many people enjoyed their first decent meal for a long time.

Figure 1.1
After the official ceremony on 1 January 1901, these schoolchildren danced for the thousands of people who had gathered to watch Australia become a nation. Where was this photograph taken?

Figure 1.2
Australia's first stamp, 1913

Think *for yourself*

1. Centennial Park was opened in 1888. Can you work out why? (Clue: 'Centennial' comes from a Latin word meaning 'hundred'.)
2. In 1988 Australians celebrated another birthday. What was it? How was it celebrated?
3. The new Australian government had the job of designing and issuing postage stamps. The first Australian stamp did not come out until 1913 (Figure 1.2). As you can see from the cartoon (Figure 1.3) some people did not like the stamp. One person wrote to the paper and called it 'a rubbishy label advertising some . . . brand of kangaroo tail soup'. What do you think? Why do you think the kangaroo was chosen for Australia's first stamp? Special stamps were also designed for the 1988 birthday. Try to find out what subjects they featured.
4. Australia did not have an official flag at the birthday celebrations of 1 January 1901. It had not yet been designed. A competition was held and almost 33 000 people sent in their ideas about how the flag should look. The prize of £200 was shared between five people whose ideas were very similar (Figure 1.4).

   Think of some symbols that would look well on the Australian flag. Try to design a new Australian flag.

Figure 1.3 This cartoon was published when Australia's first stamp was issued. Miss Australia is saying: 'It's awful: I am utterly disgusted with it'.

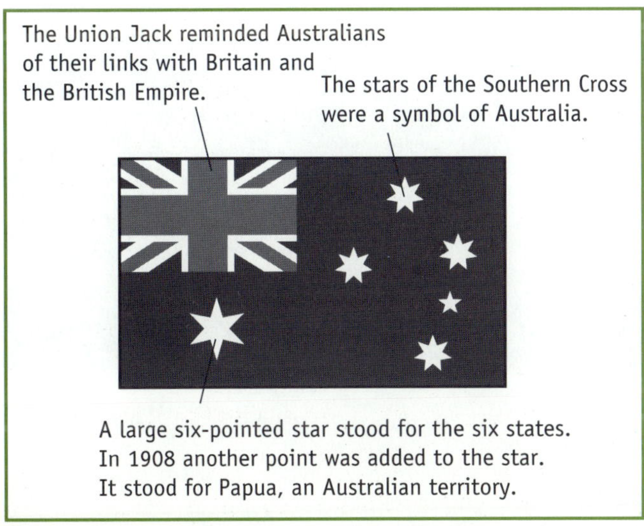

Figure 1.4 Australia's first flag. Compare it with the present flag. How is it different?

More celebrations

Sydney celebrated Australia's birthday on 1 January 1901. Only a few months later it was Melbourne's turn. The occasion was the opening of Australia's first parliament. This event was very special because the Duke and Duchess of Cornwall and York, who were members of Britain's royal family, were present. Schoolchildren nicknamed them 'corned beef and pork'.

Fourteen thousand people squeezed into Melbourne's Exhibition Building to watch the official ceremony. It was a glittering affair. That night the 'important' people went to a grand concert and the 'ordinary' people turned up in thousands in the streets to celebrate. Strings of electric lights lit up the Exhibition Building and other city buildings. Melbourne had never seen anything like it before. The streets were decorated with arches, banners and flags.

A capital for the new country

Australia now had a parliament but no capital city. As Sydney and Melbourne were the two largest cities, many people thought that one of them should be the national capital. But the two cities were such strong rivals that neither of them wanted the other to become the capital of Australia.

The search for a new capital began in 1899 and lasted until 1908. In 1902 a group of politicians visited country towns to try to find one that would make a good capital city. They had a lot of fun. Wherever they went the local people fed and entertained them and tried to convince them that their area was just right to be the capital.

Many places were seriously considered. Some of them were Albury, Orange, Yass, Bombala, Dalgety, Tumut, Armidale and Tamworth. None of them seemed quite suitable. At last it was decided that a completely new city would be built. The site for the capital was to be in the Molonglo Valley.

Figure 1.5
This is how the Australian painter Tom Roberts depicted the opening of the first Australian Parliament. Where did this event take place? Can you identify any of the people in the painting?

Figure 1.6

Politicians toured the country to find a good place for the capital city. Here they wait while Sir William Lyne, the premier of New South Wales, climbs a fence at Albury.

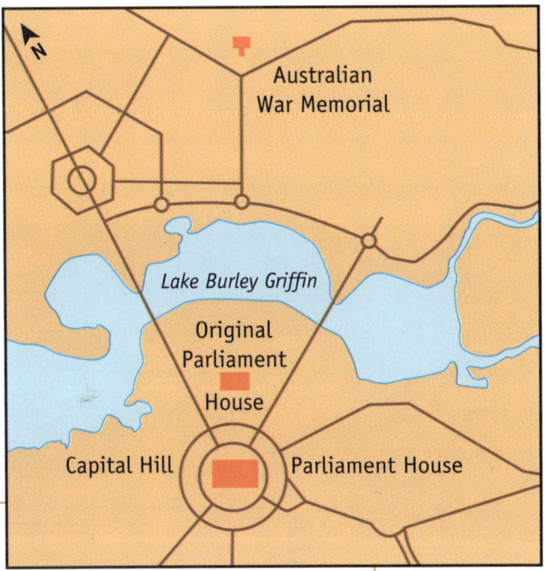

Figure 1.7

Canberra today—a simplified diagram

Planning the capital

In 1911, the prime minister, Andrew Fisher, announced a competition to choose the best design for Australia's capital city. One hundred and thirty-seven entries came from all over the world. The prize was given to Walter Burley Griffin, an architect from Chicago in the USA. Although he had not been to Australia to see where the city was going to be built, he used maps, information about weather and landforms, drawings and a survey to study the area.

In Griffin's design the main parts of the city were shaped as circles and rectangles. These main points were joined by long avenues. The city was designed so that it would fit in well with the natural landscape of the region.

Although many people liked Griffin's plan, others thought that it was too grand. They were afraid that it would cost too much money to build. The plan was changed to make it simpler. But a year later it was changed again and most of Griffin's ideas were brought back.

Canberra was given its name in 1913. Canberra is an Aboriginal word but its exact meaning is not known. Australians had suggested some odd names for their new capital. 'Woolgold', 'Sydmeladperbrisho', 'Engirscot' and 'Cooeeton' were some.

For many years Canberra grew slowly. Because parliament was meeting in Melbourne, there was no rush to build a new parliament house. People in the government argued about the amount of money that was being spent on the new city. When funds became short, there were long delays. Work almost stopped during the First World War. Gradually the city grew and its main buildings were finished.

In May 1927 the new parliament house was opened and there was another celebration. The Duke of York read the official proclamation. The famous singer Nellie Melba led the crowd in singing *God Save the King*. The official guests stood in the dust of the half-finished bush capital. At that time fewer than 7000 people lived there.

Almost sixty-one years later, on 9 May 1988, a new and much larger parliament house was opened by Queen Elizabeth II. As 1988 was the year of Australia's Bicentenary, it was an appropriate year for the opening of a grand new symbol of nationhood.

Figure 1.8
This photograph was taken in May 1927. Where was it taken? Why had large crowds gathered there? Is this building still being used?

Figure 1.9
Australia's Parliament House was opened in 1988. Where in Canberra is this building situated? Why do you think this site was chosen? What other buildings can you identify in this photograph?

CHECK the facts

Choose the right ending for each of the following sentences:

1 The ceremony at which Australia officially became a country was in
  a Canberra
  b Sydney
  c Melbourne.

2 Australia's first governor general was
  a Walter Burley Griffin
  b Duke of York
  c Lord Hopetoun.

3 Melbourne was decorated in May 1901 because
  a Australia's first parliament was opened there
  b it was the beginning of the twentieth century
  c the king of England was visiting the city.

4 Australia did not have a capital city in 1901 because
  a Canberra was still being built
  b Australia was not yet a nation
  c Sydney and Melbourne could not agree where it should be.

5 The Duke of York was in Australia in 1927 to
  a open the new parliament house in Canberra
  b judge the competition for the design of Canberra
  c open Australia's first parliament in Melbourne.

Think *for yourself*

1 If you could choose, where would you have the capital of Australia?

2 Look again at the other names people suggested for the new capital. Work out why they were suggested.

3 Parliament house was opened by the Duke of York. What relation was he to Queen Elizabeth II? (Clue: he became King George VI.)

4 One important part of Walter Burley Griffin's design for Canberra was not finished until 1963. Can you find out what it is? (Clue: it is named after the designer of Canberra.)

5 The design of Canberra came from a competition. In 1979 another competition was held to choose a design for a new building in Canberra. What was this building? Why was it needed? Where is it?

THE HISTORIAN AT WORK

The following is part of the speech made by Prime Minister, Stanley Bruce, at the opening of Canberra's Parliament House in 1927:

> Your Royal Highnesses,
>
> It is my privilege to open the door of this building, the future home of the Parliament of the Commonwealth ... In this ... hour we rejoice at your presence with us. His Majesty the King is the visible symbol of our unity. He is the centre of all our loyalties. That he should associate himself with his Australian subjects in this historic ceremony by commissioning your Royal Highness to represent him is a source of deep gratification to us all. We ask you to convey to his Majesty our devoted homage, and an assurance of our loyalty and affection to his throne and person.
>
> Twenty-six years have passed since the King was pleased to inaugurate the first Parliament of the Commonwealth ... We have emerged with a definite national consciousness. We have evolved great policies, which are so embedded in the soul of the nation that they not only govern our lives today, but point the course which we and future generations must inevitably follow.
>
> We have played our part in war, and proved ourselves worthy to endure. The sacrifices, suffering and untold trials of those who went and those who waited have bound us inseparably together. Within this period of little more than a quarter of a century a nation has been born.
>
> With humility in our hearts we render thanks to Divine Providence for all that we have done and are doing. We remember with gratitude the fostering care of the mother country and the protection we have enjoyed under the British flag. Today it is our solemn duty to reaffirm our faith in our country, and our devotion to the Crown and Empire.
>
> Great though our progress has been, Australia is but on the threshold of achievement. In the future, millions of the British race will people this land. In numbers surpassing the motherland, standing resolutely for those principles of freedom and justice upon which the Empire is based, who can tell how great may be the part our nation will play in years to come?

1 To whom is the prime minister's speech addressed? Whose representatives are they?

2 Does this speech sound to you like a speech that the leader of a really independent nation would make? How many words or expressions can you find in the speech that suggest that Australia was still dependent on Britain? What did Australia depend on Britain for?

3 What according to Stanley Bruce, was the most important thing that made Australia into a true nation?

4 Stanley Bruce makes a prediction about the future of Australia's population. What is this prediction? Did what Bruce predict actually happen?

5 Imagine that Bruce could see what Australia is like today. Try to think of several things about modern Australia that would surprise him. What aspects of Australian society today do you think he might not approve of?

6 On the evidence of this speech, name some differences between Australia in 1927 and Australia in the late 1990s.

7 What groups of people in Australian society would a modern prime minister probably refer to in a speech celebrating the nation of Australia? Why did Bruce not refer to them?

A government for the new country

When Australia became a united country in 1901, a new form of government was worked out. A set of rules was drawn up to show how the country was to be governed. This was called the **constitution**. The constitution could be changed only if the Australian people agreed to change it in a **referendum**.

The Australian constitution set up two houses of parliament whose members are elected by all voters. The House of Representatives, or lower house, makes most of the laws. The other house, the Senate, must approve the decisions made in the House of Representatives before they can become laws.

Like many other countries, Australia has a two-party system of government. This does not mean that there are just two political parties—you can probably think of four or five. But the two main parties are most important in the way government works. The party that has the most members in the House of Representatives is called the **government**. Its leader is the prime minister. The other main party is the **opposition**. Sometimes two parties may join to form a coalition so that they will be strong enough to form a government.

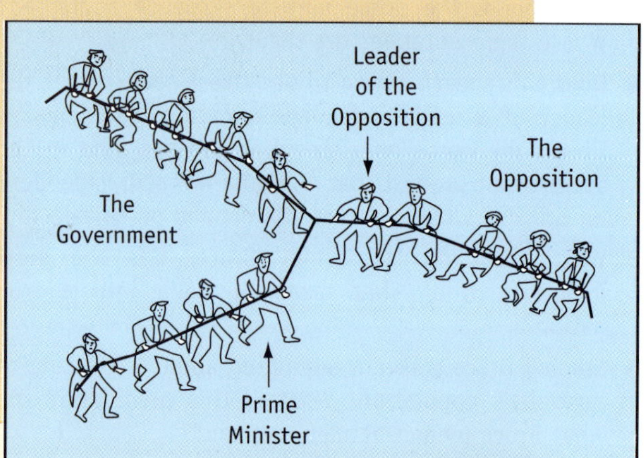

Figure 1.10
Government in Australia. In 1996, a coalition government was elected. Which two parties are in the coalition? Which party is the opposition today? Who is the prime minister? Who is the leader of the opposition?

Three political groups

Before 1914 Australia had three political groups.

The **free traders** believed that they should not have to pay customs duties or tariffs on goods coming into Australia or going out of Australia. Many farmers supported the free traders. They thought that they could sell their products more cheaply overseas if people did not have to pay customs duties on them.

The **protectionists** wanted to protect Australia's industries. They wanted to put a tariff on goods coming into Australia. This would make these goods more expensive, and people would be more likely to buy things that were made in Australia.

The **Labor Party** was Australia's first well-organised political party. It was formed in 1902 and was backed by many **trade unions**. The unions wanted men and women in parliament who would try to help working-class people.

Three leaders

Between 1901 and the beginning of the First World War in 1914, there were six Australian prime ministers. Three of them, John Christian Watson, George Reid and Joseph Cook, were in power for just a short time. The other three were:

Edmund Barton

Prime minister from January 1901 to September 1903
Previous job: lawyer
Party: protectionist
What he did: Barton's government passed the Immigration Restriction Act which stopped Asians from coming to Australia. By another Act of parliament most of the 10 000 Pacific Islanders who worked on Queensland's sugar plantations were sent home. Barton's government set up Australia's High Court.

Alfred Deakin

Prime minister from September 1903 to April 1904; July 1905 to November 1908; June 1909 to April 1910
Previous jobs: lawyer; journalist
Party: protectionist; later a 'Fusion' party of protectionists and free traders
What he did: Deakin's government set up an Arbitration Commission which tried to solve industrial problems and stop strikes. The idea of the basic wage began in 1907. In the same year, old age pensions started. In 1908 the site for Australia's new capital was chosen. The Royal Military College was opened. Boys and young men were compelled to do military training.

Figure 1.11
Why is Barton shown as a nurse? Who is the new baby?

Andrew Fisher

Prime minister from November 1908 to June 1909; April 1910 to June 1913; September 1914 to October 1915
Previous job: coal miner
Party: Labor
What he did: the government began issuing paper money. Before, this had been done by the private banks. The Commonwealth Bank was set up. Fisher had the first account. A competition was held to design a new capital city. When the First World War started, Fisher promised that Australia would support Britain.

Figure 1.12
Alfred Deakin

Figure 1.13
Andrew Fisher

CHECK the facts

Are the sentences below true or false?

1. All voters elect the members of the constitution.
2. A law must be passed by both houses of parliament.
3. Protectionists thought that customs duties would help the working class.
4. Andrew Fisher was a leading protectionist.
5. Edmund Barton was Australia's first prime minister.
6. Two of our early prime ministers had been lawyers.
7. The Labor Party started the basic wage.
8. The Labor Party formed the Commonwealth Bank.

Australia and Britain

In 1901 most people in Australia were proud to be Australians. They thought that their country was the land of opportunity, the land of the future. They looked back to what Australians had done in the last hundred years and thought of all that could be done in the future.

Although Australians elected their own parliament and made their own laws about things that happened in Australia, they did not control their own defence or foreign policy. Australia did not have its own navy and it could not make treaties or agreements with other countries. For both these things Australia depended on the 'mother country'—Britain.

Figure 1.14
This trademark appeared in 1906. What sort of things do you think it was used for?

Empire Day

On 24 May 1905, Australia celebrated its first Empire Day. Empire Day reminded people in Australia that they were part of the British Empire—at that time, the greatest empire in the world. All round Australia there were special church services. To celebrate the occasion, the cities and towns were decorated, and brass bands played in the streets.

In schools children listened to speeches, cheered, marched and acted out plays about the Empire. They learnt and recited patriotic poems and sayings such as:

> I give my mind to my country to think for it; I give my heart because I love it; I give my hands to my country to work for it.

For most people Empire Day was a day of celebration. Australians were proud of their new nation. But they were also proud that it was part of the British Empire.

Figure 1.15
These schoolchildren are dressed up to celebrate Empire Day in about 1915. Do you know who the boy and girl in the front represent? Why did Australian children get dressed up like this once a year?

Figure 1.16
Why does Mother Britain have a navy ship on her apron? Why is Australia shown as a child?

Australia was part of the British Empire. In 1907 Australia, Canada, South Africa and New Zealand became known as **dominions**. Although the British government arranged meetings to hear what these dominions thought about defence and foreign policy, Britain still kept firm control over these things.

But Australians were getting some ideas of their own. They were specially concerned about the fact that Britain did not have strong military bases in the Pacific area. This meant that Britain might not be able to defend Australia. Britain had even signed a treaty with Japan, which was a country that Australia feared. As a result of these worries, Australia decided to build up its own navy. It started to do this in 1909.

Australia and its neighbours

The continent of Australia is much closer to the countries of Asia than to Britain. In 1880 there were a few thousand Asian people in Australia. Among them were Chinese, who had come to look for gold or to work on the Overland Telegraph. There were also people from the Pacific Islands, such as the Solomon Islands and the New Hebrides, who were brought to Australia to work on sugar plantations in Queensland.

When the Commonwealth of Australia was formed in 1901, more than ninety-eight out of every hundred people were white. It was a general wish that Australia remain a country of white people. Australians believed that theirs should be a country where British people lived according to British customs.

If you look at Figure 1.19 you will read some of the opinions that white Australians expressed in 1901.

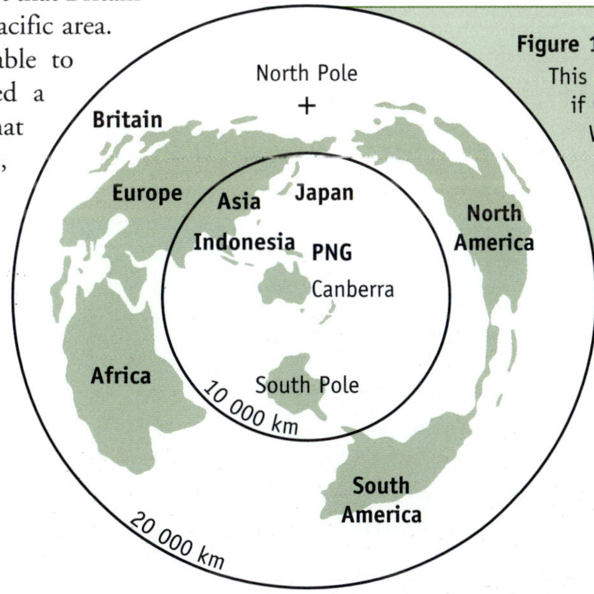

Figure 1.17
This is how the earth would look if Canberra were at the centre. Which countries are closest to Canberra? Which continent is closest?

Figure 1.18
Most white Australians in 1901 preferred to forget about the Aborigines. Since 1788 the number of Aborigines had fallen quickly. Many white people believed that Aborigines were a dying race. Most Aborigines lived on reserves or mission stations. They relied on white people to give them food, clothes, blankets and medicine. This picture, taken in about 1911, shows a white official handing out blankets to Aborigines in Queensland.

One of the first laws that the new Australian parliament made in 1901 was the Immigration Restriction Act. This Act stated that if a person wanted to settle in Australia, he or she could be given a spelling test. The spelling test could be in any European language! So a person from China or Japan who wished to come and live in Australia could be given a spelling test in French or Italian or English. If the person failed, he or she would not be allowed to come. In this way people whose skin was not white could be prevented from settling in Australia.

In 1905 the Act was changed so that the spelling test could be given in any language at all. The new law was supposed to be fairer. It did not alter the fact that Asians were still given spelling tests in languages they did not understand. Of course they failed the tests and were not allowed to come to Australia.

Figure 1.19
Some opinions given by white Australians on Asians

Think *for yourself*

Figure 1.19 gives four reasons why Australians wanted to keep Asians from settling in Australia.

The following four extracts express the same ideas. Can you match up each of the extracts with one of the reasons shown in the diagram?

Figure 1.20
This cartoon was published in an Australian magazine in 1901. Explain what the cartoon means.

What Australia values is the fact that the white man leads the world in almost everything.
Bulletin, 22 June 1901

I asked a bloke for shearing down on the Marthaguy.

'We shear non-union here,' he said. 'I call it scab,' said I.

I looked along the shearing-board before I chanced to go,

Saw eight or ten dashed Chinamen all shearing in a row.

A B Paterson, *Bushman's Song*, 1891

[Australia] objects because they intermarry with white women, and thereby lower the white type.
Bulletin, 22 June 1901

The customs of their country
Of course will then prevail;
And every English slave will have
To wear a long pigtail.
We'll all of us be fed on rice,
As true as I'm a sinner;
And 'stead of spoons we'll have to use
Those chopsticks for our dinner.

Charles Thatcher, *Chinese Immigration*, 1857

KNOW the chapter

1 The answers to these questions are either dates or numbers:
- **a** What was the official birth date of the Australian nation?
- **b** How many stars are on the Australian flag?
- **c** When was Australia's first parliament house opened?
- **d** How many prime ministers did Australia have before 1914?
- **e** When did Australia's navy begin?

2 Who was I?
- **a** I designed the city of Canberra.
- **b** I sang at the opening of Australia's parliament house.
- **c** My government passed the Immigration Restriction Act.
- **d** Before I became prime minister I was a coal miner.
- **e** I wrote a poem that criticised the way Asians were given jobs because they worked for less money than white Australians.

3 Write a sentence to answer each of these questions:
  a Why did Australians celebrate Empire Day?
  b Why did Canberra grow slowly in the early 1900s?
  c Why did trade unions support the Labor Party in the early 1900s?
  d Why did most Australians think of Britain as the 'mother country' in the early 1900s?
  e Why were Asians who wanted to settle in Australia given spelling tests in the early 1900s?

4 Each of these scrambled words has been used in this chapter. Unscramble each one.

A	R	C	B	R	E	A	N
		1		2			3

(page 5)

N	O	M	I	N	D	I	O
				4		5	6

(page 11)

I	T	H	E	W
7		8	9	

(page 11)

Now rearrange the numbered letters in the words you have formed to complete the following sentence:
The year 1901 saw the birth of a ...

			■						

THE HISTORIAN AT WORK

In August 1908 a visiting United States fleet of sixteen warships sailed into Sydney Harbour to be greeted by huge and enthusiastic crowds. A month later the same fleet received a similar reception in Melbourne. The two following extracts refer to this event.

In March 1908, the Melbourne newspaper the *Age* commented on the planned visit:

A Mr Deakin's hospitable message was ... an invitation to the people of America to admit the common trust of the two white races whose destinies are bound up in Pacific dominance. Its acceptance implies ... that America is prepared to play her part. Our statesman will doubtless discern in it as well the necessary implication that America expects us to undertake our corresponding obligation ... With America, our friend and potential ally, navally predominant in the Pacific, Australia has nothing to fear from Asia ... [But] it would be absurd to hope that America would ever bother about us if we continued to postpone the enforcement of our naval policy. It is highly probable that the American Fleet would never have been allowed to visit us if the American people were ignorant of the Australian naval aspiration ... Australia is an island continent. Our destiny lies on the sea. No friend or enemy can reach us save by the sea ... Nothing is plainer than that we must have a navy ... That is the lesson of the forthcoming visit ...

After the visit of the American fleet, Arthur Griffith, a member of the New South Wales Parliament, wrote the following:

B On the 27th May, 1905, in the Strait of Tsu Shima, an event occurred which marks a new epoch in the development of civilisation. On that momentous day, for the first time in the world's history, a battle fleet owned and manned by the coloured Orientals annihilated, in a few hours, a mighty armada of steel-clad battleships belonging to one of the great white nations [Russia] ... From the day of Tsu Shima, until a few weeks ago, the Mikado was Lord of the Pacific, and that ocean washes the shores of our island continent. Britain has not a battleship within 10 000 miles [16 000 km of Australia] ... [but] the United States of America has leapt full armed into the gap, and by the transference of her 'Great White Fleet' from the Atlantic to the Pacific has flung down the gauntlet to the Mongol ... Never before have [Australians] shown such ... enthusiasm as in the reception of the great Anglo-Saxon armada, which has just left our shores. Compared with it the ... reception given to the Heir to the British throne a few years ago dwindles into unimportance.

1 From the evidence of extract B above, what country was Russia at war with in 1905? What words make this clear?

2 Use an atlas to find out where the Strait of Tsu Shima is. Use the information in extract B to work out what happened there on 27 May 1905.

3 Why do you think some Australians felt alarmed about what happened on 27 May 1905?

4 What evidence can you find in the above extracts that Australians felt isolated in 1908? Who did they feel isolated from?

5 Do you think that Arthur Griffiths and the writer of the *Age* article would have supported the Immigration Restriction Act? What evidence can you find for your answer in the two extracts?

6 What connection does Arthur Griffiths make between the events of 27 May 1905 and the visit of the United States fleet three years later?

7 According to the writer of the *Age* article, what must Australia do quickly to help defend itself? What arguments does the writer use to support this view?

8 In 1903 was there any formal alliance between Australia and the USA? What word in the *Age* article makes this clear?

2

Australia *at* war

What did you do last Anzac Day? Did you go to the beach? Have a party? Watch television? Play sport? Did you see your local Anzac Day march?

Anzac Day is celebrated in Australia on 25 April. On that day, Australians remember a military campaign that took place in 1915. In this campaign Australian troops, with troops from several other countries, tried to capture a piece of land called the Gallipoli Peninsula. They were not successful and the soldiers who survived had to be taken away by boat.

Why should we have a holiday to celebrate a defeat that happened over eighty years ago? Why were Australians fighting in a war thousands of kilometres away? How did that war start? The answers to these questions will help us understand a lot about Australia and its place in the world in 1914.

Assassination

Date: 28 June 1914
Place: Sarajevo, capital city of Bosnia. Bosnia was a part of Austria-Hungary. Its people were Serbs.
Victims: Archduke Franz Ferdinand, next in line to the Austrian throne, and his wife Sophie. They were visiting Sarajevo.
Murderer: Gavrilo Princip, nineteen-year-old Bosnian student; Austria-hater; member of a secret society called the Black Hand.
Eyewitness report: The streets of Sarajevo were decorated that day and big crowds were out to cheer the Archduke and his wife. Although the visitors had been warned about possible trouble, they chose to drive in an open car so they could wave to the crowds. It was a sunny morning, and soon after ten o'clock, the four cars in the procession started off. The procession was supposed to go to the cathedral in the middle of the city. But just before the cars reached the turn-off, a young man in the crowd threw a bomb at the Archduke's car. It hit the folded-down hood and the Archduke was not hurt.

Franz Ferdinand was angry and decided to go straight ahead to the town hall instead of to the cathedral. That way he could miss the centre of the town. The drivers were told to speed up, but they were not told exactly where they should go. The first driver turned off towards the cathedral. The Archduke's driver did the same. When he realised that he had made a mistake, he stopped and began to reverse slowly.

As he was doing this another young man from the crowd fired two shots into the Archduke's car from a distance of four or five paces. The first shot hit the Archduke in the neck. The second hit Sophie in the stomach. In half an hour they were both dead.

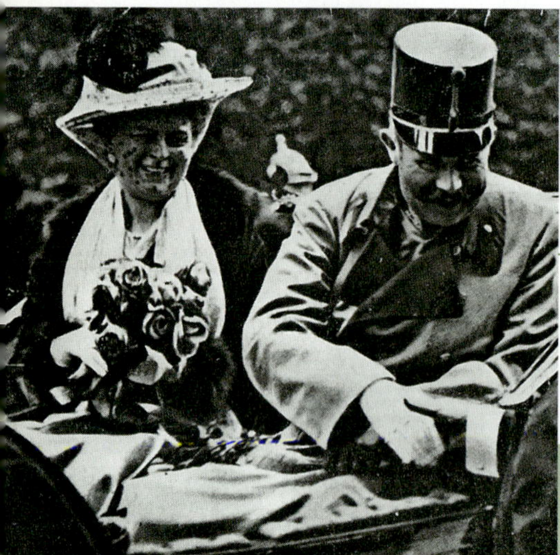

Figure 2.1
Victims of assassination, Archduke Franz Ferdinand and his wife Sophie

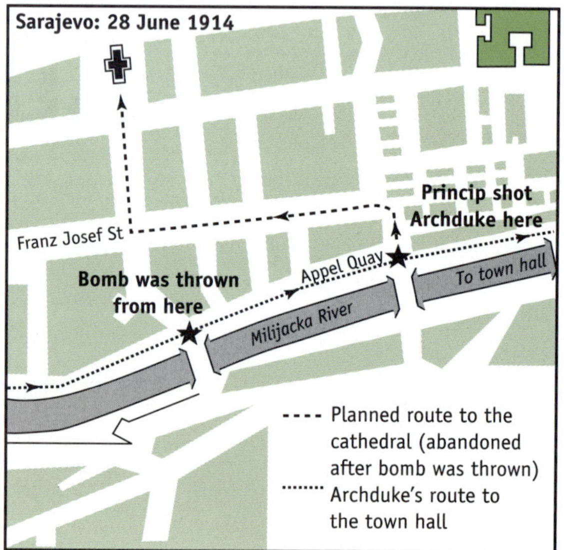

Figure 2.3
The area of Sarajevo where the assassination took place

Figure 2.2
The assassin, Gavrilo Princip

Results of murder: Gavrilo Princip was nineteen years and eleven and a half months old. By law he was two weeks too young to be hanged. He was sentenced to prison for twenty years but died of tuberculosis in 1917.

The Austrian government claimed that the Serbian government had planned the murders of the Archduke and his wife. Serbia hated Austria. Most people in Bosnia were Serbs. When Bosnia became part of the Austro-Hungarian Empire in 1908, many Bosnians wanted to break away and join Serbia. The Austrian government was nervous about Serbia; it was looking for a way of teaching

Serbia a lesson. Austria used the assassination of Franz Ferdinand as an excuse and sent an ultimatum (a list of demands), to Serbia. When Serbia refused to do everything that was demanded, Austria declared war on Serbia. This happened on 28 July 1914, exactly one month after the murders.

Why a small war became a big war

When Austria declared war on Serbia there were 810 000 men in the Austrian army. In 1918, after four years of war, at least 13 million people had been killed. Millions of others were sick, wounded, starving or homeless. Why?

You can see from the map (Figure 2.4) that there were many problems and tensions in Europe in 1914. Countries were very jealous of each other. Five times in the last eight years war had almost broken out. In fact, things were so tense that six large countries had formed groups or **alliances** to protect each other if war broke out. The groups were called the Triple Alliance and the Triple Entente.

The alliances meant that if one country went to war, others could quickly be dragged in as well. Russia was an ally, or supporter, of Serbia. Germany was an ally of Austria-Hungary. When Austria declared war on Serbia on 28 July 1914, Russia and Germany quickly became involved.

Figure 2.6 shows how the war had spread by 1917. Because of the treaties and alliances in Europe, a local war had become a world war.

Figure 2.4
Europe in 1914

Britain feared the growing power of Germany. Britain had a large empire and did not want Germany to get new colonies.

Germany was formed in 1871. By 1914 it was a powerful country. Germany was jealous of the empires of Britain and France. Germany had a strong army but was envious of Britain's navy.

Russia was worried about the new, strong Germany. Russia wanted to control the Balkans and to make sure that Russian ships could reach the Mediterranean Sea.

France had lost some rich land to Germany in 1871. Many French people wanted revenge. Others feared their strong neighbour.

Austria-Hungary had a large empire. But many of the people in the empire wanted to be free. Austria-Hungary wanted to control the Balkans. It feared Russia's power there.

These countries were 'the Balkans'. They were the 'powder keg' of Europe. Other countries tried to gain power in the Balkans. Serbia hated Austria and stirred up trouble against Austria.

Turkey, like Austria, controlled a crumbling empire. Turkey feared both Russian and Austrian power in the Balkans.

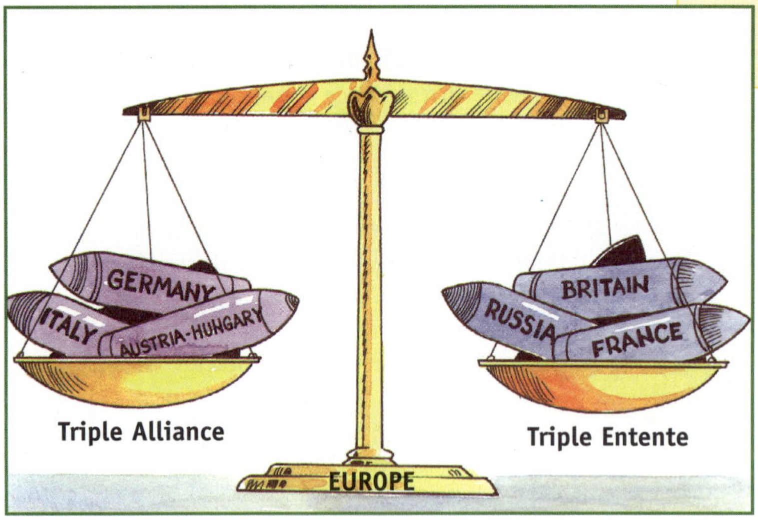

Figure 2.5
Europe in the balance

Figure 2.6
The two sides. By 1917 these countries were involved in what we now call the First World War.

CHECK the facts

Are the sentences below true or false?

1 There is no one alive today who can remember the First World War.

2 Franz Ferdinand was murdered on 28 July 1914.

3 Franz Ferdinand was heir to the Austrian throne.

4 Germany was jealous of Britain's navy.

5 Britain had a large empire in 1914.

6 Italy was a Balkan country.

7 Germany, Austria and Belgium were partners in the Triple Alliance.

9 Russia was an enemy of France.

10 Austria was the first country to declare war.

Think *for yourself*

1 Before 1914 the Balkans were called 'the powder keg of Europe'. Why were they called this?

2 Could this description still be used to refer to the Balkans? Do some research to find out what has happened in this part of the world in the last few years.

3 John Kennedy, Anwar Sadat, Indira Gandhi and Yitzhak Rabin were famous political leaders who were assassinated. Do some research to find out which country each was leader of and who assassinated them. Were any of these assassinations in any way similar to the assassination of Archduke Franz Ferdinand?

4 Can you name any other famous people who have been assassinated or whom someone has tried to assassinate? What measures are taken to protect political leaders from assassination attempts?

A plan goes wrong

When war started Germany put into action the Schlieffen Plan which had been worked out some years before.

Figure 2.7
The Schlieffen Plan

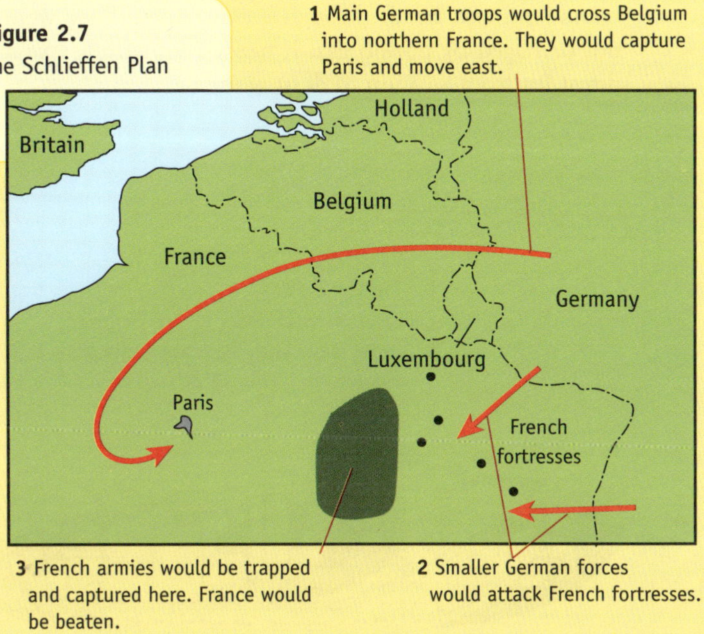

Figure 2.7 shows a diagram of the Schlieffen Plan. According to the plan, German troops would march through Belgium and into northern France. The French army would expect Germany to attack straight across the border between France and Germany where the French had built fortresses. But if German soldiers came down from the north, they could capture Paris and then catch the French soldiers in a trap. When France had been taken, German troops could then move east and attack Russia.

This was the plan. But in just over a month it had gone wrong. Troops from France and Belgium slowed the German army down. Soldiers were sent from England to help the French army. When Russia came into the war, many German soldiers were moved away to fight the Russian army.

Both sides began to dig trenches to defend the land they had won. Early in 1915 these trenches stretched right across northern France. This was called the Western Front. The trench warfare there was to last for another three years.

A new kind of war

Trench warfare was horrible. Each side dug trenches that were usually deep enough for men to stand in. Between the trenches was a stretch of ground called no-man's-land. It was guarded by barbed wire. At times there were fierce battles. In these battles one side or the other would sometimes win a little ground. When the fighting was heavy, over 60 000 men could be killed in one day.

Figure 2.8
In the trenches. Use this picture and what you have read to write a paragraph about trench warfare.

Leading off the trenches were **dugouts** where soldiers slept and ate. The dugouts and the trenches were usually muddy and were always infested with lice and fleas. After heavy rain they were often flooded. Soldiers got a disease called trench foot from standing in filthy mud for long hours. Sometimes soldiers stayed in the same trench for months. Neither side gained or lost much ground.

Day after day and night after night, the big guns fired. Shells exploded over the trenches, scattering metal and shrapnel. Then the unlucky ones were ordered to go 'over the top'. With only their steel helmets to protect them, they tried to run through no-man's-land to attack the enemy trenches. Most of them were mown down by machine guns or caught in the barbed wire of no-man's-land.

Figure 2.9
These soldiers are wearing a type of gas mask that was used after 1916. They are firing a Vickers machine gun. Why was poison gas such a deadly weapon?

Poison gas was a deadly new weapon. Chlorine was the first poison gas. Later, mustard gas was used. These gases choked, blinded or burned soldiers. At first, soldiers used wet rags or bandages to try and keep the gas away from their noses and mouths. Then gas masks were invented. Even dogs and horses had to wear gas masks in battle.

Three other new weapons were **submarines**, **tanks** and **aeroplanes**. Submarines played an important part in the First World War. Ships carrying supplies were sunk by German submarines, or U-boats as they were called. In 1917 the U-boats began attacking all ships in the war zone, even those of neutral countries that were not fighting in the war. It was this 'unrestricted submarine warfare' that brought the United States of America (USA) into the war.

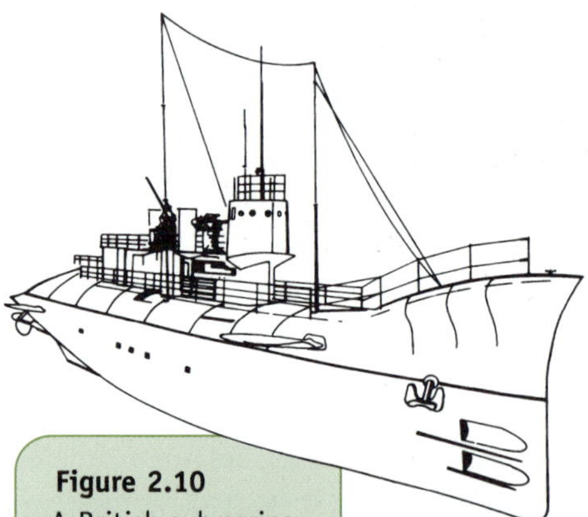

Figure 2.10
A British submarine

Tanks were invented in Britain. They were a well-kept secret until they were first used in 1916. Then thirty-six tanks helped to win a battle near the Somme River in France. Tanks were useful weapons. They could cross no-man's-land and break through enemy lines. They were not damaged by poison gas. It needed something like a direct hit from a canon to destroy them.

Figure 2.11
Each of these Mark 8 tanks carried eight men. They had two large guns and seven smaller guns.

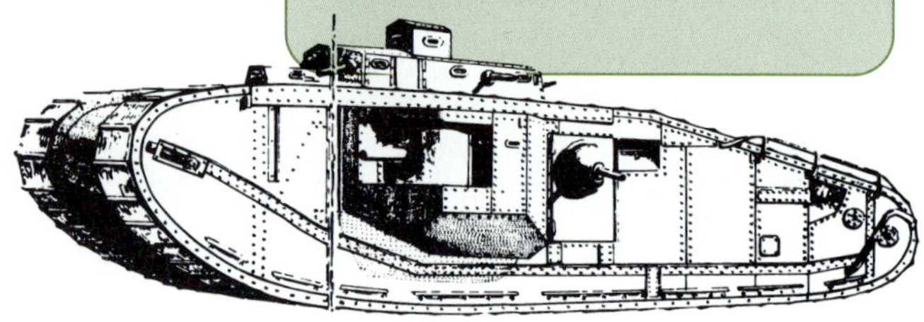

Airships and aeroplanes were used for the first time in the First World War. Early in the war, Germany used airships to spot enemy boats. Some of these huge Zeppelins, as they were called, dropped bombs on Britain. During the war, aeroplanes became faster and better. In 1914 the total number of aeroplanes for all the countries was only 2000. By 1918 they had about 10 000. Both sides used planes for air raids, spying, taking photographs and defending ships. The top pilots were called Aces. The most famous of the Aces was a German, Manfred von Richthofen. He was known as the Red Baron.

Figure 2.12
This Fokker D7 was used by the German Airforce

CHECK the facts

Match each word or expression in column A with its meaning in column B.

A	B
Schlieffen Plan	leaving a trench to attack the enemy
Western Front	a country that is not fighting in a war
no-man's-land	the battle area in northern France
going over the top	an area of land between enemy trenches
mustard gas	German plan to attack and defeat France
neutral country	top pilots
Aces	German submarines
U-boats	a poison that blinds, burns or chokes

Think *for yourself*

1 Figure 2.13 shows a recruiting poster. It was designed to encourage young men to join the army. What sort of people would it appeal to?

Try to find and copy another recruiting poster from the First World War. Books in your library about the war will help you. Design a poster of your own. Remember that you are trying to make people join the army to fight for their country.

2 The uniforms that were worn in the First World War were different from uniforms worn in earlier wars. Earlier uniforms had often been brightly coloured. But uniforms of the First World War were dull. Khaki, brown and grey were common colours. Why did this change happen?

Find pictures of First World War uniforms from library books. Draw some of these new-style uniforms in your book.

Figure 2.13
A recruiting poster

Australia joins in

Britain was at war. Australia was part of the British Empire. So Australia was at war, too. Most Australians in 1914 had no doubt that Australia should help Britain, the 'mother country'. Joseph Cook, the prime minister, said: 'Whatever happens, Australia is a part of the Empire, right to the full. When the Empire is at war, Australia is at war.'

Why did Australian men join the army to fight for Britain? There were many reasons, as you will see from Figure 2.14.

Figure 2.14
Why Australians joined up. Can you think of any other reasons?

Other ideas

Although most Australians were very excited about the war, there were some who thought that Australia should not have become involved in Britain's war.

Nothing to do with us.
Our religion says we should not kill.
Why should we fight for Britain?
Australia was told to fight, not asked if it would help.
Rich factory owners only want to make more money by selling war supplies.
How would you have felt?

Australians in war

Australia promised to send 20 000 soldiers to help Britain. They would fight wherever Britain needed them. Recruiting began on 10 August 1914. Six weeks later the new Australian Imperial Force (AIF) was ready to leave. On 1 November the first convoy of soldiers from Australia and New Zealand sailed from Australia.

They were sent to Egypt for training. It was in Egypt that they were first called Anzacs—a name made from the initials of the Australian and New Zealand Army Corps.

Because they were not sent to battle straight away, many soldiers became bored and were soon in trouble. They climbed the pyramids and scratched their names on the stones. They went absent without leave, got drunk and had wild donkey rides through the streets of Cairo. They caused a riot in the brothels. They threw drivers off their trams and took the trams for joyrides.

The strict discipline of the British army was not for the Australians. Many of them were country boys, used to making their own decisions. They disliked drill and saw no point in saluting officers. The image of the Australian soldier, as riotous, undisciplined and loutish, was born.

Figure 2.15
Sub-Lieutenant: *'Don't you know what to do when you pass an officer?—You're a soldier are you not?'*
Private ANZAC: *'No—I'm a farmer!'*
Why do the officer and his wife look astonished?

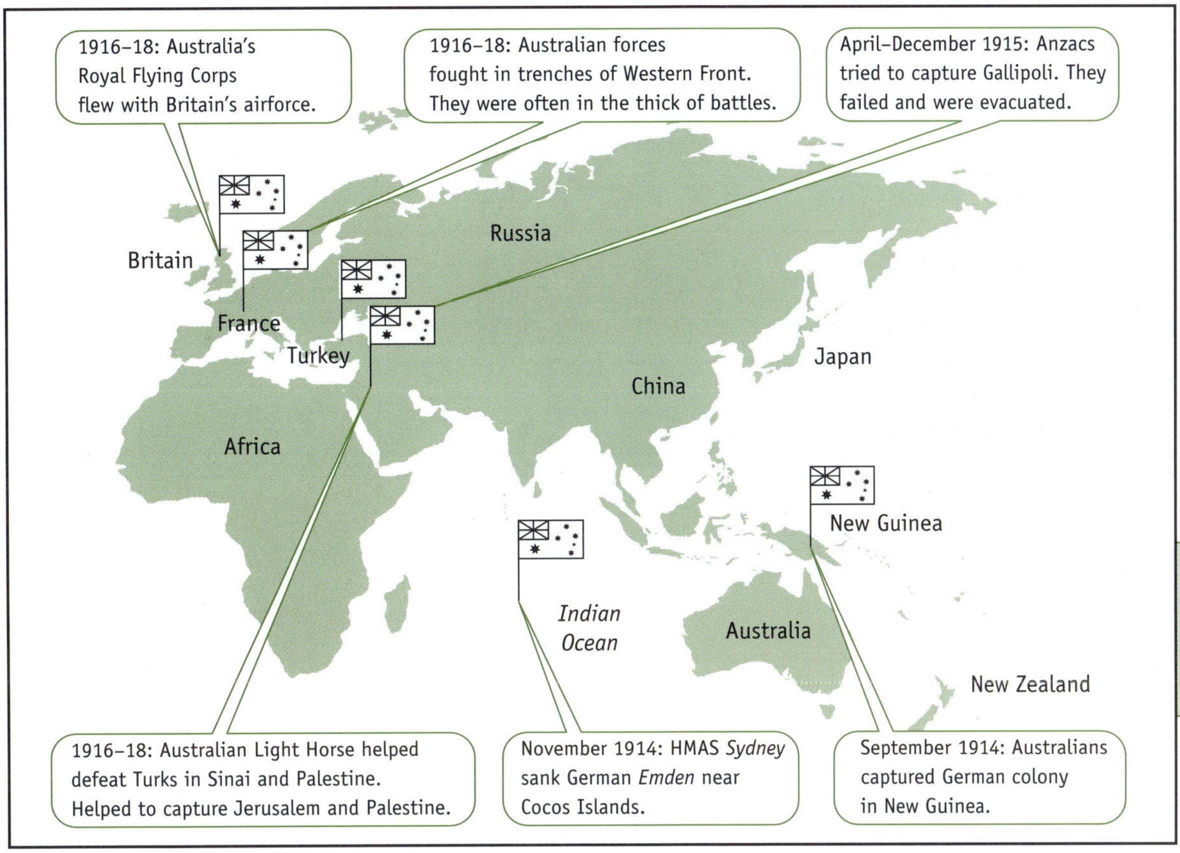

Figure 2.16 Where Australians fought

Where Australians fought

During the First World War, four out of every ten Australian men between the ages of eighteen and forty-five joined up. About 330 000 were sent overseas. Over 59 000 were killed. Another 167 000 were wounded and 4000 were taken prisoner.

The map (Figure 2.16) shows the main areas where Australians fought in the First World War.

Figure 2.17 Australian infantrymen

The Australian forces

The most obvious mark of an Australian soldier was his slouch hat made of brown felt. Foot-soldiers, or infantrymen, wore a woollen uniform tunic, brown breeches, a grey flannel shirt and khaki puttees. Puttees were a piece of woollen cloth that wound up the soldier's leg from his ankles to his knees. Soldiers disliked puttees because they were uncomfortable and stopped blood flowing properly. Each soldier carried about 35 kilograms of equipment, including ammunition, tools and spare clothes.

Men in the Australian Light Horse wore emu feathers on their hats. Their uniform was similar to that worn by the infantrymen, except they wore leggings instead of puttees. The Light Horse fought in the desert and mainly against the Turks. Desert warfare was very different from war on the Western Front. But soldiers in the Light Horse had to cope with just as many problems.

Figure 2.18
Light Horsemen

The Army Nursing Service was made up of trained volunteer nurses between eighteen and forty-five years old. Over 2000 Australian nurses served overseas and twenty-one died abroad.

They worked wherever they were needed—on the Western Front, in the Middle East, in England, Greece and Italy. Some nurses worked on hospital ships and trains. In most places they worked for long hours in terrible conditions. They rarely had enough medical supplies.

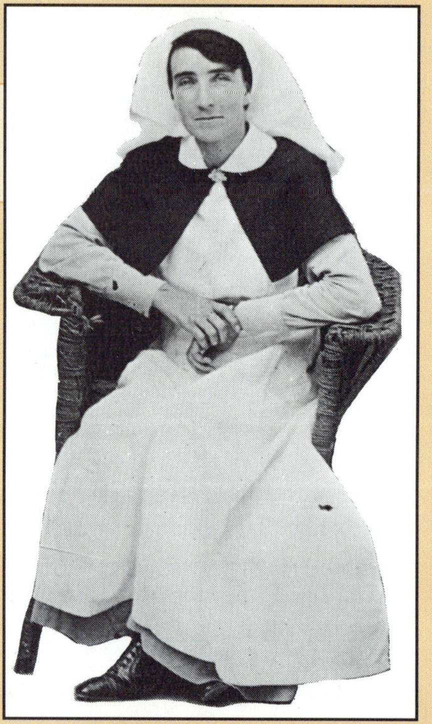

Figure 2.19
A First World War nurse

CHECK the facts

Use information from this section to complete the following:

1 Australia declared war on Germany in 1914 because ____________

2 In Egypt soldiers from Australia and New Zealand were first called ____________ This name was made from ____________

3 In November 1914 the Australian ship, *Sydney*, ____________

4 Two places where the AIF fought were ____________

5 The pieces of cloth that wound round an Australian soldier's legs were called ____________ Soldiers did not like wearing them because ____________

6 More than 2000 ____________ from Australia were sent overseas in the First World War.

Think *for yourself*

1 J. D. Burns was at school when the First World War started. He wrote a poem in his school magazine about war. Here are some lines from the poem:

The bugles of England were blowing o'er the sea,
As they had called a thousand years, calling now to me;
They woke me from dreaming in the dawning of the day,
The bugles of England—and how could I stay?

Look again at Figure 2.14 which shows why Australians joined up. Which reason is the one Burns wrote about in his poem?

2 If you have friends or relatives who are in their late eighties or older, they may be able to remember the First World War. Find out what they can recall about it. Here are some questions that you could ask:

- Do you remember when war broke out? Did you care? What did your parents or other members of your family think about the war?
- Did any members of your family join the army? Do you know why?
- What country were you living in during the First World War? What was it like living there during the war? Did the war change the lives of ordinary people?
- How did you celebrate the news that the war had ended?
- Did you understand what the war was about? Did you talk about it with your family?
- What are your clearest memories of the First World War years?
- Did you know anyone who was killed or wounded in the war?

Gallipoli

Harry Davis was not a real person. But many Australian soldiers could have told this story.

I'm Harry Davis. I joined the AIF in 1914, just after the war started. I thought it was the right thing to do. I figured that I'd see a bit of the world in the army too.

We went to Egypt first. That was a wild old time. We were supposed to be learning how to be soldiers. But after a couple of months we were all bored stiff. We were really pleased when they said we were going off to Gallipoli to fight the Turks.

I didn't really know where Gallipoli was then. I wasn't sure why we were fighting the Turks either. All I knew was that they were allies of Germany. And we all hated the Germans.

I soon learned where Gallipoli was. I've drawn a map to show you (Figure 2.21). Gallipoli is part of Turkey. It sticks out into the Dardanelles. That's the strait of water that separates the Black Sea from the Mediterranean Sea. Britain wanted to get hold of the Dardanelles. Things weren't going too well in France and nobody seemed to be getting anywhere. So the British reckoned that if they captured the Dardanelles they could send food and supplies through the Black Sea to Russia. Russia was on our side.

We went to a Greek island called Lemnos first, to get ready. Then we sailed to Gallipoli. Lieutenant-General Birdwood was our leader. We landed from small boats just before dawn on 25 April 1915. But we'd picked the wrong place. Just a narrow beach with high cliffs behind it. We didn't have a chance.

The Turks were expecting us. They stood on the cliffs and fired non-stop as we landed. There were men dying all round me. By eight o'clock that night we'd got about 8000 men on shore. But there was nowhere to go. We couldn't move the supplies or guns anywhere. There were rows of wounded men waiting to be taken away and more kept coming. All the time the Turks kept firing down at us. We were sitting ducks.

Eight months. That's how long we stayed there. Do you know how far we got in eight months? Five kilometres from the beach. We couldn't beat the Turks. They couldn't push us back. So we waited.

Figure 2.20
After the first landing on 25 April 1915, many boatloads of supplies were landed at Anzac Cove. We spent days unloading them and dragging them to our camp.

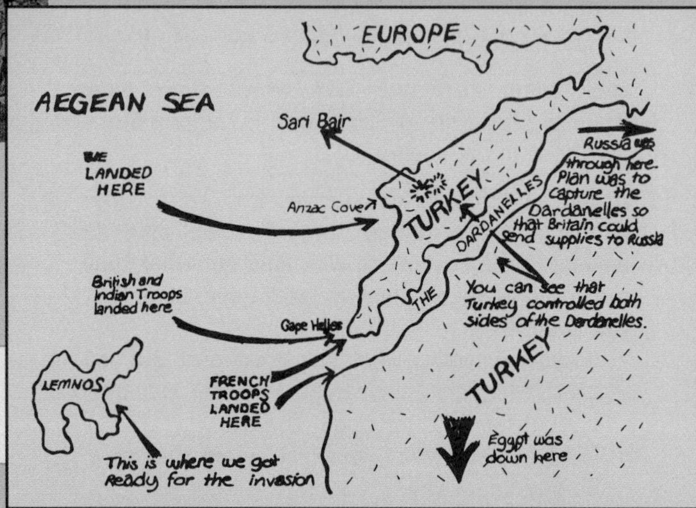

Figure 2.21
Harry Davis' map of Gallipoli

Figure 2.22
Our water came in tanks from Egypt. We had to drag the tanks up to our camp. You can see some of our dugouts in the picture.

Figure 2.23
After battles, getting rid of the bodies was always a problem

We lived in dugouts and tents in the scrub near the beach. We sniped at Johnny Turk and he sniped back at us. Then the big guns blazed and there was heavy shellfire. Sometimes we had fierce battles. In August we tried to capture Sari Bair, the ridge in front of our base. We fought hard for four days. But we ended up no better than we were at the beginning.

Every day we spent hours digging trenches and carrying water, food and supplies around. By June it was so hot that the fat in our tins of bully beef melted. Nobody had thought to give us any hot weather uniforms, so we cut our breeches down to make shorts. We were always thirsty. Most of our water came from Egypt in boats and there was never enough of it. But worst of all were the flies. They were everywhere. We ate and drank them. Almost everyone got dysentery from the flies and the terrible food.

One day at the end of November there was a terrible storm. Very soon every trench was like a river. A lot of our men died. As others climbed out, the Turks fired down at them. That night the rain turned to sleet. The mud froze over and more of our men were frozen to death by the snow and gales that followed.

At last the War Council in England realised that we couldn't win. A lot of us didn't want to give up, but we were ordered to retreat. It took twelve days for all of us to leave. During the day time we pretended that nothing unusual was happening. We even pretended to land more supplies. But every night men went quietly down to the beach and got onto the boats that were waiting there. We put sandbags and blankets on the tracks so that Johnny Turk wouldn't hear us. The boats took us out to ships waiting in the harbour.

A few of the boys stayed in the front line. They kept on shelling the Turks and lit fires all over the place so that the Turks would think we were still there. On the last night they blew up some of the stores and ammunition that were left. They even rigged up some guns that fired half an hour after we'd all gone.

We didn't get anywhere in Gallipoli. But when we got home everyone treated us as heroes. They talked about how brave we'd been and how we'd kept going when things were hopeless. They were proud of us and what we'd done. We put Australia on the map, they said.

I had a lot of good mates at Gallipoli. You have to stick together when you're in a place like that. Otherwise you'd have no hope at all.

CHECK the facts

Read Harry Davis' story and answer the questions below.

1. Harry Davis gives two reasons why he joined up. What are they?
2. Why was he pleased to be going to Gallipoli?
3. Why did Britain want to control the Dardanelles?
4. Why does Harry Davis say that the Anzacs 'didn't have a chance' when they landed at Gallipoli?
5. How long did the Anzacs stay at Gallipoli?
6. The Anzacs gave the Turks a nickname. What was it?
7. Why did the Anzacs have to carry water from place to place?
8. Why did many Anzacs drown in November 1915?
9. Why were the Anzacs forced to leave Gallipoli?
10. Why were the Anzacs treated as heroes when they went home?

Think *for yourself*

1. At the beginning of this chapter we asked why people today celebrate Anzac Day. Can you now explain why there are marches and services each year on Anzac Day?
2. The periscope in Figure 2.24 was invented by Australians at Gallipoli. How would it have been useful in the kind of fighting the Anzacs were doing?

Figure 2.24
Periscopes were used in trench warfare

3 An Anzac wrote this poem about the retreat from Gallipoli:

Not only muffled is our tread
To cheat the foe,
We fear to rouse our honoured dead
To hear us go
Sleep sound, old friends—the keenest smart
Which, more than failure, wounds the heart,
Is thus to leave you — thus to part,
Comrades, farewell!!!

foe enemy, *rouse* wake up, *keenest smart* main regret

a What did the soldier mean by 'cheat the foe'?
b How was the tread of soldiers leaving Gallipoli muffled? (Clue: look back to the story by Harry Davis.)
c The soldier gives two reasons for the 'muffled tread'. One is 'to cheat the foe'. What is the other reason?
d What is the soldier's main regret at leaving Gallipoli?

THE HISTORIAN AT WORK

Charles Bean was not a soldier, but he was with the Anzacs at Gallipoli. He kept a detailed dairy of what he observed there. After the war he returned to Gallipoli with a group of artists who painted pictures of many of the events that occurred there. The painting below is one of these. It shows the Anzacs attacking Turkish positions on a narrow ridge known as the Nek in the hills above Anzac Cove. This attack took place early in the morning on Saturday, 7 August 1915.

Figure 2.25
Anzacs watch Turkish prisoners in a prisoner-of-war compound.

Figure 2.26
George Lambert, 'The Charge of the 3rd Light Horse Brigade at the Nek, 7 August 1915', 1924, oil on canvas, 152.5 x 305.7 cm, Australian War Memorial (7965)

The following is an extract from Bean's diary:

> August 8, Sunday
>
> Today is Sunday, August 8th, fifteen weeks after we landed …
>
> I have just seen as caddish an act as I ever saw in my life. About 100 Turkish prisoners and two Germans were sitting in the pen built by the Australian Division opposite my dug out. There is an incinerator within a few yards. Some chap had poured out a tin of kerosene on the ground in front of it and laid a trail of kerosene … Some chap put a light to the trail, it flared along and when it reached the kerosene there was a huge flare of fire very uncomfortably close—if not dangerously—to the Turks. The wretched prisoners rushed to the far corner of the pen like a flock of sheep rounded up by a dog, and the fellows looked on and laughed. There were both Australians and Britishers there amongst the onlookers. I wondered someone hadn't the decency to hit the man who did it straight in the face. The same thing exactly was done yesterday.
>
> The treatment of these prisoners makes you blush for your own side. They are under the control of the Army Corps Police and APM … They have put Indian sentries over them, who are about as capable as keeping off the Australians who crowd around to stare at them as an old woman with a stick would be. Three Turkish officers are among the lot. So far as we know they have treated our captured men and officers excellently. These three officers were sent off under an Indian sentry to a vacant shell of a dug out in Australian Divisional lines. They were sent there in the morning and absolutely forgotten. No food or water was sent to them. Our Divisional interpreter happened to be passing in the afternoon, when these Turks told him. He went to the APM of Army Corps, whose business it was. APM said he was too busy—would the interpreter get some other officer to do it.
>
> The interpreter saw another officer who said he would have bully beef and biscuits sent up. Interpreter said he would not take bully beef and biscuits up—the Turks wouldn't give our officers bully beef and biscuits if their own officers were feeding better. The officer saw things in this light and sent up a decent meal. The Turks had some tea but no one provided them with any water. Interpreter had to go round for that and couldn't find any. They are now in a bare dug out, no blankets, no water proof sheet, no comforts of any sort.

1 Do some research and find out who Charles Bean was. What was his job at Gallipoli?

2 Describe Bean's attitude to the behaviour of the Australian and British soldiers. What words in the extract show how strongly he felt about what happened?

3 Use a dictionary to find the meaning of:
- bully beef
- Provost-Marshall.

What was the Assistant Provost-Marshall's job?

4 Does Bean hold the Assistant Provost-Marshall partly responsible for what happened? In what way might he have prevented the incident from taking place?

5 Using the painting as evidence, write a brief account of the Anzac attack at the Nek. Describe the weapons used and the way the Anzacs attacked. How do you think the battle ended? Why do you think this?

6 Look back at Harry Davis' account on pages 27–29. Do you think the attack shown in the painting was part of the Anzac's attempt to capture Sari Bair? Why?

7 Imagine you were one of the Australian soldiers involved in the incident described by Bean. Write an account of what happened. In your account try to imagine why you and your mates acted as you did. Could the kind of events shown in the painting have influenced the way you acted towards the Turkish prisoners?

Now imagine you were one of the Turkish prisoners in the pen. Describe what happened from your point of view.

Finally, imagine that you were one of the Turkish officers that Bean refers to. Describe how you were treated and how you felt.

8 Find out what is meant by the terms **primary evidence** and **secondary evidence**. State whether the painting, the extract from Bean's diary and the photograph in Figure 2.25 are examples of primary or secondary evidence. Explain why in each case.

9 The night before Bean wrote the above diary entry he had been wounded in the leg while observing a battle scene. If Bean had not been wounded these events may never have been described. Can you explain why? Do you think the fact that he was wounded could have affected his attitude to the way the Anzacs behaved? Discuss.

Back in Australia

When war first broke out, so many men volunteered that the army could not provide enough weapons or uniforms for them. Those who did not join the army had plenty to do.

Factories were kept busy making goods that could no longer be bought from overseas. Politicians travelled round the country making speeches to persuade even more men to join the army. Wheat farmers planted large crops because they thought that Britain would need extra supplies of food. Graziers sold wool to the government so that uniforms could be made. Families stuck pins in maps to show where the fighting was and who was winning. The government put taxes up to raise money to pay for the war.

In October 1914 a new law gave the government much greater control over people's lives. More than 3400 people were fined or sent to prison for crimes such as these:

- spreading rumours that would frighten people
- wearing a soldier's uniform without permission
- selling goods belonging to the Red Cross
- hiding a German
- dyeing army overcoats.

Over 30 000 Germans lived in Australia in 1914. In 1915 Germans and Austrians who were old enough to join the army were put into special camps. Others were carefully watched by police and neighbours. Many Germans lost their jobs. Some changed their surnames. Some were beaten up by gangs of youths. German schools and churches were closed. German music was banned. German sausage was renamed Belgian sausage. Forty-two German place names were changed as well. **Blumberg** became **Birdwood**; **German Creek** became **Empire Bay**.

Leaders of trade unions were angry about the war. They believed that factory owners were making big profits while workers were asked to work longer hours for less money. Prices and taxes were going up, and workers found that their wages would not buy as much as before. In 1916 coal miners in NSW went on strike. The strike lasted for two months. The next year railway men went on strike. They were joined by miners, seamen and others. Some people thought it was unpatriotic to go on strike. But by 1917 many people had lost any enthusiasm they previously had for the war.

Thank you, Figure 2.28
Germans and Austrians in the bar at the camp at Berrima, NSW. From the evidence of this photograph, can you suggest the kind of work these men were required to do?

Figure 2.27
These schoolgirls and their teacher spent the war years at a camp in Berrima. Why?

Think *for yourself*

1 Look at the list of crimes that people were punished for after October 1914. Why did the government want to stop people doing each of these things?

2 Why was German sausage renamed *Belgian sausage* in the First World War? (Clue: look back to the diagram of the Schlieffen Plan.)

3 Why were the names *Birdwood* and *Empire Bay* chosen to replace German place names?

4 How do you think factory owners could make bigger profits during the First World War?

5 Do you think it is unpatriotic to go on strike while your country is fighting a war?

Mutiny

On 4 February 1916, 5000 soldiers training at the AIF camp at Casula, to the west of Sydney, refused to accept another one and a half hours of drill a day. They marched to Liverpool where they were joined by thousands more from another camp. Some ransacked local hotels, others took over trains to Sydney and went on a spree. They stole beer from hotels, brawled, broke into shops and fought anyone who tried to stop them. At Central Station one soldier was killed and six were hurt in a fight with army police.

Many people blamed alcohol for the mutiny. Some said that all hotels should close at 6.00 p.m. Four months later a new law was passed to make this happen.

A chaplain who had been with the Anzacs at Gallipoli was on leave in Sydney at the time. He wrote to the paper:

We, who are on leave, are obliged to wear the uniform of the AIF. Are we to feel now that there is a stigma attached to us because fellows at Liverpool and Casula wear the same thing? For five months I lived in trenches and slept in a hole in the ground. I lost my health. God help me if I am to lose my pride, too.

stigma bad name

Think *for yourself*

1 Do you think the soldiers from Casula and Liverpool were very different from those who fought at Gallipoli?

2 What punishment do you think they should have received?

3 Was the chaplain at Gallipoli for the whole of the Anzac campaign? (Clue: read the story of Harry Davis again.)

4 Why was the chaplain worried that he and others wearing the AIF uniform would get a bad name?

Women in the war

Some Australian women wanted to be as much a part of the war as men. Eleanor Jacob formed a women's battalion which 700 women joined. They spent their time drilling and learning first aid. Other women volunteered as nurses or army cooks. But only the nurses were allowed to go overseas.

Most Australian women could only 'wait and weep'. The number of women doing full-time work grew, but only slowly. Women did not take over men's jobs in large numbers.

But women did work, and sometimes very hard, to help the war effort. They joined the Red Cross and the Australian Comforts Fund. Women and children knitted about 1 350 000 pairs of socks to send to soldiers. These socks helped to stop men in the trenches from getting trench foot. Women raised money to buy extra food, tobacco, newspapers and clothes for the troops.

Figure 2.29
How are these women helping the war effort? What other sorts of work did women do?

The women did not get any pay for all this work. But women were learning that they could manage by themselves. They developed useful skills. Many of them wanted to use these skills after the war. But when the war finished, they were expected to go back to their homes and forget about the independence they had become used to.

An important decision

In 1916 Australians had to make an important decision. By this time fewer men were volunteering to join the army. The war was taking longer than people had expected and many thousands of soldiers had been killed. Reinforcements were needed.

The prime minister, William Morris Hughes, wanted to introduce compulsory military service (called conscription), to Australia. He wanted the conscripted soldiers to fight overseas just as volunteers did. But Hughes was the leader of the Labor Party and most members of this party did not support conscription.

Figure 2.30
'I'll have you!'
Billy Hughes wanted to introduce conscription

Hughes decided to ask Australians whether they approved of conscription. In order to do this he planned a referendum for October 1916. Voters had to answer 'yes' or 'no' to the question: Should men be conscripted for overseas service?

A bitter campaign began. Hughes was a stirring speaker, and he convinced many people that conscription was necessary. He was supported by most Australian newspapers as well as by many religious leaders. His main opponent was Dr Daniel Mannix, the Roman Catholic Archbishop of Melbourne.

Hughes was defeated but the results were very close. However, a majority of Australians had shown that they did not want to send conscripted soldiers to fight overseas.

Because of this defeat, Hughes broke away from the Labor Party and formed a new party, the Nationalist Party. This party won the 1917 election and Hughes, still convinced that conscription was necessary, held another referendum. Again he was defeated—and this time even more people voted against conscription.

Women and conscription

Australian women had been given the right to vote in 1902. Both sides in the conscription battle wanted to win the votes of women. Hughes even arranged 'women only' rallies to convince them to vote for conscription.

But many women were strongly opposed to conscription. A group called the Queen's and Women's Peace Army was formed to arrange rallies against conscription. Here is one of its songs:

I did not raise my son to be a soldier,
I brought him up to be my pride and joy,
Who dares to put a musket on his shoulder
To kill some other mother's darling boy?
The nations all should arbitrate their quarrels,
It's time to put the gun and sword away.
There'd be no war today,
If mothers all would say,
I did not raise my son to be a soldier.

Think *for yourself*

1 Use a dictionary to find the meaning of 'arbitrate'. What does 'arbitrate their quarrels' mean?

2 What kind of women would this song have appealed to?

3 Why do you think many women were opposed to conscription?

4 Why do you think Hughes arranged special 'women only' rallies?

THE HISTORIAN AT WORK

Posters and Propaganda

Figure 2.31

Figure 2.32

Figure 2.33
Your turn next!

Figures 2.31 and 2.32 are posters that were produced during the conscription campaign. Figure 2.33 is a cartoon drawn by the famous artist Norman Lindsay.

1 Do you think the people who produced the poster in Figure. 2.31 were in favour of the Queen's and Women's Peace Army? Why? Would members of the Peace Army have approved of the poster in Figure 2.32? Why?

2 Which of the two posters do you think Prime Minister Hughes would have approved of? Why?

3 What kind of people do you think each of the posters was designed to appeal to?

4 Do you think either of these posters would have been successful in changing people's minds about the issue of conscription? Discuss.

5 Look again at the song on page 35. In what way is the song's message similar to the message in Figure 2.32?

6 Examine the cartoon in Figure 2.33. It was intended to make people believe something. In two or three sentences explain what the cartoonist is trying to make people believe. Explain what each of the three figures represents.

7 Do you think that the artist Norman Lindsay was in favour of or against conscription?

8 If you do not already know, find out what the word 'propaganda' means. Is the cartoon in Figure 2.33 an example of propaganda? Are the two posters examples of propaganda? Look back through this chapter and see if you can find any other pictures, or words, that could be called propaganda.

Think *for yourself*

1 Australian soldiers voted in the conscription referendum. Here are the results:
YES (supported conscription) 72 399
NO (opposed conscription) 58 894

Year	Time	Number of volunteers
1914	Aug–Dec	52 500
1915	Jan–June	56 750
1915	July–Dec	109 000
1916	Jan–June	83 250
1916	July–Dec	41 000
1917	Jan–June	27 250
1917	July–Dec	17 750
1918	Jan–June	16 000
1918	July–Nov	13 000

Table 2.1
Figures for volunteers, 1914–18

a Why do you think most Australian soldiers supported conscription?
b Imagine that you were a soldier who voted YES. Explain why you voted the way you did.
c Imagine that you were a soldier who voted NO. Explain why you voted the way you did.

2 Look at Table 2.1 which shows how many Australians volunteered to join the army between 1914 and 1918. Draw a column graph based on these figures. One centimetre or one line of your page should stand for 10 000 volunteers. On the base line one centimetre can stand for six months. Colour the highest column red. Which period is it? Now answer these questions:
a Which year had the most volunteers?
b Which year had the fewest volunteers?
c The Gallipoli campaign was between April and December 1915. Do you think this had any effect on the number of volunteers that year?
d What was the total number of volunteers?
e In one six-month period the number of volunteers fell by over 40 000. Which period was it? Can you suggest why this might have happened? How did the prime minister try to make up for the fall in the number of volunteers?
f Why are there no figures for July 1914? Can you guess why there are none for December 1918?

How the war ended

By 1917 the war in Europe had been bogged down in the mud of the trenches for over two and a half years. It seemed as though it would go on forever. But in 1917 two important events happened which changed the war.

The USA joined the war on the side of Britain and her allies. Before 1917, the USA had lent Britain over $2.25 million and had sent many supplies to help Britain. But in 1917 German submarines began attacking passenger and cargo ships, as well as warships. It was this 'unrestricted submarine warfare' that convinced the USA that it should join the war. Over 1 million American soldiers were sent to Europe. Both sides knew that the USA could provide many more millions of men as well as guns and supplies.

There was a revolution in Russia in 1917. As a result a communist state was set up. The new leader, Lenin, wanted to change Russia quickly. He could not afford to keep Russian troops fighting in Europe while he was strengthening his own power in Russia. So in 1918 Russia signed a treaty with Germany and left the war.

Germany was now free to put all its efforts into winning on the Western Front. But this effort failed and the German troops were pushed back out of France. Germany's allies, Austria-Hungary and Turkey, could not support Germany. By 1918 these countries had been badly weakened. They could no longer continue with the war effort. Germany and its allies had to accept defeat.

Figure 2.34
Coming home

In November 1918 fighting stopped and a truce or **armistice** was signed. In Australia (and in other countries on the winning side) it was a time of wild excitement. Crowds gathered in the streets, dancing, drinking, singing and cheering. In Melbourne the mob derailed a tram and caused it to crash through an office window.

Making the peace

When fighting stopped in 1918, it was clear that the world would never be the same again. The leaders of the winning countries met in Versailles, just outside Paris in France. But they found it hard to agree about what they wanted to demand from Germany.

Figure 2.35
These children were dressed up in 1918 to celebrate the end of the war. Why does one of them carry an American flag? Compare these children with the children in Figure 1.15. In what ways are they alike? How are they different?

Figure 2.36
Three different ideas about the peace treaty

The Treaty of Versailles, which Germany had to sign, was a compromise. Parts of it suited each country, but nobody was completely satisfied with it. Here are some of the results of the treaty:

- Germany lost 13 per cent of its land in Europe and all its colonies.
- Germany had to pay for the war.
- Germany could not build tanks, warships or aeroplanes. It was allowed only six ships in its navy and 100 000 men in its army.
- Germany had to take the blame for starting the war.
- New countries were formed in Europe out of the old German empire. Other treaties broke up the empires of Austria-Hungary and Turkey.
- A League of Nations was set up to try to stop wars from happening. Nations agreed to meet and discuss their problems instead of fighting about them.

How the war changed Australia

Conscription split the Labor Party. There was no Labor Party government for another thirteen years.

Hughes went to the peace conference at Versailles to represent Australia. Australia was given control of the German colony in New Guinea.

About 65 per cent of Australia's soldiers were either killed, wounded or taken prisoner in the war. Those who came back often found it hard to settle down.

New industries grew up during the war. The BHP steelworks in Newcastle was opened in 1915.

Government took greater control of industry and banking. A government shipping line was set up.

Ending of Australia's isolation. Planes and radios brought Australia closer to the rest of the world.

Think *for yourself*

All cities and most towns have a war memorial. Do you know where you local war memorial is? Visit the memorial and find out the following.

1. Was the memorial built before the First World War? How can you tell?
2. Write down the main inscription (message) on the war memorial.
3. Does the memorial list the names of people from your area who died in the First World War? Are some surnames listed more than once? What does this mean?
4. Draw a picture of your local war memorial in your history book.
5. Some war memorials have an inscription to 'The Unknown Soldier'. What does this mean? Why is 'The Unknown Soldier' remembered?
6. In some places there are memorial swimming pools or libraries. Do you think it is better to remember the dead through things such as this or in statues and stone memorials? Why?

Figure 2.37
Some results of the First World War

KNOW the chapter

1 The words below have been used in this chapter. From the list of words, choose one to match each explanation

assassination alliance
patriotism volunteer
conscription armistice
referendum ultimatum

a A truce between enemy countries
b The murder of an important or well-known person
c Forcing people to join the army
d Group of countries that join together to support each other
e Person who joins the army without being forced to
f A list of demands sent by one country to another
g Asking the people in a country what they think about a suggested change
h Love of one's country.

2 Place these events in the right order.
— First conscription referendum in Australia
— Armistice
— USA enters the war
— Assassination of Franz Ferdinand
— Versailles Peace Treaty
— Austria-Hungary declares war on Serbia
— Anzacs land at Gallipoli

3 Name the countries referred to in the following:
a declared war on Serbia on 28 July 1914
b was allied with Italy and Austria-Hungary in the Triple Alliance
c German troops marched through this country in 1914 on their way to France
d fought against the Anzacs at Gallipoli
e some of this country's soldiers wore emu feathers in their hats
f joined the war in 1917
g experienced a revolution in 1917 and left the war the year after
h its spokesman at the peace talks after the war was Clemenceau
i had to take the blame for starting the war
j after the war gained control of the German colony in New Guinea.

4 Use the clues below to fill in the word puzzle. You can find all the words you need in Harry Davis' story about Gallipoli.
a The Anzacs were trained here.
b At Gallipoli the Anzacs showed great __________ and determination.
c The Gallipoli peninsula juts out into the __________
d The Turks fired at the Anzacs from the __________
e A fierce battle happened here.
f The Gallipoli campaign was fought so that __________ could be sent to Russia.
g The commander of the Anzacs.
h Dysentery was one of the diseases caused by __________
i After eight months, boats took men from Gallipoli to __________ in the harbour.

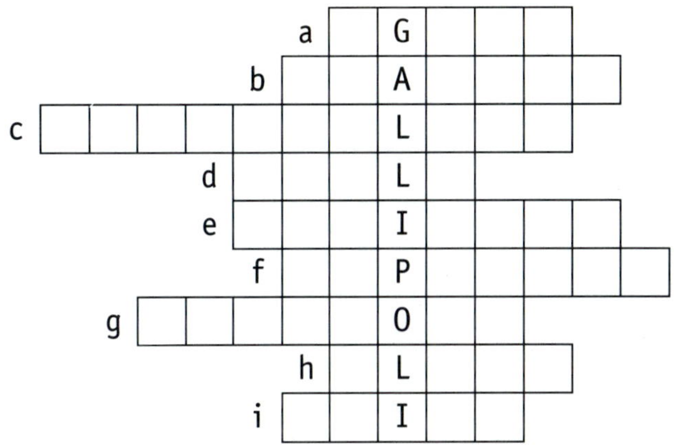

Fig. 2.38
This school at Condobolin built memorial gates after the First World War. Eighty-one ex-pupils and teachers fought for Australia. Ten ex-pupils and one teacher were killed.

THE HISTORIAN AT WORK

Roy Whitelaw was a young Australian who joined the First AIF in 1915. Between October 1915 and the end of the war, he wrote many letters to his family in Melbourne. Here are extracts from three of those letters.

8th October 1917

Dear Everybody,

Just a few lines with this mail, with a promise of a much longer letter next week.

We have been very busy the last few weeks, on the go all day and most of the night, sometimes doing seventeen to eighteen hours without a spell …

Thought the Somme was hard enough last year, but it's child's play compared with this lot … Why, the other day I was detailed to take two lorries loaded with bombs as near to the trenches as possible, along the road we are fighting for. It was some trip believe me, we only got as far as the field guns for ten lorries were blown up and burning on the road in front of us … This was at a place called Hooge along the Menin Road.

I will try and give you an idea of what my job is.

First of all we are parked near Poperinghe (which Fritz bombs nearly every night), from there we receive orders for lorries to proceed to railhead Ypres and convey ammunition to advanced dumps. At railhead there may be 120 to 150 lorries, here we take over the ammunition from the R.O.O. in charge of the train. I go on the first lorry to whichever dump we may be delivering to, of course this is early in the morning.

On arriving at the dump I have to report to the officer in charge, get five or six lorries in, seeing that they keep a fair distance apart in case a shell should get one of them. Then my work starts for I have to check the number of rounds, the make and size, for some are eighteen pounders and others are four and a half.

I keep going at the dump till the 150 or perhaps 200 lorries are finished which is usually 10 or 11 p.m. This seems a long while … but … the shells are in boxes which must be opened, shells taken out, and the boxes … have to be returned empty to railhead. If we were to leave the boxes Fritz would see them from his balloons and soon blow dump, lorries and everything up …

5th November 1917

My Dear 'Folks at Home'

Expect this letter should arrive somewhere about Christmas at your end … Sincerely hope that fate decrees that this stunt will be finished with, and that we may be home to celebrate the occasion with you all next year, if not sooner.

We've been having rather a rough time of it this last few weeks … Still we have the satisfaction of knowing we are doing our share of helping and enduring in this testing of strength against Fritz, but at what a price. Gee! It would break your heart to see the slaughter and suffering, and we have had our share of both.

Only last Saturday I was detailed in charge of seven lorries to convey a working party up as near to the lines as possible, but owing to the shell holes on the road, one never knows if he can get as far as the detail orders. Anyway, after packing them up and proceeding on our way (it was about 5 a.m.) we reached this point. Just daylight, and we were travelling very slowly on account of the horse and mule traffic. This is near where we worked one night a little while back with gas masks on, and gas shells plonking around the dump, quite a cheerful spot I can tell you. While we were crawling along, a Fritz plane came over fairly low, dropped a flare which lit everything up like day … He eventually caught sight of the dump for he dropped several big bombs and up she went—ammunition, men and mules. Talk about a bedlam, we could see mules and men running in all directions into boggy shell holes, in fact anywhere out of range of exploding shells.

Then it was our turn, for he caught sight of the lorries on the road. Over he came, my it's a funny, creepy feeling waiting for your numbers to go up. I ran along from the leading lorry to tell the working party to hop off and take cover when bang, bang, zip bang, four bombs on one side of the road, then bang and six more on the other side …

14th January 1918

Dear Old Dad,

... Things are much the same here, plenty of work and the usual slogging away at Fritz. Of course, it's winter just now, and with a vengeance, bitterly cold winds, snow and frost. The trouble is that every now and then it thaws which makes the roads ... practically impassable.

All M.T. traffic is closed, horse wagons are doing most of the work. This means a spell for us, but we would much rather have the frozen roads for everything is mud, mud and water.

I had a touch of trench feet last winter and, as it never troubled me during the summer, thought it had left me but sure enough it came on again. My toes are absolutely dead and when the blood begins to circulate, gee, it gives me hell. Still, our A.M.C. cpl. has it in hand and seems to be curing it.

At present I am living in a dug-out with my cpl., it is about twenty feet [6 metres] long by five feet [1.5 metres] wide, dug well into the earth and covered with bomb-proof iron and sand bags. We have made it very comfortable inside, just the two beds, fire drum and table, rats and mice are our only trouble ...

Well owing to censor etc., I must finish, but will write again next week ...

1 What country was Whitelaw in at the end of 1917 and the beginning of 1918? Where had he been a year before? (An atlas will help you to answer these questions.)

2 What job was Whitelaw doing at this stage of the war? Can you find any evidence that he was doing something different during the previous winter?

3 Why was Whitelaw's job an important one? Who relied on Whitelaw and the other people who were doing this job?

4 Whitelaw returned to Melbourne in 1918, but he was lucky not to have been killed or seriously wounded. List several ways in which he might easily have been killed.

5 Apart from enemy weapons, what other factors made life dangerous and unpleasant for Whitelaw and other soldiers in this part of the war?

6 Use evidence from these extracts and the picture in Figure 2.39 to suggest ways in which the fighting and conditions in this part of the war were similar to the fighting and conditions at Gallipoli. In what ways were they different? What weapons were used here that were not used in Gallipoli?

7 From the evidence in these extracts and in the picture in Figure 2.39, what role do you think animals played in this part of the war? Why do you think they were used?

8 Who would have read Whitelaw's letters before they were delivered to his family? Do you think this was necessary? Why?

9 Would it be true to say that Whitelaw had mixed feelings about the war? Write a couple of sentences describing his attitude to the war. Do you think that, on the whole, he was glad he had joined the army?

10 Explain the following words and terms that Whitelaw uses: Fritz, balloons, M.T. traffic, A.M.C. cpl.

Figure 2.39
This painting shows the town of Ypres during a battle that took place there in 1914

How people *lived* 1901–39

In the early 1900s motor cars were still a novelty. Only very well-off people could afford them. Public transport, too, was not nearly as well developed as it is today. Railways, for example, did not travel to suburbs that were a long way from the centres of Australia's capital cities.

It was not very convenient for people to travel long distances to work. People needed to live close to where they worked. Most factories were in the inner-city areas and the workers' houses were built close to them. These houses were usually single-storey terraces.

Figure 3.1
A row of nineteenth-century terraces

A roof over your head

In the city

Terraces (Figure 3.1) were part of most Australian cities before the First World War. Workers' terraces were tiny houses built almost on the street. Each terrace was only about 5 metres wide, and long rows of them were joined together. The front room, or parlour, was only used on special occasions. It was usually kept very clean and tidy, ready for visitors. There was no toilet in the house. It was in a wooden hut in the yard. Once or twice a week, council workers came to empty the pans.

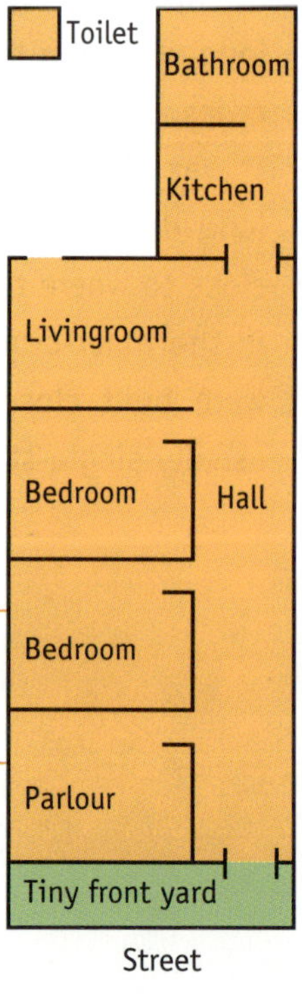

Figure 3.2
Plan of a worker's terrace

Richer people lived in two- or even three-storey terrace houses. The bedrooms were upstairs. In the 1920s and 1930s, blocks of flats were built in Sydney and Melbourne. They were usually three or four storeys high.

Think *for yourself*

1 What do you think the main disadvantages of living in a terrace house in the inner city would have been? What advantages would there have been?

2 The houses in Figure 3.3 were built in the 1980s. In what ways are they different?

3 If you live in a capital city, look in newspapers and find some advertisements for terrace houses for sale. Why have these houses become popular again? In what ways have they been changed since the early 1900s?

Figure 3.3
Townhouses at Macquarie Fields, NSW

Homes for the soldiers

There were 16 000 houses built between 1919 and 1921 by the War Service Homes Commission (Figure 3.4). This scheme was set up by the Australian government to provide cheap homes for ex-soldiers. The Commission built houses and sold them to soldiers. Each house was built on a separate block of land. In this way people were encouraged to move out of the inner city.

Figure 3.4
A house built in the period 1919–21

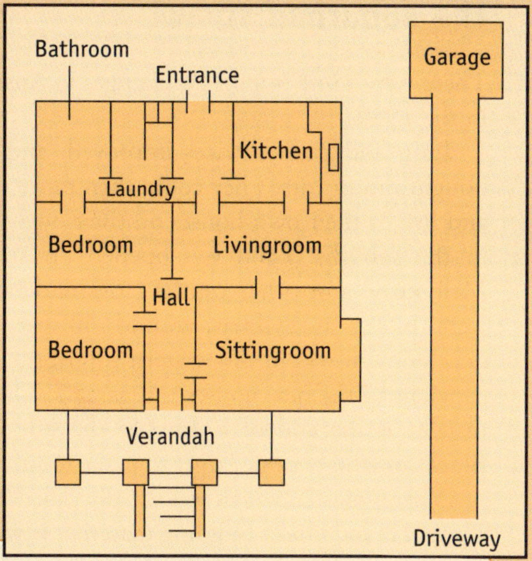

Figure 3.6
A typical house plan in the 1920s. How does it differ from the terrace house in Figure 3.2?

Figure 3.5
The lounge room of a War Service home in 1924

Figure 3.7
An advertisement for the newest kind of refrigerator in 1925. How does it differ from a modern refrigerator?

Think *for yourself*

1 Do you think the government should help ex-soldiers to buy houses? Why?

2 How did this War Service house (Figure 3.4) differ from the terrace houses in Figure 3.1?

3 Figure 3.5 shows the lounge room or sitting room of a War Service home in 1924. In what ways is this lounge room different from the lounge room of a modern house?

The suburban sprawl

There were some important changes in Australian houses in the 1920s.

Train and tram services improved, and some people bought motor cars. They could then move out of the city and live in their own houses on their own blocks of land in the suburbs. Land was opened up around Sydney, Melbourne and other capital cities and housing estates were built. In Sydney, around 40 per cent of this development was in the western suburbs.

Many of the new houses had garages. The garages were usually at the end of a drive at the side of the house. Blocks of land became larger to make room for the garage.

Fibrous plaster, which was usually called 'fibro', became a popular and cheap building material. It was invented in New Zealand and came to Australia in 1916. Houses could be built cheaply and quickly with this new material.

The new houses in the suburbs were bigger than terrace houses. The kitchen and bathroom were inside the house, they were not stuck on the back, although toilets were often still in the garden. In the 1920s and 1930s electricity was installed in many new houses.

Think *for yourself*

1 Draw a plan of your house. Is it similar to the plan of the suburban house in Figure 3.6? How is it different? When was your house built?

2 Most Australians live in single-storey houses. Can you think of some reasons to explain why?

Changing fashions

In the 1920s and 1930s there were changes in the way houses looked. These were some of the most popular styles.

Californian bungalow

This style was the most popular of all. The roof had two or three gables, and the front verandah or porch was supported by thick columns, which were sometimes covered with concrete or pebbles.

Spanish mission

In spite of its name, this style came from America. Architects thought that courtyards, balconies and big windows would suit Australia's climate. Most Spanish mission houses in Australia did not have courtyards and balconies. But they did have arches and columns, which were often painted white.

Figure 3.8
A Californian-style bungalow popular in 1920s and 1930s

Figure 3.9
Spanish mission style house

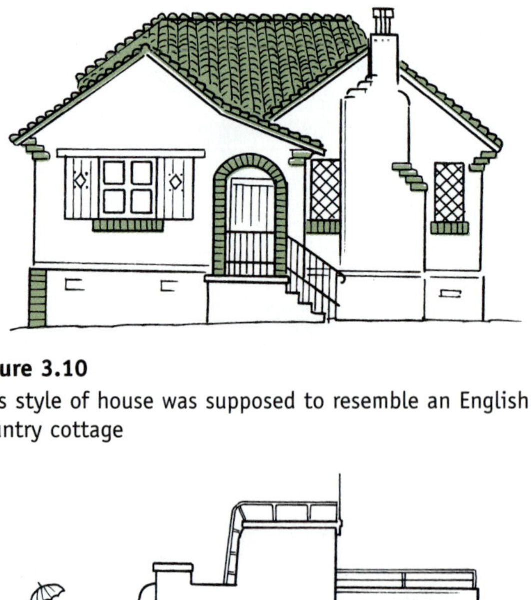

Figure 3.10
This style of house was supposed to resemble an English country cottage

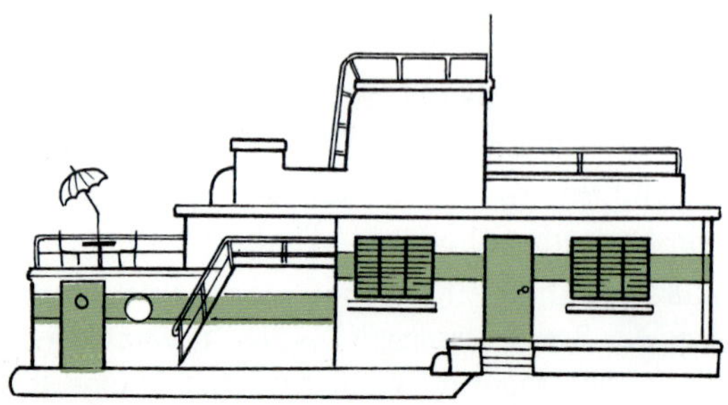

Figure 3.11
International-style house, 1930s

English cottage

These houses were supposed to look like English country cottages. Their owners often used shutters and patterned bricks to make the houses look quaint. Sometimes dark beams were used to give the houses an old-fashioned look.

International

This was also called the 'P & O style'. With their porthole windows, flat roofs and curved walls, the houses looked rather like the huge ocean liners of the 1930s. These were the most modern houses built between the wars. They were designed to get rid of all the frills and decorations of older houses. They used modern materials such as chrome, glass and metal.

Think *for yourself*

1 Do you think that any of these styles of houses are suited to the Australian climate? Why?
2 Why do you think that most Spanish mission style houses did not have courtyards and balconies?
3 Can you think of a reason why the Californian bungalow style was so popular in Australia?
4 Why would some people have wanted to live in houses that were like cottages in England?
5 Where did the 'P & O' style get its name?

School days, school days

Ideas about schools change. At different times people have different ideas about who should go to school and how long they should go for, about what they should learn and how they should be taught. Between 1900 and 1939 there were many changes in schools. But some things remained the same.

Think *for yourself*

1 Use a dictionary to find out what the subjects in this poem were about.

Ram it in, cram it in—
Children's heads are hollow!
Slam it in, jam it in,
Still there's more to follow:-
Hygiene and history,
Agronomic mystery,
Algebra, histology,
Latin, etymology,
Botany, geometry,
Greek and trigonometry—
Ram it in, cram it in,
The exam will follow.

Frank Lintaber, *An Examination Idyl*, 1893

2 Figure 3.12 shows what was considered to be an ideal classroom in the early 1900s. Look at the photograph carefully. How can you tell that it was posed for the camera?
3 Read these statements about schools before the Second World War.
   a Children were expected to learn a lot of facts.
   b Classrooms were overcrowded.
   c Exams were very important. Most people thought that the main job of a school was to prepare pupils to pass exams.

Use the poem and Figure 3.12 to find evidence for these statements. Think about your school. Using your school as evidence, would you say that the three statements are true today? In what ways have schools changed since the early 1900s?

Figure 3.12
Cleveland Street Public School, Sydney

What pupils learnt

Reading, writing and arithmetic were called the Three Rs. They were thought to be very important, and children spent at least half of each day learning and practising them. But there were other subjects as well, and some teachers tried to make them interesting.

Secondary schools

After 1911 different types of secondary schools were set up in NSW. To see how the system worked, look at Figure 3.15.

Many people thought that children should not be put into such tight 'boxes' at the age of eleven or twelve. Others thought that students should have more choice of subjects. Many believed that only the brightest children should be sent to secondary school. They thought that it was a waste of time and money to send everyone to secondary school.

Think *for yourself*

Look at Figure 3.13 carefully and answer the questions.

1 What subject do you think these children are learning?
2 Do you agree with the message on the blackboard? Why?
3 In the 1930s pupils in NSW were allowed to go on only three excursions a year. The Education Department believed that pupils would learn more quickly from a good textbook than by going on visits. What do you think?

Look at Figure 3.14 and answer these questions.

4 What subject do you think these girls are learning?
5 How is this scene different from a lesson in the Home Economics Department of your school? In what ways is it the same?
6 After 1911 'domestic science' schools were set up to train girls to look after a home. Do you think this was a good idea? Why?

Figure 3.13
Kurri Kurri Public School, 1910

Figure 3.14
Burwood Domestic Science School, 1930s

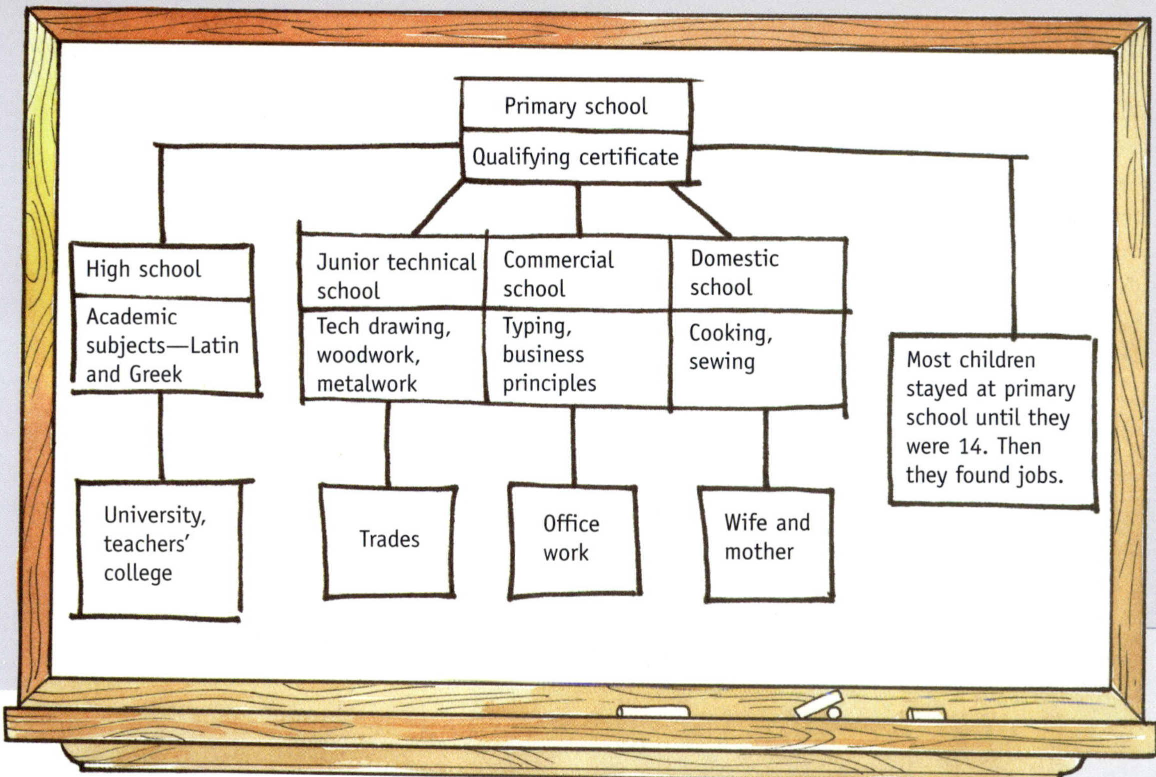

Figure 3.15
How the secondary-school system worked after 1911

Think *for yourself*

1 Draw a diagram to explain how your school system works. Do you think it is fairer than the 1911 system? Why?

2 Some people today think that secondary students should spend less time at school and more time working in the community. What do you think?

In the country

In 1901 a teacher was appointed to travel around south-western Queensland to give lessons to children in isolated areas. In 1908 a travelling school was set up in NSW to provide schooling for children in remote regions. The teacher travelled around the state and spent about one week in each place she or he visited. There were three travelling schools in NSW. The last one closed in 1949.

In 1914 the Victorian Department of Education pioneered the idea of sending out lessons by post to children who could not travel to a school. This was Australia's first correspondence school. The idea soon became popular and by 1922 there were correspondence schools in all Australian states.

Many country schools had only one teacher who had a class of children aged between 5 and 12. Country schools were often rough buildings with very little equipment. Even worse were the Provisional Schools that were set up when there were fewer than twenty children in an area. The school room and teacher's quarters were provided by the parents. They were often of a poor standard.

Figure 3.16
The travelling school. How long did schools like this last? What sort of problems would the teacher have faced? What sort of schooling do you think the pupils got?

Most Aborigines got little or no education in state schools. Some went to mission schools where they were taught to read and write. Because Aborigines were expected to become stockmen or servants, it did not seem worthwhile to teach them too much. White people did not bother to learn about Aboriginal customs or culture.

Figure 3.17
Chakola School, 1918. How many pupils went to this school? How many teachers would there have been? Do you think these children went on to high school? Why?

Teachers

Until 1905 many teachers were trained by the pupil-teacher system. Pupils who were reasonably clever were 'apprenticed' to experienced teachers. During the day they taught younger pupils. At night they studied so that they could pass exams and become 'qualified'. Teachers' colleges were later set up, but qualified teachers were in short supply until the 1930s.

Figure 3.18
Percentage of teachers in NSW, 1900–35

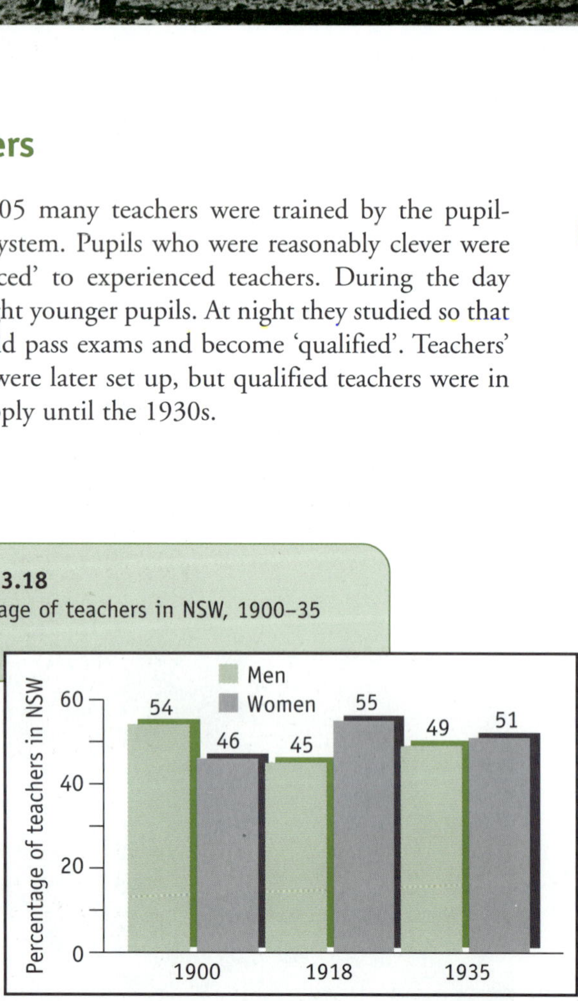

Think *for yourself*

The graph (Figure 3.18) shows the percentage of men and women teachers in 1900, 1918 and 1935. Use it to answer the following questions.

1 Insert the words 'men' and 'women' three times each to fill in the blanks.

In 1900 there were more __________ teachers than __________ teachers. But in 1918 there were more __________ than __________ . By 1935, although there were still more __________ than __________ , the numbers were almost equal.

2 Why do you think there were more women than men teachers in 1918? (Clue: look back to the section on 'Women in the war' in chapter 2.)

3 Why do you think the percentage of women teachers had fallen again by 1935?

THE HISTORIAN AT WORK

Earning a crust

Before the Second World War Australians earned their living in many different ways, just as Australians do today. The extracts below tell about the work done by four different Australians. Read them carefully, look at the pictures and answer the questions about each one.

A farmer's wife in 1902

> Inside the cottage, the house-mother began work before the sun rose. She milked, fed calves, pigs, fowls, got breakfast consisting of cold salt beef, porridge, and tea; washed up, sent children to school, carried water in kerosene tins from the dam for the day's use, set the house in order, made bread, scrubbed or washed, for washing-day must be frequent when the supply of clothes is small. The washing, too, must be done outside in the broiling sun, the clothes boiling in ever-useful kerosene tins. Dinner must be prepared—mutton, potatoes, rice, and tea. Then she must help outside with planting potatoes, or with finding the pigs that have escaped into the scrub. Then milking time, then tea time—cold beef, bread and butter, tea, but if times are bad, neither butter nor beef, merely bread, dripping, and tea. After tea, clothes to make, or maize to shell, or potatoes to cut for the morrow's planting …

1 What kind of farming is carried on at the farm described in this extract?
2 From the description and Figure 3.19, would you say that the farm is doing well or badly? Why?
3 Which jobs in this extract would not need to be done on most farms today?
4 This woman had a very hard life. Which of the jobs that she had to do would be done by machines today? Which jobs would still have to be done by hand?
5 Look at Figure 3.19. If you were not told the date when it was taken, how would you be able to tell that it is an old photograph?

A maid in 1911

Maids worked in people's homes and in hotels and boarding houses. There were 154 000 servants in Australia in 1911. Most of them were aged between fifteen and twenty-four.

> At two or three places that I have been in, you work from half past six in the morning till half past four in the afternoon without ceasing. There was a boarding house. I was a waitress there … I would have half an hour to get dressed. Then I would have to go upstairs, lay five tables, wait on the tables, wash up and clean knives, and then finish all up, and then stop on till ten o'clock answering the telephone or the door … We had three nights in the week off; after I had finished washing up and cleaning the knives and putting the gas out it would be half past seven … Then we had every second Sunday and every second Saturday off. I got my Sunday afternoon off; but after finishing waiting at table, cleaning knives and leaving everything ready for tea, it would be half past three.

Figure 3.19
The farmer's wife had a hard life in 1902

Figure 3.20
Maids spent a lot of time cleaning and polishing silver. Do you think their clothes were suitable for the type of work they did?

1 What was a boarding house? The young woman who told this story was a waitress. What jobs did she have to do?
2 What other kinds of people would have been employed in boarding houses?
3 Use the evidence you can find in this extract to work out how many hours a week this waitress worked.
4 Gas is mentioned in this extract. What do you think it was used for? Would this boarding house have had electricity? (Clue: look back to the section called 'In the city' in this chapter.)
5 What aspects of the maid's working conditions would not be tolerated by workers today? Which aspects of their jobs are no longer necessary today?

A factory worker in 1911

I went to work at a well-known factory in the city, making overcoats from 8 o'clock in the morning until 5.30 at night. After hours I took work home, and kept at it until my eyes wouldn't hold up. The most I could earn was £1 in any week. I used to bring home a dozen blouses, and finish them in six or seven nights, working up till 12 o'clock. For that I received 3s, and if it hadn't been for the help of mother I couldn't have earned that much. And when they found that I was taking £1 in a week from their till, they stopped me on piece work and gave me a wage of 17s. 6d. a week.

I was one of a team of four making ladies jackets, which were sold in the shop at £2 10s. and £2 15s. each. The four of us, working till we nearly dropped dead, could finish a dozen a week. For that the team between them received £2 2s …

Figure 3.21
A rouseabout

1 Use the evidence in this extract to work out how many hours this girl worked each day in the factory. How many hours a week would you estimate she worked at home?
2 How much did she earn a week when she was making overcoats during the day and blouses at night?
3 Did she earn more or less when she was part of the team making ladies' jackets?
4 How much profit did the employer make in a week if he sold a dozen jackets at £2 10s each?
5 Do you think this worker was fairly treated by her employer? Why?

A rouseabout in 1941

He rose at 6 a.m. and fed the horses … had breakfast, 'brushed up' and harnessed the team … which were then handed over to the boss. He then harnessed the pony and rounded up the cows from whichever paddock they were grazing, sometimes two miles away, milked them, separated the milk, and took the cows to their paddock again. He then returned to the homestead, in time to take 'lunch' (mid-morning lunch) out to the men, either stayed with them until dinner time, taking a turn with the team, or did some odd job—staining a fence or cutting thistles.

After mid-day dinner he had a snooze until afternoon lunch, or sometimes chopped a bit of wood for the missus; after taking out the men's lunch he would round up the cows. After the cows had been turned out again, it was time to unharness the team when the men returned.

1 From reading this extract, how would you described what a rouseabout was?
2 How would you describe the place where the rouseabout worked? Is it larger or smaller than the one described in 'A farmer's wife in 1902'? How do you know?
3 What do you think the homestead would be like compared to the building in Figure 3.19?
4 Who was the 'missus'? Do you think her life would have been harder or easier than the life of the farmer's wife?
5 Do you think the rouseabout had to work as hard as the farmer's wife? Explain your answer.
6 Are there jobs that people do today that are similar to the job done by the rouseabout? What are they? How are they similar to and in what ways are they different from the rouseabout's job?

New servants

In 1901 one Australian worker in every eight was a servant of one kind or another. But between then and the end of the 1930s, two new servants took over much of the work that had been done in the past by maids, housewives, cooks and laundry workers. The new servants were gas and electricity.

Gas came to Sydney's homes in the 1890s. At first only rich people could afford it. They used gas for lighting their homes, for heating water and for cooking. Gas was cleaner than candles and lamps. It did not make soot and it was cooler than the big fuel stoves that were kept going all day. A gas stove did not need as much cleaning as a fuel stove. Families with a gas stove or heater did not have to spend hours chopping wood and carrying it into the house.

Electricity was not used in homes until the 1920s. By 1929 over half of Sydney's houses were connected to the electricity supply. Electric lighting was fashionable. People saved up to buy all kinds of electrical appliances such as jugs, radios, irons and toasters. Even more useful were electric refrigerators and washing machines. With all these appliances, a woman had to spend less time on household chores.

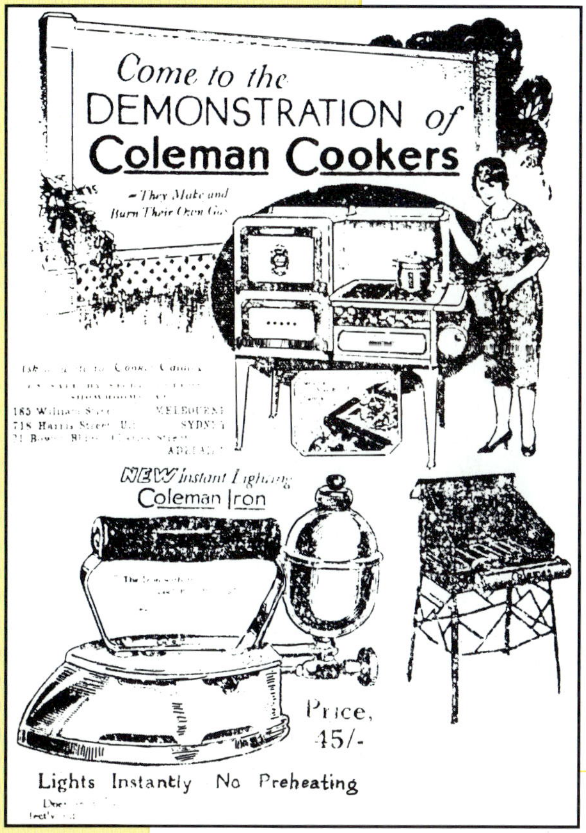

Figure 3.23
An advertisement for gas appliances in the 1930s. What appliances are advertised here? How did gas make these things easier to use?

Figure 3.22
A modern electric kitchen of the 1930s looked like this. How many electric appliances can you see?

Fun and games

Figure 3.24
Swimming costumes in 1907

Swimming and surfing have always been popular in Australia. Women on the beach were usually well covered, but some had begun to wear the then fashionable 'neck-to-knee' costume. Many people thought that these costumes exposed too much of a woman's body.

> What we saw … was disgusting! Some of these surf-bathers are nothing but exhibitionists … Women are often worse than the men, putting on light gauzy material that clings when wet too much to be decent.
>
> Mayor of Waverley, after inspecting swimmers at Bondi Beach, 1907

Radio came to Australia in the 1920s. The first sets were large and bulky, and had large, bell-shaped loudspeakers. At first, radio reception was poor and crackly. By 1939, 1 million Australians had radio sets. Serials and quiz shows were popular.

Australia's first moving pictures were made early in the 1900s. They were silent films accompanied by a pianist who played music to suit what was happening in the film. More than 250 silent films were made in Australia. 'The talkies' came in the 1930s. Most of the films that Australians went to see came from the USA. Some films, however, were made in Australia. Between 1931 and 1940 Cinesound, an Australian company, made seventeen talking films.

Dancing was popular. At family gatherings the carpet was rolled back and people danced to the music of a piano or, perhaps, a gramophone. Many dances were held in public halls and ballrooms. In the 1920s two new dances came from the USA. They were the tango and the charleston. These dances were considered very daring.

> They obey the (rule) that no liquor must be brought into the hall; but they keep the taxi outside for the evening, and there is a secret hoard of liquor in the taxi, to be drunk between dances … These taxis and many private cars are nothing else than private drinking bars.
>
> *Australian Christian World*, 1924

Figure 3.25
Radio came to Australia in the 1920s

Figure 3.26
Dancing was very popular in the 1920s

Figure 3.27
Poster for an early Australian Cinesound film

Terrible Death Dive—Page 3

163 PHILLIP STREET

CITY FORECAST: Warm and Sultry

CHAMPION TOBACCO

DAILY TELEGRAPH PICTORIAL

NET SALES EXCEED 141,048 DAILY

Reckitts Blue — for pure white linen

No. 15,624 SYDNEY: TUESDAY, JANUARY 7, 1930—28 PAGES ONE PENNY

DON BRADMAN, BREAKER OF WORLD'S CRICKET RECORDS

HOW DON BRADMAN, CRICKET HERO, WAS ACCLAIMED by Queenslanders and the Cricket Ground crowd yesterday after his amazing innings of 452, not out. It broke the world's record highest score of 437, made by Ponsford against Queensland in December, 1927. Curiously enough it was in December, 1927 that Bradman, the Bowral youth, played his first Sheffield Shield match. He scored 118 in his initial appearance in first-class cricket, and has since become Australia's most prolific and forceful run-getter. Thirteen centuries is his record in first-class cricket, and there is no saying what new records he will create before 1930 draws to a close.

Figure 3.28
The great Donald Bradman

Don Bradman was the hero of Australian cricket lovers. Between 1928 and 1948 he played in fifty-two test matches. Bradman scored 6996 runs, including twenty-nine centuries. In the 1932–33 cricket season, English bowlers used a new kind of speed bowling to try and stop Bradman from getting so many runs. This was called bodyline bowling.

> If we don't beat you, we'll knock your bloody heads off.
>
> Bill Voce, English fast bowler

Phar Lap, the horse that won the 1930 Melbourne Cup, was the idol of many Australians. Phar Lap cost £160. He won over £66 000. Phar Lap won thirty-nine races out of the fifty-three he ran.

Fig. 3.29
The great Australian racehorse of 1930, Phar Lap

Fun and games quiz

Match each name in column A with the description in column B that best suits it. Some of them have been mentioned in this section. To answer the others, you may have to do some research in the library.

A	B
Don Bradman	wrote *The Songs of a Sentimental Bloke,* one of the most popular books of the 1920s
Andrew ('Boy') Charlton	also called 'The Red Terror', won the 1930 Melbourne Cup
Phar Lap	has been a popular cartoon character since the 1920s
C J Dennis	won five Olympic gold medals for swimming between 1924 and 1932
Errol Flynn	was considered the world's greatest billiards player of his time
Ken Hall	was Australia's 'Queen of Opera'
Annette Kellerman	scored 6996 runs in test cricket
Walter Lindrum	was a well-known long-distance swimmer and was arrested in 1910 for wearing a one-piece swimming costume
Norman Lindsay	also called 'Our Glad', was a popular musical comedy star
Ginger Meggs	was an artist and writer who published *The Magic Pudding* in 1918
Nellie Melba	produced films for the Cinesound company
Gladys Moncrieff	was an Australian actor who became successful in Hollywood

In sickness and in health

Plagues and epidemics

Bubonic plague broke out in Sydney in 1900. It soon spread to other states. In the next seven months, 300 people caught the disease. One hundred of these people died. The disease came to Australia on ships from other countries, so the area around Sydney's docks was quarantined. People could not move in or out of the area. The plague was spread by rats so the government offered to pay for each rat that was caught. This was called the rat bounty. Some men who had no other work became rat catchers. You can see from Figure 3.30 how successful they were.

Figure 3.30
A day's catch. What sort of people do you think became rat catchers?

A much worse epidemic broke out in January 1919. This time the disease was a kind of influenza. It was called Spanish influenza and killed millions of people throughout the world. Spanish influenza was brought to Australia by soldiers who came back from the First World War. Between 1919 and 1920 it killed more than 11 500 Australians. Fortunately, the government was prepared for the epidemic and was able to take steps to stop the disease from spreading. Otherwise many thousands more would have died.

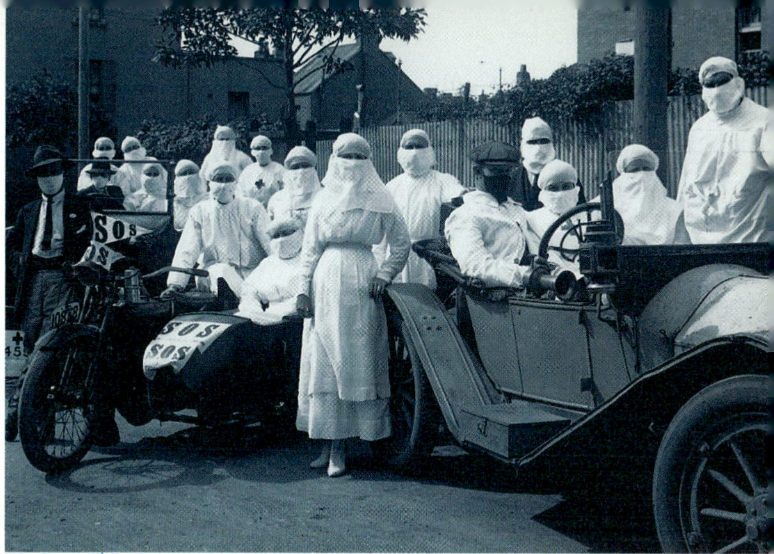

Figure 3.31
This photo was taken in 1919. Why are the people wearing masks? What sort of job do you think these people had?

Because influenza was spread from one person to another, the government tried to stop people from gathering in groups. In NSW, schools, libraries and billiard rooms were closed, and horse races were stopped. At first, churches were closed too. When they were reopened people had to sit a metre away from each other. Shops could stay open but they were not allowed to have bargain sales. Can you think why? Everyone was supposed to wear a mask when they were out of their homes.

Killer diseases

In 1901 the biggest killer disease in Australia was tuberculosis or TB. In that year ninety-four out of every 100 000 Australians died of TB. By 1940, thirty-six people in every 100 000 died of TB. Today, because we have found drugs to cure the disease, only one person in every 100 000 dies of TB.

In the early years of this century many young children died of diseases. Many of them died from an illness called gastroenteritis. This was caused by bad food and infected milk. Other children were killed by diseases such as diphtheria, whooping cough, polio and pneumonia. Many of these diseases hardly ever occur today.

Doctors and nurses

Before the 1890s people did not know about germs. They did not understand what caused diseases. They did not realise how important it was to have clean houses, clean hospitals and clean cities. Even when these things were known, it was often hard to change people's ways.

The First World War made quite a lot of difference. New vaccines were developed to help stop diseases from spreading. Soldiers were given medical examinations and check-ups. Doctors became better at doing operations. But after the war, they still knew very little about how to cure common diseases—the ones that killed thousands of people at home.

Many people looked down on the nurses. They wondered why girls from 'good' homes wanted to spend their lives looking after those who were sick. Nurses usually worked for long hours in terrible conditions. They got very little pay for their work. But during the First World War, nurses showed how important their work was. Slowly their conditions began to improve. They received better training too. After 1925 nurses in NSW had to pass exams and be registered before they could work.

Quacks and fakes

Because many doctors did not really know how to cure diseases, people often turned to false doctors or 'quacks'. Quacks were really 'con' men who sold all kinds of products. Some of these products were supposed to cure diseases. Others were supposed to improve the way people looked. Newspapers and magazines were full of advertisements for products such as 'Dr Williams' Pink Pills for Pale People', 'Bile Beans' or 'Clarke's World Famed Blood Mixture'. Many of these mixtures and pills were made from cheap alcohol. Some were just coloured syrup. 'Cigares de Joy', which were advertised as a cure for asthma, were made from marijuana!

Figure 3.33
An early advertisement for milk. Although milk may have been safe when it left the farm, much of it was infected by the time it was bought from the milkman.

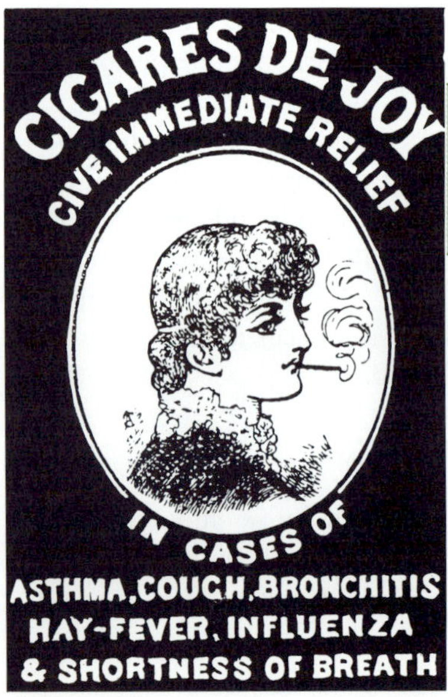

Figure 3.32
An early advertisement for marijuana.

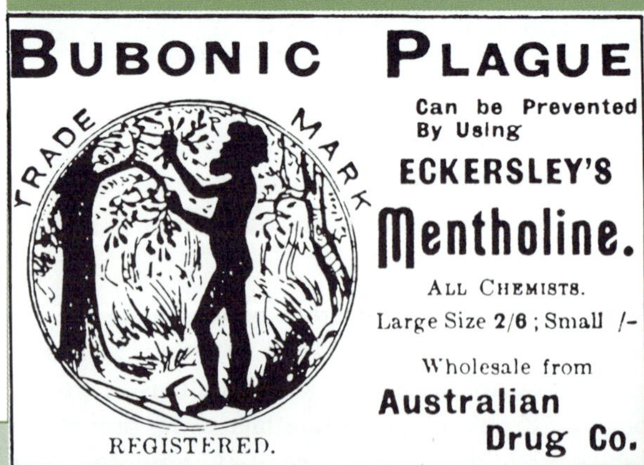

Figure 3.34
What really caused bubonic plague? Could it be prevented by medicines such as the one advertised here?

Quacks claimed that their products could cure all kinds of diseases and problems, from bubonic plague to pimples. Many people would have been a lot healthier if they had used the money they spent on quack medicines to buy fresh fruit and vegetables. But vitamins were not discovered until after the First World War, and people did not realise how important these foods were.

Figure 3.35
Australian slums. In what ways were buildings such as these unhealthy places to live in?

Public health

Slums such as in Figure 3.35 were part of every city. Today people realise that dirty streets and overcrowded houses that have no sewerage or proper water supply help to cause and spread disease. But at the beginning of the century there were not many people who cared about these things. Even when laws were made to clean up the cities, it was hard to make people obey them.

But things slowly improved. Governments became concerned about the health of children. A program was started to teach parents how to take better care of their babies. By 1939 there were over 200 Infant Welfare Centres in NSW. Doctors and nurses also started to visit schools to check the health of pupils. Often they were horrified at what they found. By the end of the 1930s governments were spending more money on health.

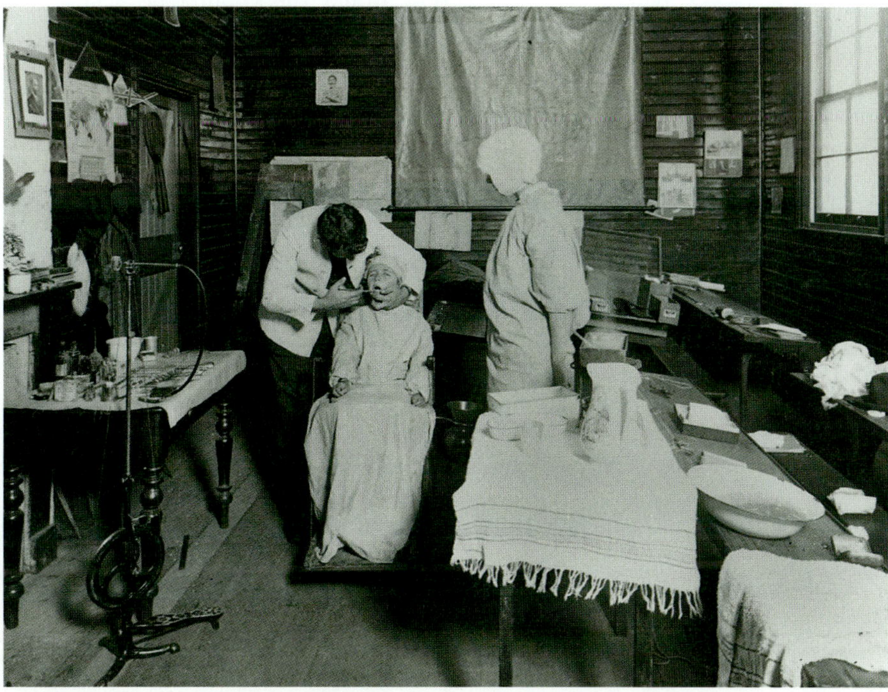

Figure 3.36
The school dentist comes to Budgee Budgee school, near Mudgee. Where did he set up his surgery? How did visits such as this help children's health?

Think *for yourself*

1 Look at these facts and answer the questions below.
- — in 1880, 120 babies out of every 1000 died before they were 1 year old
- — in 1910, 70 babies out of every 1000 died before they were 1 year old
- — in 1980, 16 babies out of every 1000 died before they were 1 year old.

a From what you have read in this section, explain why so many babies died in 1880 and 1910.

b Complete this sentence:
These figures show that **infant mortality** has (risen/fallen) in the last hundred years.

2 If you were a quack doctor, how would you go about advertising your medicine today? Design an advertisement that you think would encourage people to buy it.

3 After the First World War immunisation became more common.

a What does 'immunised' mean?

b What diseases are most Australians immunised against today?

c How has immunisation helped to improve the health of Australians?

4 Before the Second World War, some diseases were caused by bad food and infected milk. Why is milk safe to drink today?

5 The diseases that killed people in 1910 do not usually kill people today. Why not? Which diseases do kill people in the 1990s? Can you suggest why?

6 People in the outback benefited from a new medical service that started in 1928. It still exists today. Can you guess what it was? Use an encyclopaedia to check whether you were right.

On the move

In 1900 Australians could travel in many different ways. By the end of the 1930s new ways of getting from place to place had been developed.

Think *for yourself*

1 In what areas would camel trains have been used? What sort of goods do you think they would have carried?

2 Imagine that you were a busy country doctor. How would you have travelled in 1900? How would you have travelled in 1939?

3 In the 1920s, Sydney's train system was changed from steam to electricity. Electricity was cleaner and cheaper than steam. How do you think this change influenced the growth of Sydney? (Clue: look back to the section called 'The suburban sprawl' in this chapter.)

4 How would the coming of a railway line have changed life in a country town?

5 Sydney's ferries were especially important before the 1930s. Can you guess why?

6 Air travel was particularly important to country people. Think of some reasons why.

The horseless carriage

In the early 1900s people who could afford their own transport travelled in horse-drawn buggies. People today complain about how much it costs to run a car. But in those days it was not cheap to run a horse and buggy. The horse had to be stabled, fed, shod and groomed. Harness equipment had to be bought. If a person had more than one horse, he or she usually employed a stable boy to look after them.

Figure 3.37
Ways of travelling in Australia in 1900

Figure 3.38
Ways of travelling in Australia by the end of the 1930s

Figure 3.39
Bondi in the 1920s. How did cars change the way Australians spent their leisure time?

In 1900, cities and towns had water troughs, hitching rails and manure collectors. The horse was part of everyday life. But by 1930 the car was to become as common a sight as the horse was in 1900.

The first car was brought to Australia in 1897. Cars were considered a novelty. Rich people showed off by taking their friends on short car trips. There were no service stations and petrol was sold by chemists and grocers. Looking after a car was hard work. They had to be cranked to start them. Roads were often just rough tracks and the rides were bumpy and dangerous. Breakdowns were always likely and there were almost no spare parts. Car owners had to learn to be mechanics or employ a chauffeur who could fix the car as well as drive it.

Australians had started making cars soon after cars were invented. Colonel Harley Tarrant built one of Australia's first successful cars in 1901. While it was being tested, a mechanic rode behind on a bicycle so that he could do repairs on the spot. The car's first road test was made at night so that the noise it made would not disturb horses.

Besides making cars, Tarrant was also an agent for overseas car makers. He soon realised that he could make more money by bringing cars from overseas or by bringing engines from overseas and only building the bodies in Australia.

Before the First World War, cars were expensive. Only one Australian in every 900 owned a car in 1914. But in 1909 in the USA, Henry Ford made a new, cheaper car. It was called the T Model Ford. The price and design of this car suited Australian conditions. In 1917, 10 000 T Model Fords were bought to Australia. In 1925 the Ford company set up a factory at Geelong to assemble T Models in Australia.

Figure 3.40
The early days of motoring were not always a pleasure. In 1924, 400 people died in car accidents in Australia. In 1939, there were 1400 deaths.

Figure 3.41
The Tarrant Motor Company published this advertisement in 1909. Was it for Australian-made cars or for cars brought to Australia from overseas?

Figure 3.42
Fashionable clothes for motoring in 1909

Other Australian companies tried to cash in on the success of the T Model Fords by building a cheap Australian car. Some of these cars had strange names such as 'Roo', 'Wege', 'Eco' and 'Bateup'. The most successful early Australian car was the 'Australian Six'. This car was designed by Louis Chevrolet, an American engineer. It was put together at a factory in Sydney. Three-quarters of the car's parts were made in Australia. The Australian Six was produced between 1919 and 1926.

Think *for yourself*

1 Figure 3.42 shows the latest in motoring clothes in 1909.
   a Why did motorists need to wear such warm clothes?
   b Why were the goggles needed?
2 Look at the drawings of carriages and early cars in Figure 3.43. Use them to finish this sentence: The shape of early cars __________

Figure 3.43
From horse-drawn carriages (above) to early cars (below)

In and out of fashion

In 1901 Australians copied the kind of clothes that were being worn in England. They were not at all suitable for our warm climate. They were not comfortable either. Figure 3.44 shows what a well-dressed couple in 1901 would have looked like.

Why were such clothes not suitable for Australia? Why were they uncomfortable? Under her dress the woman would have worn layers of underclothes. Next to her skin she would have worn a corset stiffened with whalebone or steel. This pushed her waist in to make it fashionable. Figure 3.45 shows a corset. What was it stiffened with?

Figure 3.44
A well-dressed couple in 1901

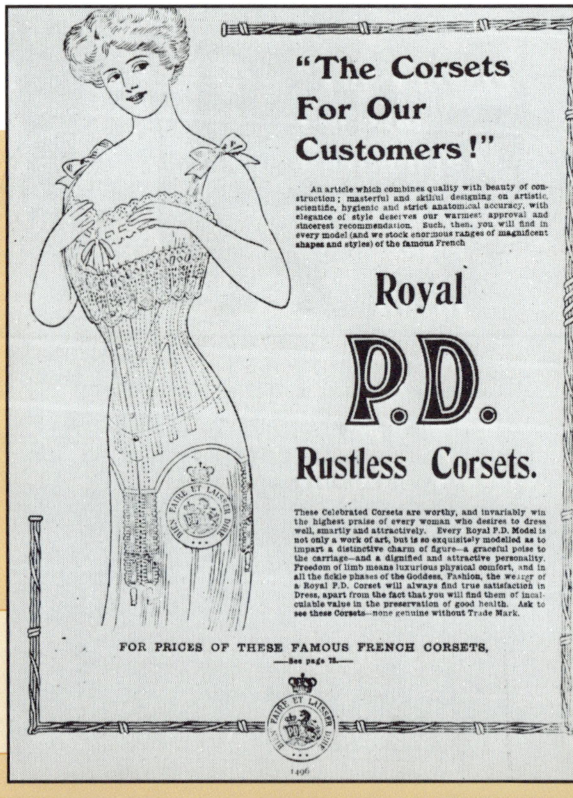

Figure 3.45
The underclothes women wore in 1915

Women's fashions had changed by 1914. Sewing machines had become more common by then, and women could make their own clothes at home. Large shops sold clothes 'off the peg'. Women could go and choose what they wanted from racks of ready-made clothes instead of having clothes specially made for them or making them themselves. Both these things helped to make styles simpler.

Figure 3.46
Fashion in 1914

Figure 3.46 shows what a fashionable lady might have looked like in 1914. But men's clothes had not changed much. Most men still wore dull suits and waistcoats. Some had started wearing more comfortable soft shirts instead of stiff starched ones. Some liked straw hats or floppy felt hats better than the hard bowler hats that had been worn in 1901.

By the end of the First World War fashions had changed again. Women did not want to go back to old-fashioned, tight and uncomfortable clothes like the ones their mothers had worn. They wanted clothes that suited their freer, more active life. Figure 3.47 shows how a young woman might have looked by the middle of the 1920s.

At first only daring young woman would have worn clothes such as these. But by the end of the 1920s many older women were also wearing this style.

Figure 3.47
In the 1920s young women dressed like this

Figure 3.48
In the 1930s fashion changed again

In the 1930s, fashioned changed once again. Hemlines went down and waists went up. Women tried to look tall and graceful. They wore high heels and straight skirts, sometimes with pleats. Some women liked dresses and coats with padded sleeves. Men still wore suits, but by this time bowler hats had gone and felt ones had taken their place.

Poor people did not follow all these fashions. They had hard-wearing clothes that would last a long time. These clothes were usually made from rough and heavy material. Women wore aprons and girls wore pinafores to keep their clothes clean. Some women, as we have seen, worked very long hours at home making clothes for fashionable ladies. They were paid only a tiny amount for each garment. The clothes were then sold in shops for much more.

Think *for yourself*

Look through old photograph albums at home. Can you find any photographs of people between 1901 and 1939? What kind of clothes are they wearing? Are they like the clothes shown on these pages?

THE HISTORIAN AT WORK

Figure 3.49
Austin Advertisement

Figure 3.50
Australia invites the British Domestic Girl

Figure 3.51
Australia for the British Boy

Examine these advertisements and posters from the 1920s and 1930s and answer the following questions:

1 What was the purpose of each of these pictures?
2 Look closely at figures 3.49 and 3.50 and work out whether each of them was produced during the 1920s or the 1930s. (The pictures on page 67 should help you here.)
3 What kind of life do figures 3.50 and 3.51 suggest that young immigrants will find in Australia? Could these types of advertisements be used today? Why or why not?
4 Look again at Stanley Bruce's speech on page 7. In what ways do figures 3.50 and 3.51 reflect Australia's immigration policy in the 1920s and 1930s?
5 What are the 'Three Engineering Masterpieces' referred to in Figure 3.49?
6 Find some modern car advertisements. In what ways are they similar to the advertisement in Figure 3.49. How are they different? What kind of people was the advertisement in Figure 3.49 designed to appeal to? Discuss
7 From the evidence of Figure 3.49 do you think the Austin was a cheap or an expensive car? Why?
8 Write three or four sentences of advertising copy to go with each of these pictures. In each case think about the kind of person the advertisement is aimed at.
9 From the evidence of figures 3.49, 3.50 and 3.51, in what ways did Australia still depend upon Britain in the 1920s and 1930s?

4
Down *and* out

When Digger Smith came home after the First World War he knew exactly what he wanted:

You coots at 'ome 'as small ideer
Uv what we think and feel.
We done our bit an' seen it throu',
And all that we are askin' you
Is jist a fair, square deal.
We want this land we battled for
To settle up— an' somethin' more.
We want the land we battled for
To be a land worthwhile.
We're sick uv greed, an' 'ate, an' strife,
And all the mess that's made of life.

Many other soldiers felt the same as Digger Smith. They had fought for Australia. Now they wanted a bit of the land for themselves.

'A fair, square deal'

The government agreed that the returned soldiers deserved 'a fair, square deal'. It also thought that the soldiers could help Australia to develop by opening up and farming land that was not being used.

A soldier settlement scheme was worked out. The state governments provided land for soldiers' farms, and the federal government lent money to help the soldiers get established. In NSW most of the land was in the Riverina district. In Victoria it was in the rough Mallee country.

Figure 4.1
This drawing was on the cover of a Sydney magazine in 1919. Why are the farmer and the soldier shaking hands?

Some soldier settlers did well. Most did not. Over 37 500 took up farms, but by 1929 almost half of them had given up and left their land. Although they had started with such high hopes, many of the men and their families had lived in poverty for ten years. Figure 4.2 shows some of the reasons why this happened.

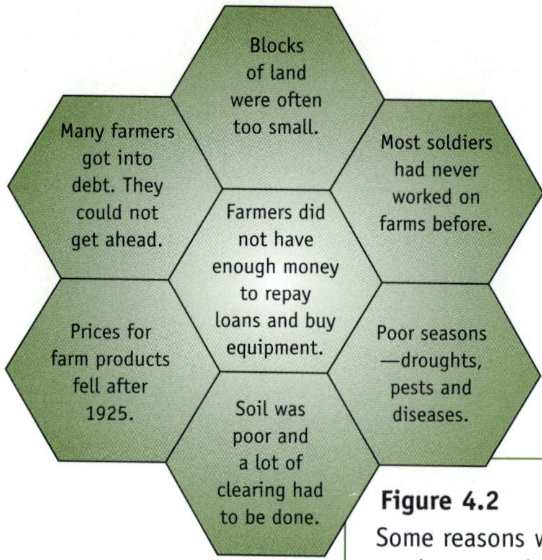

Figure 4.2
Some reasons why the soldier settlement scheme failed

Harry Davis in the Mallee

In chapter 2 you read about Harry Davis at Gallipoli. This is what happened to him after the war.

> I came back from the war and, like my mates, really believed that I deserved a chance. The government found jobs for some of the boys or trained them for new work. I'm a city boy myself, but I've always wanted to have a go at farming.
>
> The government put some land aside for us soldiers. It seemed like a good idea so I took up 350 acres [140 hectares]. It was in the Mallee, about 300 miles [450 kilometres] from Melbourne. We somehow had the idea that the land would be ready for us when we got there. That was a joke! It took us two days to get there on the train. There were no fences and no house either. We lived in a tent for months until we built a wooden shack. For a while we had to get all our water from the railway station—and that was 3 miles [5 kilometres] away. The baby always seemed to be sick.

Figure 4.3
We couldn't stand it any longer. We just cleared out.

The first year we cleared about 200 acres [80 hectares]. It was the hardest work I've ever done. My wife did as much as I did—more, in fact, because she looked after the baby too. We built the hut and sowed some wheat. That year we got over 1500 bags of wheat. The price was pretty good and we thought we might make a go of it. The next couple of years were hard, but we struggled on. The government had lent us some money to buy the land and a bit of equipment. But we had to pay it back—and pay with interest as well. So we never really felt that we were getting anywhere.

By 1925 we'd cleared the land. We bought a couple of hundred sheep too. We'd had two more babies by then. It's no fun for a woman to have a baby in a rough shack out in the bush. One of the babies died. That really set us back.

We had one bad season after another. In 1927 we only got 800 bags of wheat from the whole farm. It was dry and the soil was poor. We never had the money to buy enough fertiliser or good tools that would have made our work easier. The drought really hit hard in 1930. Dust was blowing everywhere. It really got us down. There was no food for the sheep and we got no wheat at all that year.

We couldn't stand it any longer. We just cleared out and went to Melbourne.

Think *for yourself*

1. How was Harry Davis like Digger Smith?
2. Make a list of all the things that explain why Harry Davis was unsuccessful as a soldier settler.
3. Do you think Harry Davis should take any blame for his failure? Why?
4. What might he and his family have done when they got to Melbourne?
5. Find out what the Mallee country in Victoria is used for today.

Figure 4.4
Clearing the land was the hardest work I've ever done

'Men, money and markets'

In the 1920s Australia was called 'the greatest undeveloped country in the world'. In 1924 the prime minister, Stanley Bruce, said that three things were needed to develop Australia and make it rich. They were men, money and markets. For all these things Australia depended on Britain.

Migrants were encouraged to come from Britain and settle in Australia. The government paid most of their fare. Like the soldiers, some migrants were helped to set up farms. But, like the soldiers, they too were often disappointed. They were told that they would do well in Australia. But they were not told about the problems they would have to face—problems such as finding a job or a home and settling down in a new country. About 212 000 migrants came from Britain. Most of them ended up in the cities.

The government needed a lot of money in the 1920s. It needed money to give pensions to ex-soldiers and to pay for the soldier settlement scheme. It needed money to build railway lines, roads and schools. It needed money to supply new houses with electricity and water. It also needed money to pay the interest on loans that it had raised during the First World War. During the 1920s the government borrowed most of the money it needed from Britain.

In the 1920s Australian farms and factories produced more than ever before. There were fewer than 6 million people in Australia to use these goods, so many of the goods had to be sold overseas. Australia had to find markets for them. The countries in the British Empire (including Australia) agreed on a system that would help them to sell products to each other. Member countries paid less customs duty on goods that they bought from other Empire countries. This helped to make the goods cheaper. Britain bought most of Australia's wool and a lot of Australia's other farm products.

Think *for yourself*

1 Do you think that today Australia could still be called 'the greatest undeveloped country in the world'? Why?

2 Imagine that you were a young single person living in London in 1922. Explain why you decided to migrate to Australia and what you expected to find when you arrived.

3 Read the information about 'men, money and markets' again. Write a sentence about each of these three things. In your sentences, explain how Australia depended on Britain to provide each one.

Figure 4.5
Australian wool, fruit and wheat were sold to Britain in the 1920s. Many advertisers used Australian symbols to sell their products. Which Australian symbols are used in these advertisements?

The end of the 1920s

For many people the 'Roaring Twenties' were good years. But by 1929 things did not seem to be going so well. Food prices were falling and farmers found it hard to sell their goods and make a living. In the cities, almost one worker in every ten was out of a job. There were a lot of strikes as trade unions tried to get higher pay for those who had work. As we have already seen, many migrants and ex-soldiers were having a hard time.

Then, at the end of 1929, came the Great Depression.

How the Depression started

The Depression began in the USA. In the 1920s the USA was booming. Many people invested their savings by buying shares on the stock market. A lot of investors made fortunes. But in 1929 people started selling shares. As large numbers of shares were sold, the prices of shares went down. As share prices dropped, more people panicked. They wanted to sell their shares before the price went even lower. Then, on 24 October 1929, the stock market crashed and the price of shares fell much lower than ever before.

This was the beginning of the Depression. You can see from Figure 4.7 how it spread to many other countries.

Figure 4.6
After the collapse of the Wall Street Stock Exchange, crowds of Americans rushed to Wall Street to try to recover their savings. Were they successful?

Figure 4.7
How the Depression spread

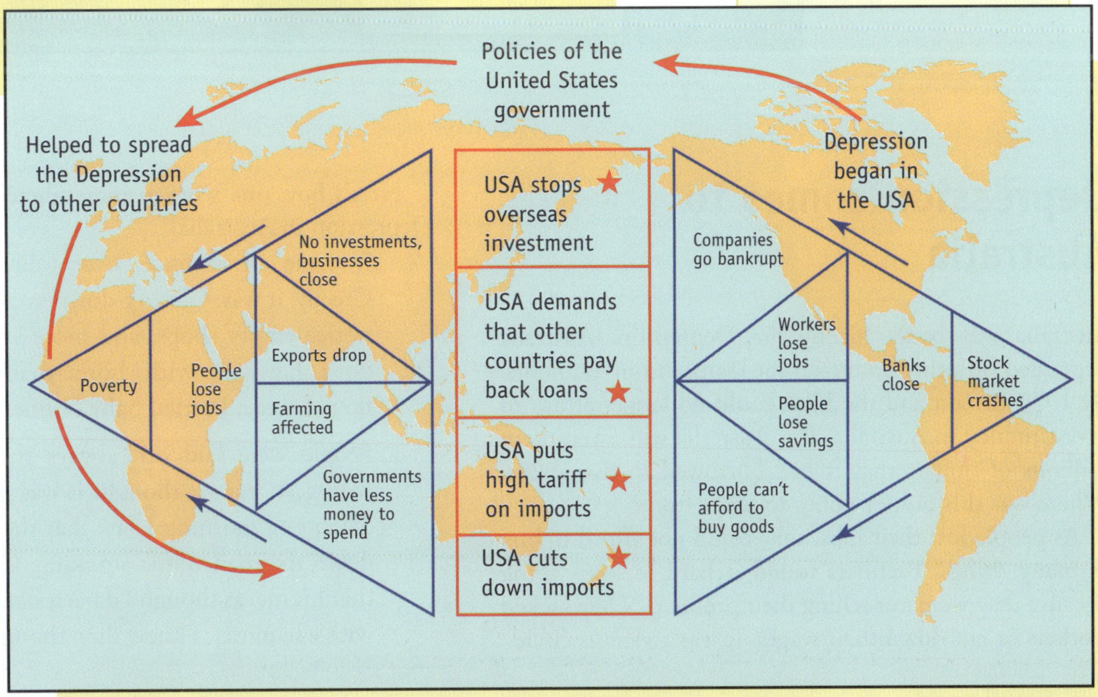

CHECK the facts

Are the sentences below true or false?

1 Many ex-soldiers from the city took up land in the 1920s.
2 Land for soldier settlers was carefully chosen so that it would make good farms.
3 Migrants from Greece were helped to come to Australia in the 1920s.
4 In the 1920s Australia borrowed most of the money it needed from the USA.
5 In the 1920s Britain bought most of Australia's wool.
6 By 1929, six workers out of ten in Australia had a job.
7 The Depression started when the stock market in Britain crashed in 1929.
8 After October 1929 the Depression spread to many other countries.

Figure 4.8
How Australia raised money. Although the government found the money to pay off its loans, many Australians lost their jobs. They spent the 1930s living in poverty.

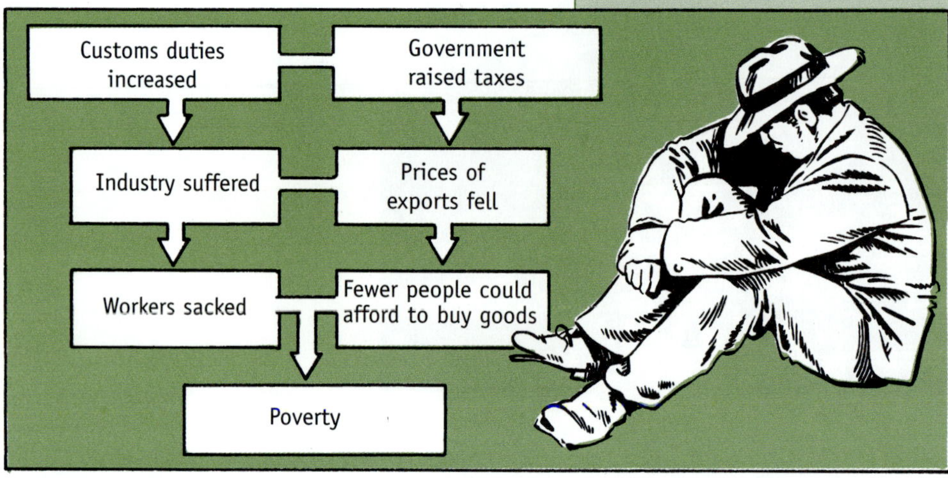

Depression comes to Australia

Australia was badly hit by the Depression. Australia depended on other countries for loans and investments. By 1930 Britain and the USA could no longer afford to invest money in Australia. But Australia still owed them millions of dollars that it had borrowed in the 1920s. Where was this money going to come from?

As people lost their jobs, they could not afford to buy as many things. Factories found it hard to keep going because they were not selling their products. They sacked workers or cut down their wages. It was a vicious circle.

Here's how one woman remembered the start of the Depression in Australia:

> It came all at once, over four or five months. Creepy, it was. Closing-down sales first. Then you'd notice empty shops, and more and more door-to-door hawkers with home-made clothes, pegs, flower seeds, knitted baby bonnets.
>
> People were laid off, always the oldest and the youngest, but we thought it was just temporary … Then one morning I saw that the factory chimney down the road wasn't smoking. Can't tell you how that hit me, as though I'd been slammed in the chest with a hammer. I knew then though. We were for it.

Figure 4.9
A family in the 1930s

Think *for yourself*

1. Why were closing-down sales a sign of the coming of the Depression?
2. What is a hawker? Why do you think hawkers were a sign of the coming of the Depression?
3. Look at the things the hawkers were selling. Where do you think they might have come from?
4. Why was this woman so upset by the fact that the factory chimney was not smoking?
5. If you have older relatives or friends, ask them what they remember about the Depression. They may have some interesting stories to tell about their own lives in the 1930s.

THE HISTORIAN AT WORK

Unemployment in the Depression

Unemployment was the worst problem of the Depression. The graphs in figures 4.10, 4.11a, 4.11b and 4.12 contain information about unemployment in Australia and some other countries. Look closely at these graphs and then answer the questions.

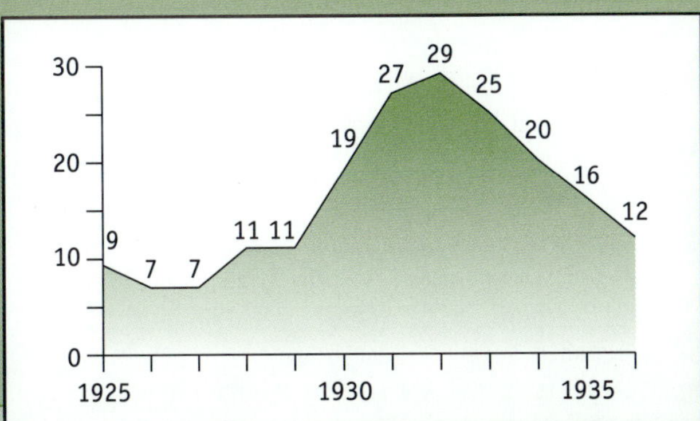

Figure 4.10
Percentage of trade union members out of work in Australia, 1925–36

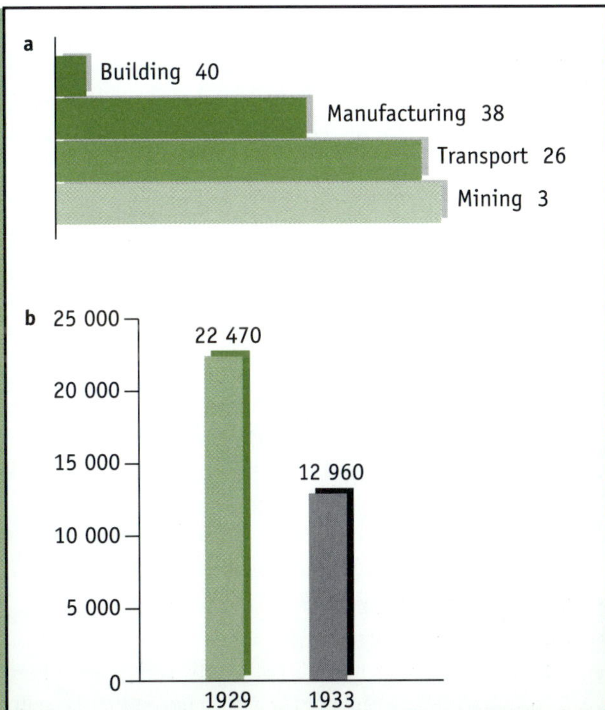

Figure 4.11a
Percentage of unemployed trade union members in Australia, 1932

Figure 4.11b
Number of coal miners in NSW

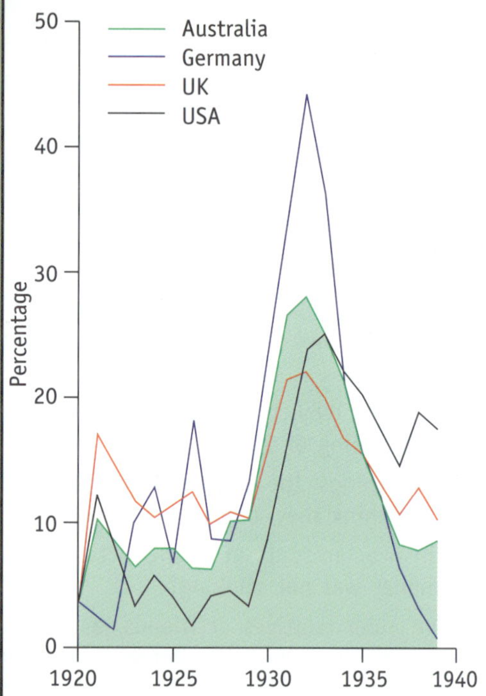

Percentage of work-force unemployed

Figure 4.12
Unemployment rates in four countries, 1920–39: Australia, Germany, United Kingdom, USA

1 a In Australia, which years between 1925 and 1936 had the lowest percentage of unemployed people?
  b How did unemployment in Australia compare with unemployment in Germany, the United Kingdom and the USA in these years?

2 a In Australia, which year between 1925 and 1936 had the highest percentage of unemployed people?
  b How did unemployment in Australia compare with unemployment in Germany, the United Kingdom and the USA in that year?

3 From the information in figures 4.10 and 4.12 would you say that the Depression in Australia was over by 1936? What happened to unemployment in Australia between 1936 and 1939?

4 Was the Wall Street crash of 1929 the first sign of economic hard times? Use the evidence in Figure 4.12 in answering this question.

5 Complete these sentences:
  a In Australia the number of trade union members out of work rose by __________ per cent between 1929 and 1930. It rose another __________ per cent between 1931 and 1932. In Australia between 1929 and 1932 the number of trade union members out of work rose by __________ per cent. In Germany during the same period the number of people out of work rose by __________ per cent.
  b In Australia in 1932 the unemployment rate among trade union members was __________ per cent. This means that __________ trade union members out of every 100 were out of work. In the United Kingdom in the same year __________ out of every 100 people in the workforce were out of work, and in the USA __________ people out of 100 people in the workforce were out of work.
  c In Australia the unemployment level in 1929 was (higher/lower) than in 1934. This is (true/untrue) for the United Kingdom, the USA and Germany.
  d From the graph in Figure 4.12 we could say that in Australia the four worst years of the Depression were from _____ to _____.
  e In Australia in 1932 the highest rate of unemployment was in the __________ industry, where __________ trade union members out of every 100 were out of work.
  f Between 1929 and 1933 the number of coal miners in NSW fell by almost (10 000/15 000/2000).

6 a What does 'manufacturing' mean?
  b Why do you think the rate of unemployment in manufacturing and building industries was so high during the Depression?
  c Can you suggest how the high unemployment rate in the manufacturing and building industries could cause many people in the transport industry to lose their jobs?
  d Why do you think that unemployment in the mining industry was not as bad as in some other industries during the Depression?

7 From the evidence of the graph in Figure 4.12, would you say that the Depression in Australia was more or less severe than the Depression in each of the other countries shown?

8 a The unemployment rates for Australia shown in figures 4.10 and 4.12 are slightly different. Can you explain why? (Clue: carefully read the label beneath each of these graphs.)
  b What is meant by the 'workforce'? What kinds of people would not be counted as members of the work force?

9 Which of the countries shown in Figure 4.12 had the lowest rate of unemployment after 1936? Can you suggest why? (You may need to look at the next chapter before you answer this question.)

Down and out

What was it like to be out of work in the 1930s? At first many people found it hard to accept that they had been sacked. Their pride was hurt. One woman remembered:

> My husband was ashamed to tell me when he was put off; it was six weeks before he confessed there was not even any money for the rent. All that time he'd been taking money from his bank and pretending it was his wages. He just broke down when he told me. It was a blow to his pride, dreadful.

Suddenly people who had been used to having work and money found themselves poor, hungry and, sometimes, without a home.

> At age 27 ... I stood at the back of an Adelaide restaurant and waited for the rubbish tins to be put out. Half-chewed meat, vegetable peelings, hunks of bread, all slopped up with cold gravy and tea leaves and burned fat. It makes you spew to think of it. Yet there might have been thirty or forty men waiting there in the dark, night after night.

Figure 4.14
'Well, things are brightening up. Last week I only got enough out of this for the dog; this week there's enough for me, too!'

Figure 4.13
Men like this tramped the streets looking for work. Would you have given this man a job?

Often women and teenagers were given jobs because their wages were lower than those of older men. In many families, sons and daughters supported their parents.

Sometimes work was rationed out. People worked part-time so that all the workers in a company could keep their jobs. Although their wages were smaller, at least these people had jobs. They didn't have the dispiriting task of searching for work each day.

Looking for work

Jack was an unemployed bricklayer.

> Many a day I walked along the street with my shoes falling apart, trying to keep the top part on, and the other part flapping. You'd cut cardboard soles, but you'd get that way that there'd be no sole at all, just upper. It was nothing to walk twenty or thirty miles around the city areas looking for work ... You mostly got your jobs on the hoof, walk around everywhere ... Frightened to take a tram because you might pass a street where there was a job.

There were thousands of people like Jack who tramped about looking for work. Trade unions couldn't help much. Jack's union had run out of money because its members couldn't afford to pay their fees. A few jobs were advertised in the papers, but for each one there were dozens, or even hundreds, of applicants.

Think *for yourself*

1 Try to find out what Australia's unemployment rate is today.

2 The picture in Figure 4.15 was published in a workers' newspaper in 1933. Use it and what you have read in this chapter to write three or four sentences about the way unemployment affected people's lives.

Figure 4.15
The despair of poverty

Helping yourself

Many people remember the Depression as a time when people worked out all kinds of ways to earn enough to stay alive. Bert and his father sold fish outside pubs.

> I used to go hawking with the old man. He'd borrow a few bob and go to the fish markets. A lot of the fish would be condemned. Too small, or too big; they weren't bad. We'd meet the bloke who was taking them to the tip around the back of the market, and give him a few bob. He'd tip the lot into the back of our T Model Ford and we'd hawk it from a basket outside pubs.

They raffled chickens inside the pubs as well.

> My father would buy up old chickens, take them home and soak them in the trough; try and make them look a bit plump. You'd powder them with flour to hide the bruises, and take them round and try to raffle them in pubs on a Friday. If they were very old, you'd break the breastbone and shove a lump of corn beef inside to bump up the weight.

Figure 4.16
Busking was common during the 1930s

Others became door-knockers. Men, women and children tramped around from house to house selling all sorts of things, from pins and needles to shampoo made out of soap powder. Busking was also popular. Wherever people gathered there would be a few singers or musicians trying to entertain them and then passing the hat around.

Think *for yourself*

1. What does Bert mean by 'borrow a few bob'?
2. Why would Bert and his father have had a T Model Ford rather than any other kind of car? (Clue: look back to 'On the move' in the last chapter.)
3. Which was cheaper in the 1930s—chicken or corn beef? How can you tell?
4. Do you think Bert and his father were crooks?
5. What does 'busking' mean? Why was it popular in the 1930s?

Figure 4.17
A relief card like this had to be shown when unemployed people applied for 'the susso'

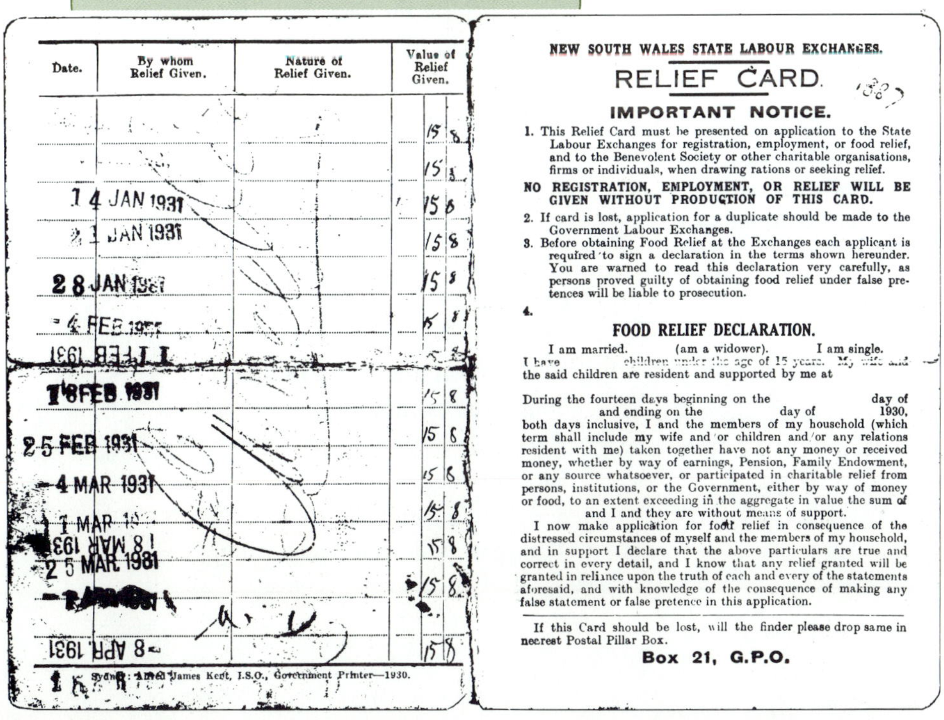

Date.	By whom Relief Given.	Nature of Relief Given.	Value of Relief Given.
			15 8
			15 8
14 JAN 1931			15 8
21 JAN 1931			15 8
28 JAN 1931			15 8
4 FEB 1931			15 8
[illegible]			[illegible]
18 FEB 1931			15 8
25 FEB 1931			15 8
4 MAR 1931			15 8
11 MAR 1931			15 8
18 MAR 1931			15 8
25 MAR 1931			15 8
[illegible]			[illegible]
8 APR 1931			15 8

Sydney: Alfred James Kent, I.S.O., Government Printer—1930.

NEW SOUTH WALES STATE LABOUR EXCHANGES.

RELIEF CARD.

IMPORTANT NOTICE.

1. This Relief Card must be presented on application to the State Labour Exchanges for registration, employment, or food relief, and to the Benevolent Society or other charitable organisations, firms or individuals, when drawing rations or seeking relief.

NO REGISTRATION, EMPLOYMENT, OR RELIEF WILL BE GIVEN WITHOUT PRODUCTION OF THIS CARD.

2. If card is lost, application for a duplicate should be made to the Government Labour Exchanges.
3. Before obtaining Food Relief at the Exchanges each applicant is required to sign a declaration in the terms shown hereunder. You are warned to read this declaration very carefully, as persons proved guilty of obtaining food relief under false pretences will be liable to prosecution.
4.

FOOD RELIEF DECLARATION.

I am married. (am a widower). I am single. I have children under the age of 15 years. My wife and the said children are resident and supported by me at

During the fourteen days beginning on the day of and ending on the day of 1930, both days inclusive, I and the members of my household (which term shall include my wife and/or children and/or any relations resident with me) taken together have not any money or received money, whether by way of earnings, Pension, Family Endowment, or any source whatsoever, or participated in charitable relief from persons, institutions, or the Government, either by way of money or food, to an extent exceeding in the aggregate in value the sum of and I and they are without means of support.

I now make application for food relief in consequence of the distressed circumstances of myself and the members of my household, and in support I declare that the above particulars are true and correct in every detail, and I know that any relief granted will be granted in reliance upon the truth of each and every of the statements aforesaid, and with knowledge of the consequence of making any false statement or false pretence in this application.

If this Card should be lost, will the finder please drop same in necrest Postal Pillar Box.

Box 21, G.P.O.

On the Susso

We're on the susso now,
We can't afford a cow
We live in a tent,
We pay no rent,
We're on the susso now.

Children in the 1930s sang this song. 'Susso' was short for 'sustenance'. Look up 'sustenance' in the dictionary. What does it mean?

In June 1934 almost 674 000 people in Australia were living 'on the susso'. Each state had its own way of giving the unemployed and their families enough food to keep them alive. But many politicians felt that the Depression would not last long, so they did not work out a really effective way of helping people. The 'susso' gave people food coupons. It did not usually provide money for rent, clothes, medicine or bills. People often had to rely on charities and churches for help with these things.

In Sydney and other cities in NSW, people had to be out of work for two weeks before they could get 'the susso'. They had to report to a depot. Then they were given coupons that allowed them to get food from certain shops. They had separate coupons for milk, bread, meat and groceries. In the country, people without work reported to the police station to get their dole coupons.

The government was afraid that workers would not try hard enough to get a job if they could get food from the government. The dole coupons therefore did not provide enough food for a family to live on. But most workers hated to go 'on the susso'. They did not want to accept handouts. Many refused to take the dole even when they were out of work.

Think *for yourself*

1 How was 'the susso' of the 1930s different from the dole of today?

2 If you know anyone who is out of work, ask him or her how it feels to be unemployed. Do you think people today feel the same way about unemployment as people did in the 1930s?

3 In April 1933 a married couple with three children could get food coupons worth 18s. ($1.80). Here are some food prices at that time:
1 rabbit 9d. (8c)
1 lb stewing chops 3d. (3c)
1 dozen eggs 9d. (8c)
1 lb sugar 4d. (3c)
20 lb potatoes 1s. (10c)
1 bottle Foster's beer 1s. (10c)
tin golden syrup 6d. (5c)
1 lb tea 1s. 6d. (15c)
1 pint milk 3d. (3c)
1 loaf bread 10d. (9c)
pie and sauce 3d. (3c)
ice-cream cone 3d. (3c)
1 lb butter 1s. 10d. (19c)
1 lb cheese 1s. 6d. (15c)
milk shake 4d. (3c)
12d. = 1s, 1lb = 500g, 1 pint = 600 mL
   a Imagine that you had to feed a family of two adults and three children for a week on your 18s. ($1.80). Make up a weekly budget using the prices listed above as a guide.
   b What foods would your imaginary family be short of in your weekly plan?

4 Why might many out-of-work people have refused to apply for the susso during the Depression? Do you think this was a sensible attitude? Why?

5 Find out how much a married couple with three children could get on unemployment relief if they were unemployed today? Draw up a weekly budget for the household. Could they cope better than the 1933 family?

Depression songs

The songs below were sung in the 1930s.

The moon belongs to everyone,
The best things in life are free.
The stars belong to everyone,
The best things in life are free.

Why were songs such as 'The moon belongs to everyone' popular? What sort of people would have sung this sort of song?

(Sung to the tune of 'My Bonnie Lies Over the Ocean'):

I'm spending my days in the doss house,
I'm spending my days on the street,
I'm searching for work but I found none—
I wish I had something to eat.
Soup, soup, soup, soup,
They gave me a plate of
loop-the-loop,
Soup, soup, soup, soup,
They gave me a big plate of soup.
I went and I fought for my country,
I went out to bleed and to die,
I thought that my country would help me,
But this was my country's reply:
Soup, soup, soup, soup,
They gave me a plate of
loop-the-loop,
Soup, soup, soup, soup
They gave me a big plate of soup.

1 What is a doss house?
2 'They gave me a big plate of soup'. Who do you think 'they' might have been?
3 Read again what Digger Smith wanted at the beginning of the chapter. In what way was Digger Smith like the person who wrote this song?
4 Which expresses more hope for the future: this song or the Digger Smith poem? Why do you think this is so?

Figure 4.18
Soup kitchens like this were common in the Depression. They were usually set up by clubs, charities or church groups. Who is running this soup kitchen? Why was the soup made in such large pots?

Travelling around

Here is another Depression poem. It is about people who travelled from place to place looking for work.

There ain't no work in Bourke.
No lucre at Echuca.
Damnall at Blackall.
Things are crook at Tallarook.
Got a feed at the Tweed.
No feedin' at Eden.
Everything's wrong at Wollongong.
Might find a berth in Perth.

lucre money

Try to make up rhymes like this about the places near you.

Many hundreds of people went to the country where they thought work would be easier to find. On the way they begged, trapped rabbits, and if they were lucky, picked up odd jobs to keep them going.

Figure 4.19
Jumping the rattler. What sort of men did this? Why was it so dangerous?

Figure 4.20
These swagmen had found their way to Sydney. Why do you think they left the country? What might have happened to them in Sydney?

Some of these men took the risk of jumping on to a moving train to get them from place to place more quickly. This was called 'jumping the rattler'. As well as being very dangerous, it was against the law. The hoboes, or 'boes' as they were called, liked to travel in wheat trains because they could snuggle down in the wheat and keep warm. But if they went down too far they could easily be suffocated. Some men slipped or lost their grip when they jumped on to the trains. Others were crushed under heavy loads or knocked over when the train went under the bridge.

When they arrived in a town, with their swag and worn-out shoes, men were given food. But they were not allowed to stay long in one town because they took work from local people.

Relief work

Local and state governments sometimes arranged special work for unemployed people. After 1934 the federal government also organised this 'relief work'.

The work was usually hard and boring. Men built railways, bridges, roads and footpaths. They planted forests, laid sewer pipes, made irrigation channels, put up rabbit-proof fences and built public buildings. Look around your town or suburb. If you see a building which has a 1930s date on it, it may have been built as a relief project during the Depression.

Figure 4.21
These relief workers are building a road in a newly developing part of Sydney. It is now the busy suburb of Kogarah. Why did men take on relief jobs such as this?

If people refused to take a relief job, they were not allowed to get the dole. Special camps were built close to the work, and men who had never been out of the city were often sent to the bush. They were far from home and rarely had enough money to go and see their families.

Tom worked on relief jobs in the Victorian bush.

> We camped on top of a mountain in mid-winter in these little six by eight tents, cooking for ourselves, planting pines. There was no mess room or shelter, and one of the fellows took bad with pneumonia ... He was dying and we had to go on strike to get him out of the camp. We made a stretcher and carried him down seven miles on our back.

Relief work helped some people to feel better about being out of a job. But sometimes councils used relief workers, who did not get trade union rates of pay, and sacked their regular workers. Relief workers sometimes went on strike to get better wages and conditions.

Figure 4.22
Tents in a relief workers' camp. This photograph was taken in Western Australia. Why did workers get pneumonia in camps like these?

Somewhere to live

The winter of 1931 was a hard one. More and more people were losing their jobs. People were hungry and worried. Children were sick. Many unemployed families could not pay their rent. When this happened, landlords could turn them out of their homes, or evict them.

Friday, 19 June 1931, became known in Sydney as 'Bloody Friday'. On that day there was a battle between forty police and eighteen workers at Newtown. The workers were all members of the Unemployed Workers Movement, an organisation that was linked with the Communist Party. They had taken over a house in Newtown. When the police tried to evict them, they put barbed wire and sandbags around the house and hurled rocks and bits of iron at the police. Hundreds of people gathered to watch. After about an hour the police managed to break the door down with axes and hammers. All the workers were arrested and dragged into police vans.

When people were evicted, their clothes, furniture and everything they owned were dumped out on the street. Often these would be sold off for almost nothing. Sometimes unemployed people who had been evicted got their own back by burning or pulling down the landlord's house. But often there were rows of houses left standing empty while thousands of people had nowhere else to live.

Figure 4.23
Arrests after Newtown riots

Some families became squatters and lived in these empty houses. If enough people did this, it was hard for the owners to evict them. Some families moved in with friends or relatives. Many moved to the country, hoping to find work there. Others kept moving from house to house. Sometimes they sneaked out in the middle of the night before they could be evicted.

Figure 4.24
Shacks like this were common in the shanty towns of the 1930s. What sort of problems would the people who lived here have to cope with? Do Australians still live in conditions like these?

Shanty towns grew up as the number of homeless people increased. By 1934 there were 400 people living in the sandhills at La Perouse. They lived in humpies, shacks and tents. The settlement was given the name 'Happy Valley'. Hundreds more people lived in tents at Lidcombe. There were similar settlements in all the main towns and cities. Shacks were made from flour bags, scrap iron, old wood, bark, packing cases and anything else people could scrounge.

Think *for yourself*

Use the memories of these two people, Figure 4.25, and what you have read in the rest of this chapter to write a paragraph on each of these topics:

- Women in the Depression
- Children in the Depression

Women and children

Shirley lived in a tent in a camp of relief workers.

> My mother … mended and unpicked and re-made things all the time to keep us clean and tidy … She almost blinded herself at nights, sewing by a hurricane lamp … I was the only kid from the unemployed camps at high school … It was tremendously hard on my mother … She used to bleach flour bags to make school blouses.

Miriam grew up in Melbourne in the Depression.

> We had a lot of fun … A favourite playground was the Melbourne Cemetery. We'd find a poor run-down grave and look after it, clean it up, find a jam bottle and put soursobs in it. We'd go to the Carlton Baths for threepence … We had plenty of mates and a great deal of freedom … We had a lot of games and a lot of songs. We used to sit round in the streets and gutters just making up stories. We had a much better time than much more privileged kids these days.

Figure 4.25
Did children have more fun in those days?

Depression? What depression?

Not everyone suffered in the Depression. Although most people had their wages cut, the price of food, clothes and other goods fell as well. People who were in work were able to buy things more cheaply. Some people made their fortunes by buying land and houses when they were very cheap. Although many small businesses had to close, larger ones were able to survive and some even made bigger profits in the 1930s than they did in the 1920s.

The poor and unemployed were bitter about those who were doing well in the Depression. Many joined political organisations that promised a solution to their problems. Two of these were the Australian Communist Party and the New Guard.

The Communist Party believed that if workers joined together they would be strong enough to take over factories and businesses from the rich people who owned them. Then, instead of working for low wages, the workers could share the profits of these factories and businesses. Instead of having a few rich people and a lot of poor people, money would be shared fairly and evenly.

The New Guard was started by Colonel Eric Campbell. Many of its members had been soldiers in the First World War. The New Guard hated communists. Its members wanted a strong, tough government that would stamp out communists and others they considered to be trouble-makers.

Finding a solution

In 1929 a Labor Party government was elected in Australia. Prime Minister James Scullin had the difficult job of getting the country going again. People expected the government to find a way to end the Depression. But there were different ideas about how this could be done.

The two main ideas were **deflation** and **inflation**.

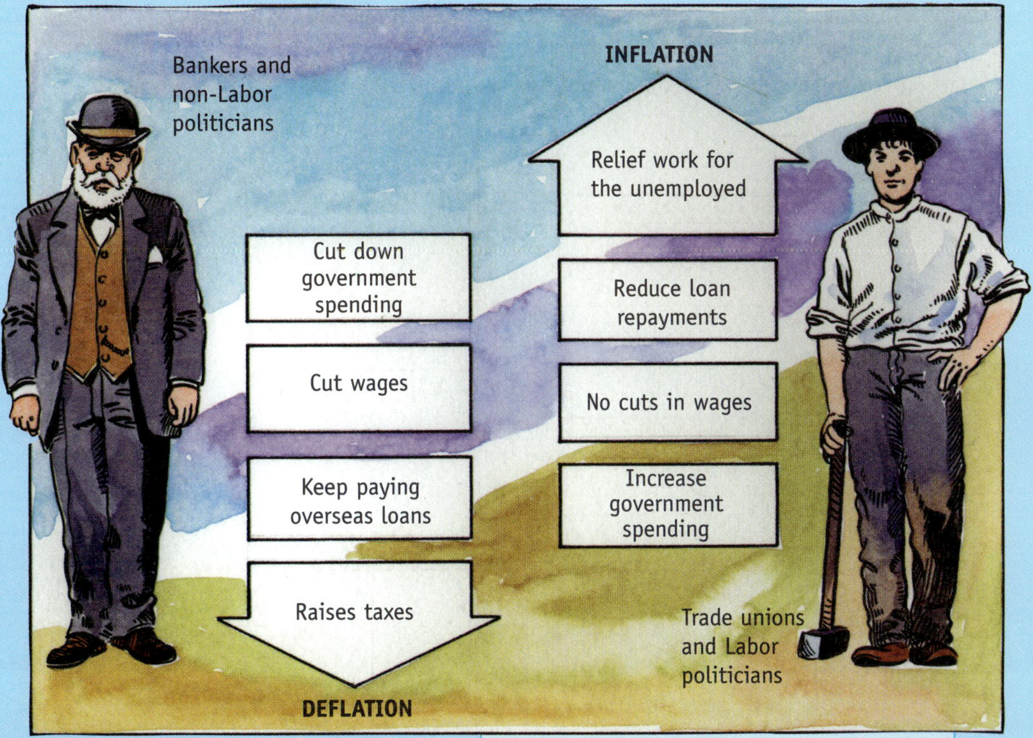

Figure 4.26
There were two main ideas on how to end the Depression—deflation and inflation

CHECK the facts

Match each word or expression in column A with its meaning in column B.

A	B
susso	special jobs created to give work to the unemployed
jumping the rattler	forcing people to leave their homes
relief work	system of giving food coupons to the unemployed
eviction	organisation that hated communists
shanty town	hitching a ride on a train
New Guard	settlement of shacks and tents

In June 1930 the government asked a British banker, Sir Otto Niemeyer, to come to Australia and help to find a solution. Niemeyer suggested that the government should follow a deflation policy. He said that Australia should keep on paying back the money it owed to other countries.

The government could not agree about what to do. Some politicians thought that Niemeyer's ideas were good ones. Others wanted to follow an inflation policy. In June 1931 the government finally decided to accept most of Niemeyer's ideas. Government spending was cut, wages and pensions were reduced, taxes were increased and Australia continued paying back its loans.

Figure 4.27
A cartoon of the 1930s. What is the Bank of England doing to Australia? Why? Do you think the person who drew this cartoon supported Jack Lang? Why do you think this?

Jack Lang gets the sack

Jack Lang was the leader of the Labor Party for NSW. In November 1930 he became premier of NSW.

Lang disagreed completely with Niemeyer's advice. He said:

> Niemeyer's chief purpose seemed to be to see to it that Australia met its overseas interest payments on due date, without regard to the suffering and misery it would cause in this country … Sir Otto Niemeyer was determined to squeeze the last drop of blood out of Australia.

Early in 1931, Lang's government in NSW stopped paying the interest on its overseas loans.

The federal government decided that if Lang's government would not pay its debts, the federal government would pay the debts and then take money from NSW banks. It passed a law forcing banks to hand over money that belonged to the NSW government.

Lang's next move was to withdraw government money from the banks so that they could not give it to the federal government. Money collected by NSW—such as taxes, tram and train fares—was not put into the banks. Instead, it was taken straight to the treasury building. The building was guarded so that the officials of the federal government could not take the money.

In May 1932 the governor of New South Wales, Sir Philip Game, dismissed Lang for defying the federal government. Parliament was closed and new elections were arranged. There were riots and street fights as Lang's supporters fought with his enemies. Lang was bitterly hated by the New Guard. They accused him of being a communist.

In the elections, Lang's government was easily defeated.

Figure 4.28
Jack Lang.
In the elections, Lang's government was easily defeated.

Think *for yourself*

1 What sort of people supported **deflation** as a way of ending the Depression? Look at the picture in Figure 4.26 and explain why these people thought that deflation was the best policy.

2 What sort of people supported **inflation** as a way of ending the Depression? Look at the picture in Figure 4.26 and explain why these people thought that inflation was the best policy.

3 Why did Jack Lang oppose the ideas of Sir Otto Niemeyer?

4 Why did Lang put money into the treasury building instead of into the bank?

5 Why was Lang dismissed by the governor of NSW?

Figure 4.29

Workers' houses are pulled down to make way for the Sydney Harbour Bridge. The little girl in the middle has got dressed up in her mother's shoes

'The Old and the New' by Harold Cazneaux

Sydney's bridge

One of the few bright spots during the Depression years was the opening of the Sydney Harbour Bridge. Work on the bridge had started in 1923. More than 720 houses had to be pulled down to make room for the approaches to the bridge. The main arch was started in 1928 and from then on people in Sydney could watch as the two halves grew closer together. There were plenty of jokes about them not meeting in the middle. To many people the bridge was one of the wonders of the world. One newspaper wrote that: 'The building of this gigantic bridge is just as much a national milestone as Anzac'.

Figure 4.30

This painting, by the Australian painter Roland Wakelin, shows the Sydney Harbour Bridge being built in 1928–29.

The bridge was opened in March 1932. Jack Lang made his speech. But before he could cut the ribbon, Captain de Groot, a member of the New Guard, rode up on a racehorse and cut the ribbon 'in the name of the decent and loyal citizens of NSW'. He was arrested and later fined.

A new ribbon was quickly found and the ceremony continued. Then there was a great procession across the bridge. There were school children, bridge workers, Aborigines 'specially selected for the occasion' and, of course, hundreds of politicians and officials. There were dozens of floats. The Bondi lifesavers forgot their sandshoes and people wondered why they seemed to be dancing along the road.

When the procession finished, the crowds swarmed over the bridge. They were given until midnight, when cars started crossing. In the evening there was a huge fireworks display.

Fifty years later, in 1982, there was a similar scene on the Sydney Harbour Bridge when, as part of the fiftieth anniversary celebrations, the bridge was closed to traffic and thousands of people thronged the roadways to walk across the harbour.

Think *for yourself*

1. There was almost no fuss when over 720 houses, mostly belonging to working people, were pulled down to make way for the bridge. Do you think people would accept this today for a similar project? Why?
2. Why do you think the New Guard used the opening of the bridge as a time to make a protest?
3. The Sydney Harbour Bridge is still one of the most popular items on Australian souvenirs. Design a souvenir showing the bridge. Why has it become such a popular symbol of Australia? What other symbols are there?

Figure 4.31
Captain de Groot is arrested after his unofficial opening of the Harbour Bridge

Figure 4.32
Crowds of people walked across the bridge after the opening ceremony on 19 March 1932. Three days earlier 50 000 school children had been allowed to walk over the bridge on Children's Day.

The Depression fades

By the late 1930s more people had jobs and wages had increased. Factories were producing more and trade was picking up. But when the Second World War broke out in 1939, Australia had not fully recovered from the Depression.

The Depression caused a lot of suffering. It also had important effects on Australia. For several years Australia's development almost stopped. The productivity of industries and farming declined. There was almost no immigration to Australia, and fewer babies were born than ever before. Many people, who had suffered poverty and hardship for years, lost their faith in what governments could do to help them. They became cynical.

Figure 4.33
Harbour Bridge souvenir, 1981

KNOW the chapter

1 All these people are mentioned in this chapter. Write a sentence or two about each person. Say who he was and why he was important.
Stanley Bruce
Eric Campbell
Sir Philip Game
Jack Lang
Sir Otto Niemeyer
James Scullin

2 Match each date in column A with an event in column B.

A	B
24 October 1929	Bloody Friday
November 1930	opening of Sydney Harbour Bridge
19 June 1931	Jack Lang becomes premier of NSW
March 1932	New York stock market collapses
May 1932	674 000 Australians 'on the susso'
June 1934	Jack lang is dismissed

3 Each of these scrambled words has been used in this chapter. Unscramble each one.

D	O	L	E	S	I	R
				1	2	3

(page 72)

S	K	A	T	E	R	M
				4	5	6

(page 74)

R	O	B	R	O	W
		7			8

(page 80)

G	A	R	M	I	N	T	S
	9	10		11	12	13	

(page 74)

Y	E	M	O	N
	14	15		

(page 74)

Now rearrange the numbered letters in the words you have formed to complete the following sentence:

The years between 1920 and 1929 were sometimes called the

4 Use the clues below to fill in the word puzzle. All the words are in this chapter.

- **a** Many shops had to hold __________ sales at the end of the 1920s. (2 words)
- **b** A person who sold things from door to door.
- **c** The unemployed were given food __________.
- **d** He unofficially opened the Harbour Bridge. (2 words)
- **e** The government employed some men on __________.(2 words)
- **f** Some unemployed men would sleep here. (2 words)
- **g** Many poor people lived in __________ towns.
- **h** The government followed this policy to try to end the Depression.
- **i** 1932 was the year of highest __________.
- **j** Jack Lang refused to pay these.

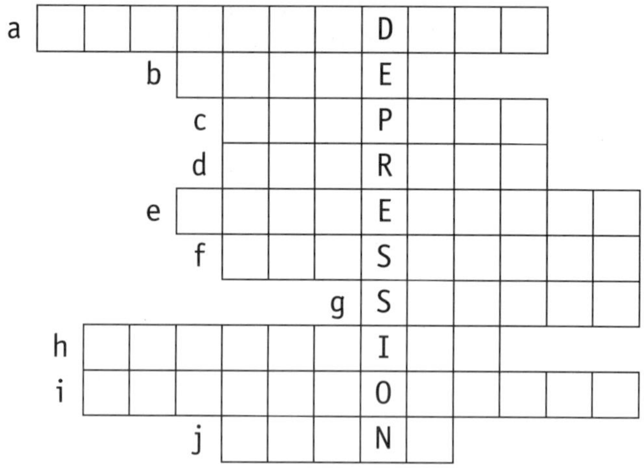

THE HISTORIAN AT WORK

The following letter was written to the 'Mayor and Council' of Richmond, a suburb of Melbourne, on 9 June 1931.

A Dear Sirs,

The recent decision of the Richmond Council that all moneys raised for the local unemployed must be handed into the Mayor's fund. I guess that it would go the same as the Million Penny Fund to a few of the pets. Cr [Councillor] Lightfoot opposed it strongly. I am not surprised at that because if he has to hand the money in from the Picture night then there would be mighty few boots for the women and children and none for his pets. Then again we see that Cr Lightfoot wants auditors to go into the Books. Did Cr Lightfoot have his books looked over by auditors and let the ratepayers see how he juggled his money [?] It would be a good thing for the unemployed if that was done. Now we get to another statement. Cr O'Connell talks about the communists. They must be his nightmare as he abuses them whenever he gets the chance. In the past when the U.W.M. asked the council for any concessions the first question Cr O'Connell slings—are you a communist[?] I am no communist but I would rather be a communist than a twister. Cr O'Connell says that everything must be fair and above board in regards to unemployment. I can bring proof regarding how fair and above board the work is given out at the Reserve. 1 Man has had 6 days in 6 months 2 Men 6 days in 10 months and myself 2 days since August last … I think it is run crook as it can be, and as it has been run althrough the piece. As the Town Clerk stated that he did not care if a man was registered for 2 years it was all fair and above board. I think he is in the swim as well.

I am yours etc,

E. Barry

The following passage is a description by a member of the U.W.M. of an event that occurred in Richmond in August 1931.

B We had a very good organisation to fight evictions and one particular Wednesday there was an eviction in Burnley and we got an awful bashing from the police. People were batoned down. So we called a meeting and decided to do something about it. The eviction was instigated by the estate agents on behalf of the owner. They never let you know who owned the houses and we didn't know how to find out for ourselves, so we decided to take on the Richmond estate agents. On the Friday we met at a certain place and divided up into groups of two people to each estate agent. It was late shopping night and at a quarter to nine there were two of us outside each of nine estate agents in Richmond. One chap in each group had a watch and they were all synchronised. At a quarter to nine, 'Bang!' We wrecked every estate agent's window in Richmond with lumps of bluemetal. There was hell to pay the next day. The papers were full of it. Even Mr Sidney Myer came out with a statement that it wasn't right that people should be evicted because they were out of work, and the government should do something. Well, the government announced the rent subsidy of eight shillings a week. If you had an eviction order you could apply for this money. This took the sting out of the eviction fights.

1 What do the initials U.W.M. stand for. (Look back to page 85.) Do you think E. Barry (document A) was a member of the U.W.M?

2 List the accusations that E. Barry makes against members of the Richmond Council (document A). What evidence, if any, does he produce to support these accusations? What do you think he means by each of the following expressions:
- pets
- juggled his money
- twister
- in the swim?

3 From the evidence of E. Barry's letter (document A), what measures were being taken in Richmond in 1931 to help unemployed people?

4 Try to imagine how E. Barry (document A) felt while he was writing this letter. How can you tell this from the letter? Why do you think he felt this way?

5 Why did the members of the U.W.M. decide to attack the real estate agents' offices (document B)?

6 What was the attitude of the police and the Richmond Council towards the U.W.M? What evidence for this can you find in both documents?

7 Do some research to find out who Mr Sidney Myer was (document B). Would he have been a member of the U.W.M? Why?

8 What do you think the members of the U.W.M. hoped to achieve by attacking the estate agents' offices (document B)? Were they successful? Explain.

9 What do you think E. Barry hoped to achieve by writing his letter to the Richmond Council (document A)? Do you think his letter would have achieved its purpose? Discuss.

10 Look back to the description of what happened on 'Bloody Friday' on page 85. What similarities and differences can you find between what happened then and the events described in document B?

5

War *again*

When the First World War ended in 1918 people said that it had been the war to end all wars. The suffering and waste convinced many people that the world could never again afford to fight another war. They looked forward to a time of peace.

And yet, another, more destructive war started only twenty years later. The Second World War killed more people, caused more damage and cost more money than any other war in history. When it ended in 1945 a frightening new weapon, the atomic bomb, had been created.

Figure 5.1
Australian war graves in New Guinea. More people died in the Second World War than in any other war in history.

Figure 5.2
Like millions of other Germans, these people had no work and nothing to do. They felt defeated and helpless. Why did people like this support Hitler?

Causes of the war

In many ways the causes of this second war are clearer than the causes of the first war. In Europe the war was caused mainly by the policies of Germany and her ally, Italy. In Asia it was caused mainly by the policies of Japan. Adolf Hitler, the German dictator, must take much of the blame for the Second World War. To understand why the Second World War happened we must find out why Hitler became Germany's leader, what his ideas were, and how he went about getting what he wanted.

Germany in the 1920s

During the 1920s a lot of Germans felt angry and bitter. They were angry that they had lost the war. They were bitter about the Treaty of Versailles which they had been forced to sign in 1919.

The following story tells how many German people felt in the 1920s.

> My name is Helga Schmidt. I can remember what it was like living in Germany in the 1920s. It was bad enough losing the war. But the Treaty of Versailles made things almost impossible for us.

We Germans lost all our colonies. They were given to other countries to control. We even lost some parts of our own country too. How could we feed our people if our farming land was taken away? How could we rebuild our factories if our coal and iron were taken from us? Germany wasn't allowed to have any submarines or aeroplanes, and we couldn't have more than 100 000 soldiers in the army. I ask you, what chance would we have if we were attacked?

One of the worst things was that we had to take the blame for causing the war, even though a lot of other countries were just as much to blame as Germany was. We had to agree to give the winning countries millions of dollars to pay for the war damage. How could we get on our feet again with all that money going out of our country?

We had a new government after the war. It was supposed to be a democracy, but it didn't really have much of a chance. There was no one who seemed to be able to do anything. All they did was talk, talk, talk in parliament. What good did that do? Many other people felt just like I did. We wanted a strong leader, someone who would show the other countries that they couldn't push Germany around. That's why we let Adolf Hitler get so much power.

Figure 5.3
Adolf Hitler

Think *for yourself*

1 Helga has given a number of reasons why she felt bitter about the Treaty of Versailles. What are they?

2 If you had lived in Australia in the 1920s, would you have agreed with any of Helga's criticisms of the treaty? Would you have thought the treaty was fair? Or was it too harsh?

3 Do you agree with Helga when she says that the German government after the First World War 'didn't really have much of a chance'? Why?

4 What reason does Helga give to explain why Hitler became so powerful?

Adolf Hitler

Adolf Hitler was a soldier in the German Army in the First World War. After the war he joined a small political group. He soon became the group's leader. Under Hitler's control the group grew into a well-organised political party called the Nazi party. In 1923 Hitler tried to take over the German government. He failed and spent the next nine months in prison. There he wrote a book, *Mein Kampf* ('My Struggle'). In this book Hitler set out his ideas about how Germany could become a strong united country.

Hitler gains power

Like Helga Schmidt, many millions of Germans were angry about the Treaty of Versailles. Early in the 1930s their anger grew stronger. The Great Depression hit Germany hard. Over 6 million people were out of work.

Figure 5.4
Hitler's ideas

Others struggled to make a living. Hitler promised to make things better. In 1933 his Nazi party was voted into power. Hitler became Germany's chancellor, or prime minister. Within a year Hitler had got rid of the democratic government. The Nazis had complete control of Germany and Hitler was a dictator. He was now ready to carry out the ideas he had written about in *Mein Kampf*.

Think *for yourself*

1 What is a dictator?
2 Look at Figure 5.5 and answer the questions below.
   a Why do you think Hitler arranged public meetings such as this?
   b Why did they appeal to Germans in the 1930s?

Figure 5.5
Adolf Hitler addresses a Nazi rally

A good idea but ...

'The war to end all wars'. That was what people had called the First World War. To make sure that another war did not break out, the countries that had won the First World War set up the League of Nations. The League was an association of countries whose main aim was to keep the peace. The countries which belonged to the League believed that nations could solve their problems and disagreements by talking about them instead of fighting.

Figure 5.6
The League of Nations in the 1920s

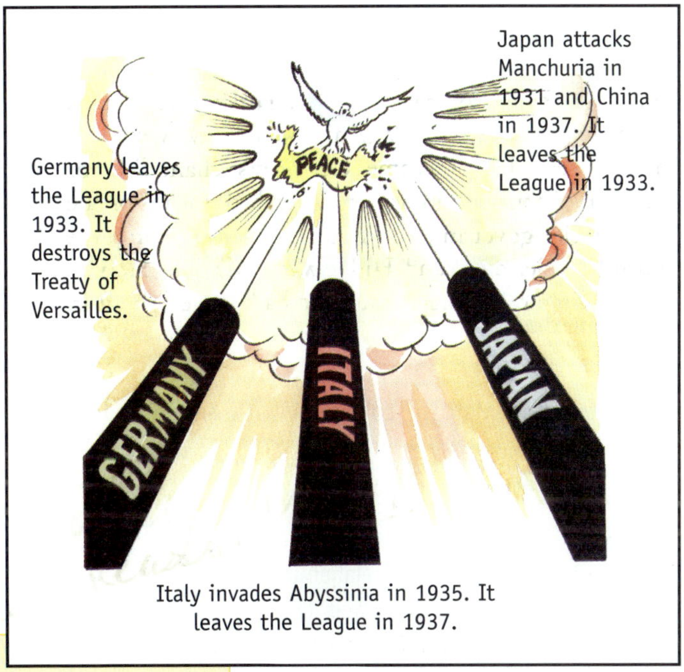

Figure 5.7
The League of Nations in the 1930s

The League of Nations was quite successful during the 1920s. You can see from Figure 5.6 that it helped people in many useful ways. But by the 1930s it was clear that the League was not going to work. Although countries talked about what a good idea it was, they did little to support it. The League of Nations had no army of its own. When countries disobeyed it, there was very little it could do. By the middle of the 1930s three countries were disobeying the League of Nations. They were Germany, Italy and Japan.

In Germany Hitler had set up a one-party government. He broke the rules of the Treaty of Versailles. He built up Germany's army and navy and began conscripting soldiers. He refused to pay Germany's war debts. He sent troops to the Rhineland area between Germany and France. He was ready to begin expanding outside Germany's border.

Mussolini had become dictator of Italy in 1922. Like Hitler he set up a one-party government. Italy was ruled by the Fascist party. Mussolini wanted to strengthen Italy's power and to take over more land. He wanted to make Italy a powerful nation.

In Japan Emperor Hirohito was the head of a government that was controlled by the army. Like Germany and Italy, Japan wanted to expand. It wanted more space and more materials for industry. In 1931 Japan attacked Manchuria in the north of China. In 1937 Japanese troops invaded China.

In 1937 Germany, Italy and Japan signed an agreement to support each other. Once again, as they did before the First World War, countries were grouping together, building up their armies and navies. They were preparing for war.

CHECK the facts

1 Are the statements below true or false?

- **a** The USA joined the League of Nations in 1919.
- **b** The League of Nations helped refugees in the 1920s.
- **c** Japan left the League of Nations in 1933.
- **d** Mussolini was the leader of the Italian Communist Party.
- **e** Millions of Germans were out of work in the 1930s.
- **f** In the 1930s Hitler built up Germany's army and navy.
- **g** Hitler allowed communists to become powerful in Germany.
- **h** In the 1930s the army was very powerful in Japan.

2 Match each date in column A with an event in column B.

A	B
1919	Mussolini becomes leader of Italy
1922	Japan attacks Manchuria
1931	Germany, Italy and Japan sign a treaty
1933	Germany signs Treaty of Versailles
1935	Hitler becomes chancellor of Germany
1937	Italy invades Abyssinia

Think *for yourself*

Use the information in Figures 5.6, 5.7 and the text to make a list of reasons why the League of Nations failed to stop the Second World War.

War comes to Europe

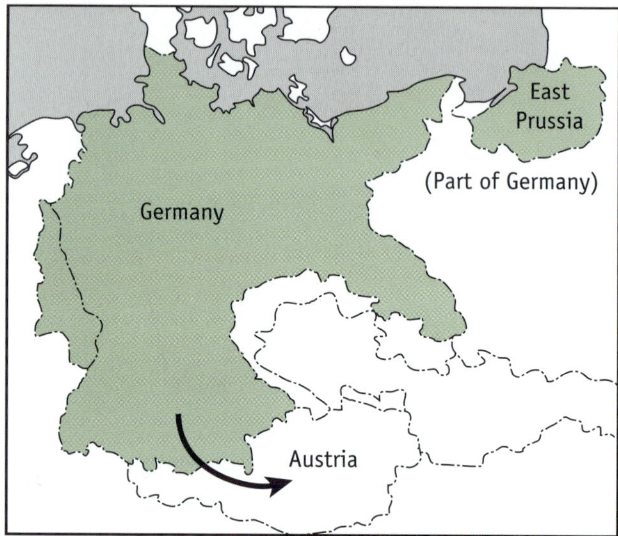

Figure 5.8
German troops enter Austria

February 1938

Hitler demands that Germany and Austria should be united. He forces the Austrian chancellor to resign and sends German troops into Austria. Britain and France are worried about what has happened, but they believe Hitler when he says that he wants no more land.

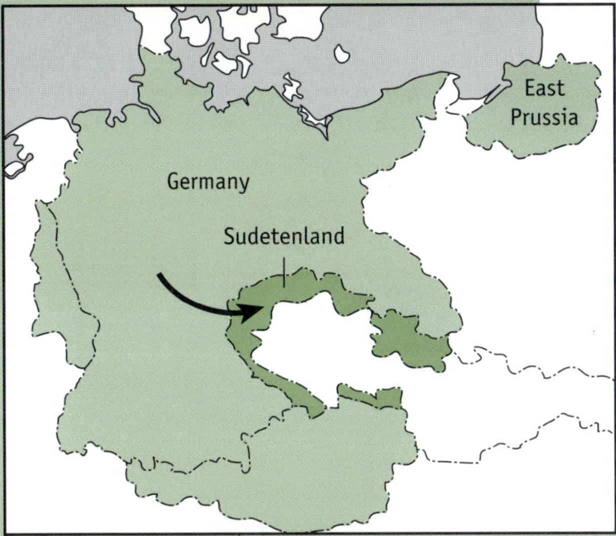

Figure 5.9
Germany takes part of Czechoslovakia

October 1938

Hitler claims part of Czechoslovakia where 3 million Germans live. He sends German troops to the border. The leaders of Britain and France meet Hitler at Munich. They agree to let Hitler take part of Czechoslovakia. They are trying to **appease** Hitler. By giving him what he wants, they hope he will be satisfied. This way they think that they will be able to avoid another large war.

Figure 5.10
German troops take the rest of Czechoslovakia

March 1939

Hitler is not satisfied. German troops march into the rest of Czechoslovakia. Britain and France realise that Hitler cannot be trusted. They know that Poland will be the next victim because Poland separates a group of German people from the rest of Germany. Britain and France agree to support Poland if Hitler attacks.

Figure 5.11
Blitzkrieg! German troops move into Poland on motorbikes and armoured cars. Planes have already bombed the city buildings. Why was blitzkrieg so successful?

Blitzkrieg!

Blitzkrieg means 'lightning war'. In 1935 Hitler said:

> If I were to attack an opponent … would do it suddenly, like a flash of lightning in the night.

Hitler used *blitzkrieg* tactics to conquer Europe in 1939 and 1940. *Blitzkrieg* relied on surprise and speed. Before dawn, German bombers attacked and destroyed planes, railways and army bases. Paratroopers captured bridges and airfields. Then came the tanks, thundering through the country and destroying what was in their way. Behind them came soldiers in cars and trucks.

Figure 5.12
The two allies: Benito Mussolini and Adolf Hitler

Figure 5.13
Germany attacks Poland

1 September 1939

Germany attacks Poland.

3 September 1939

Britain and France declare war on Germany. By the end of September Germany has conquered Poland; Warsaw, Poland's capital, is in ruins.

Then, for a few months, the war seems to stop. It is the period of **phoney war**. But Britain and France are preparing their armies and Germany is strengthening its troops on the French border.

April 1940

Germany attacks and conquers Norway and Denmark.

May 1940

Hitler's troops capture Luxembourg, Holland and Belgium. Blitzkrieg works again. German troops move into the north of France. The British and French soldiers are pushed right back to the French coast.

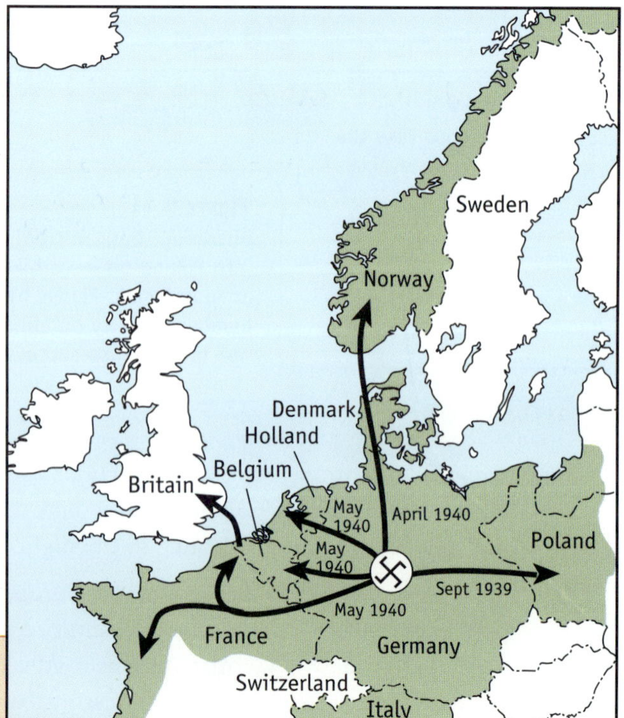

Figure 5.14
Blitzkrieg 1939–40

Daily Telegraph

SYDNEY, MONDAY, SEPTEMBER 4, 1939.

This Is Why Great Britain Is At War

BRITAIN has been forced into the war that she has for three years tried hard to avert.

Germany is really attacking the Western Powers, though her aggression was directed against Poland.

Without a declaration of war, and after Poland had agreed to take no action on the frontiers that would jeopardise discussions, German bombers rained death on Polish cities.

At the same time long-mobilised German forces crossed the borders.

Poland, with whom Germany concluded a 10-year non-aggression agreement in 1934, was subject to all the horrors of totalitarian war, already tried out on a small scale in Spain.

Even then the British Government made a last effort to save the world from another great war.

Britain appealed to the Nazis to withdraw their forces from Poland on the understanding that if she did so Britain would regard the position as restored to what it was before the invasion.

When he received this ultimatum the German Foreign Minister, Herr von Ribbentrop, added insult to the deadly injury already inflicted on Poland.

He crudely and cruelly replied:—"Germany is not guilty of aggression."

In the face of this staggering lie Britain and France could do nothing else except honor their pledges to Poland and enter the struggle.

Figure 5.15
The front page of a Sydney newspaper after war had been declared

Figure 5.16
A propaganda poster produced in the USSR during the German invasion. What was its purpose? What symbols can you find in the picture? What do they represent?

25 May–2 June 1940

Hundreds of small boats sail from England across the English Channel. At Dunkirk, on the north coast of France, they rescue 224 000 English and 95 000 French troops and take them to England.

14 June 1940

Paris is captured by the Germans.

25 June 1940

France surrenders to Germany. Fighting stops again.

August 1940

Battle of Britain begins. The German airforce, or *Luftwaffe*, starts attacking British ships. British and German planes have 'dogfights'. German planes attack British aircraft bases.

7 September–3 November 1940

London is attacked every night by German bombers. Hundreds of people are killed and much of London is in ruins. But Britain's airforce fights back and Hitler does not defeat Britain.

22 June 1941

Germany begins its invasion of Russia. At first the German army is successful.

CHECK the facts

1 Put these events in the right order. Start with the one that happened first.
- — Battle of Britain starts
- — Hitler conquers Norway
- — Germany invades Russia
- — Hitler takes over Austria
- — British and French soldiers rescued from Dunkirk
- — Hitler invades Poland
- — Hitler becomes chancellor of Germany
- — Munich conference
- — Hitler controls all Czechoslovakia
- — France surrenders to Germany.

2 What does **appeasement** mean? How did Britain and France appease Hitler in 1938? Why did they do this?

3 What does the German word ***blitzkrieg*** mean? Suggest some reasons why Hitler used *blitzkrieg* to invade Europe in 1939 and 1940.

4 What does **phoney** mean? Why is the time between October 1939 and April 1940 called the phoney war?

Figure 5.17
British soldiers climb across boats to reach safety at Dunkirk. When was this photo taken? Why did these soldiers need to escape? How did they escape?

Figure 5.18
Women and children leave their bombed London home

Think *for yourself*

1 The cartoon (Figure 5.19) was published in an Australian newspaper in 1939. What does it mean? Why did Hitler attack Poland? Why did the attack on Poland bring Britain and France into the war?

2 Figure 5.20 shows Londoners spending the night on an underground railway station. When do you think this photograph was taken? Why?

3 Fig. 5.21 shows young men waiting at a recruiting office in 1939. How can you tell that this is not a modern photograph?

Figure 5.19
POLAND, OCTOBER, 1939

Figure 5.20
Spending the night in an underground railway station in London

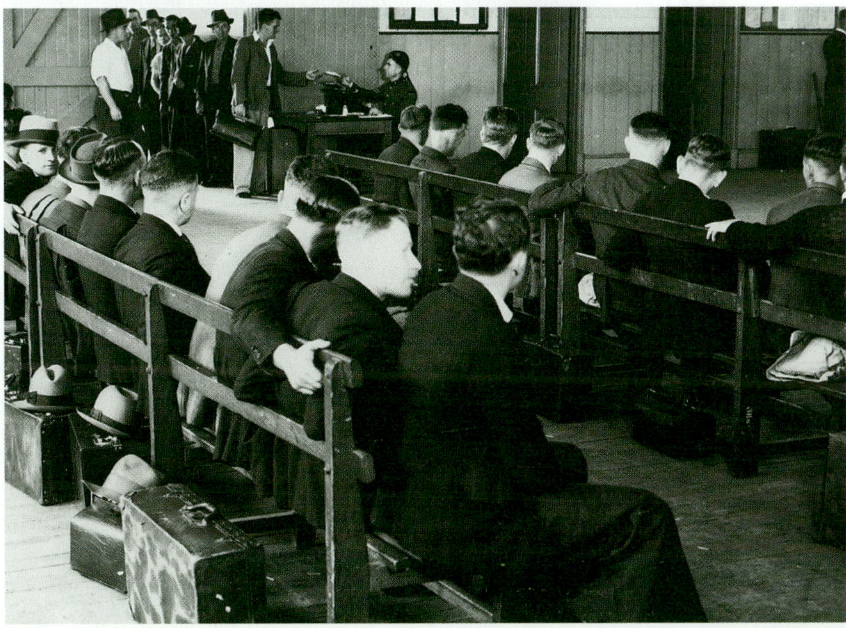

Figure 5.21
Recruits waiting to enlist for the Second World War

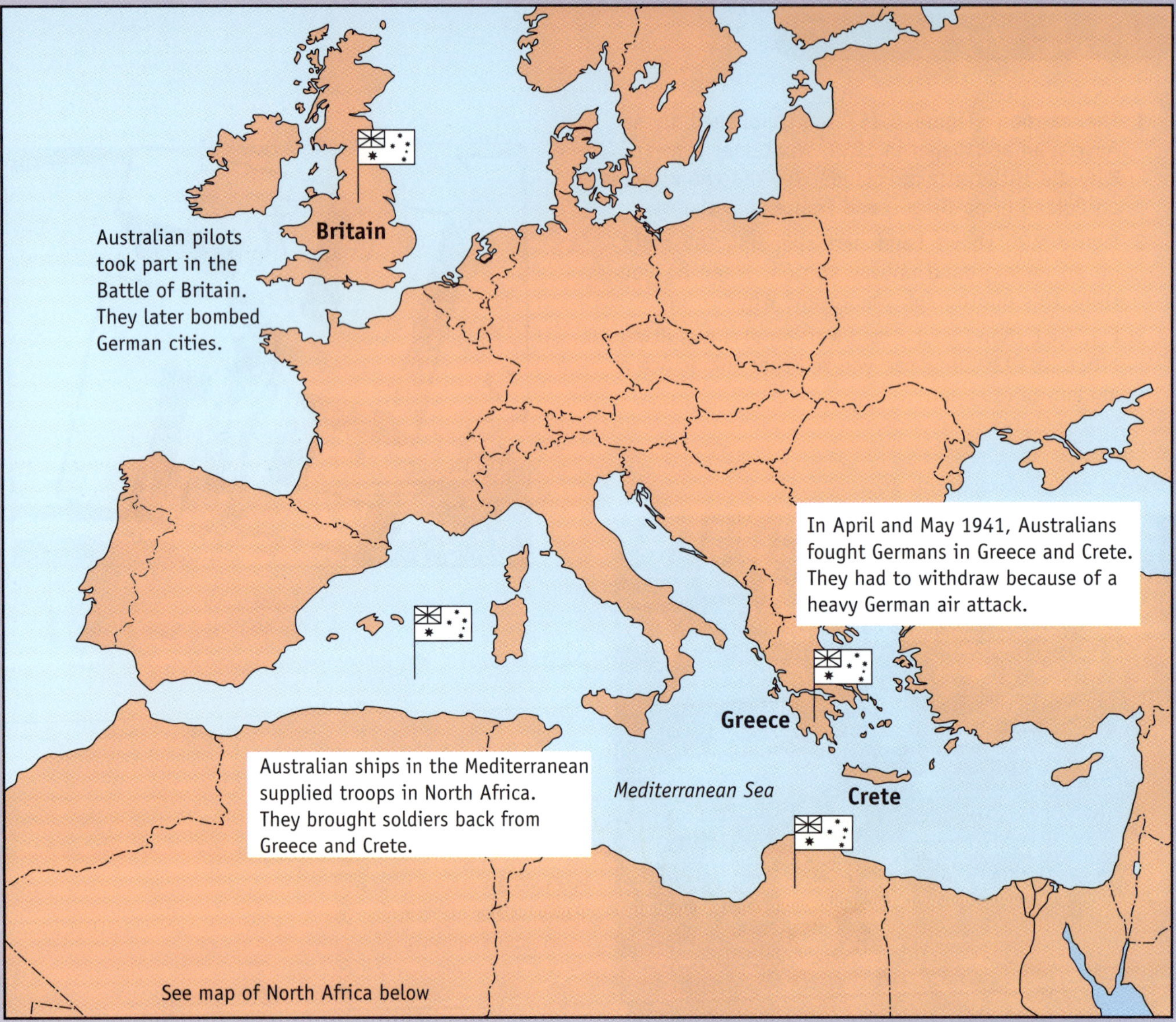

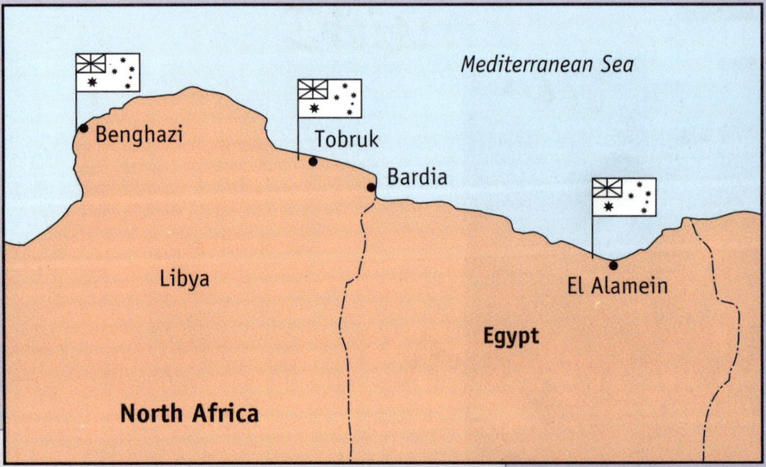

Between January and March 1941 Australians helped to defeat Italians in North Africa. They drove Italians from Bardia, Tobruk and Benghazi.

From April to September 1941 thousands of Australians held Tobruk against German troops. They were called 'the Rats of Tobruk'.

In October and November 1942, Australians fought in the Battle of El Alamein. German troops were defeated. They were soon pushed out of North Africa.

Figure 5.22
Where Australians fought—Europe and North Africa

Australia joins in—again

Australia declared war on Germany on 3 September 1939—the same day Britain did. Prime Minister Robert Menzies made a radio broadcast in which he told Australians:

> Fellow Australians. It is my melancholy duty to inform you officially, that, in consequence of the persistence by Germany in her invasion of Poland, Great Britain has declared war upon her, and that, as a result, Australia is also at war.

Australia was now an independent member of the British Commonwealth of Nations. It did not have to join the war to support Britain. But most Australians believed that if Britain was in trouble, it was Australia's duty to help.

Getting ready

As the phoney war dragged on, many Australians lost interest in the war that was so many thousands of kilometres away. But during this time Australia prepared its fighting forces. Young men were conscripted into the army so that they could be trained to defend Australia. Conscripted soldiers could not be sent to fight overseas.

The war with Japan

On 7 December 1941 Japanese bombers attacked the United States naval base at Pearl Harbor in Hawaii. Out of the whole United States fleet, there were only four aircraft carriers that were not in port. Most of the ships were moored together in 'Battleship Row'. The attack came as a complete surprise. Within half an hour the fleet had been almost completely destroyed. More than 2300 men were killed.

Figure 5.23
This painting shows the surrender of the British army at Singapore. When did this scene occur? What two flags can you see in the picture? What do they symbolise?

On the day after the attack, the USA and Britain were at war with Japan. Australia, too, declared war on Japan. For the first time Australians feared that their own land would be invaded. Prime Minister John Curtin (who had been elected two months earlier) called it 'the gravest hour of our history'.

Japanese victories

Japanese forces moved quickly into Hong Kong, Borneo and the Philippines. British and Australian troops in Malaya had to retreat to the British naval base at Singapore.

Singapore was well protected from an attack by sea. But it was not well protected from an attack through Malaya. Thousands of Japanese soldiers moved into Malaya. They moved southwards. Many of them rode down the peninsula on bicycles. On 9 February 1942 Japanese troops attacked Singapore. On 15 February the British forces there surrendered. Singapore had fallen. When Singapore fell more than 13 000 Australians were taken prisoner. Many spent the rest of the war in Japanese prisoner-of-war camps, the most notorious being Changi. Others were forced to build the 'death railway' between Burma and Siam (Thailand). Only one-third of POWs were alive at the end of the war.

Figure 5.24
A small boat goes to help sailors trapped on a ship that was bombed at Pearl Harbor. Why was the Japanese attack so successful?

Figure 5.25
Why Japan attacked Pearl Harbor

Figure 5.26
Japanese planes bombed Singapore many times. Here a mother weeps as she sees her child killed in an air raid.

Australia is threatened

When Singapore fell, Prime Minister Curtin said:

> The fall of Singapore opens the Battle of Australia … He would be a very dull person who does not accept the fall of Singapore as involving a completely new situation … Protection of this country is no longer that of a contribution to a world at war, but the resistance to an enemy threatening to invade our own shore … Hours previously devoted to sport and leisure must be given to duties of war … As things stand in Australia, brains and brawn are better then either bets or beer.

Figure 5.27
LONG-DISTANCE THINKING.
This cartoon was published in an Australian newspaper of 1942. Who do the three figures represent? What point is the cartoon making?

Think *for yourself*

1 What did Curtin mean by 'the Battle of Australia'?
2 Write down three examples of Australia's 'contribution to a world at war' before the fall of Singapore.
3 Why did Curtin think the fall of Singapore changed Australia's part in the war?
4 What did Curtin mean by 'brains and brawn are better than either bets or beer'? How did he want Australians to change?

A new ally

Britain was fighting for its life in Europe. Japan was moving quickly into Asia and the Pacific. Australia's most experienced fighting men were in Europe. Australians felt afraid. Australia had joined the war to help Britain, but now it was Australia that needed help. Would Britain allow Australia to be invaded? Could Britain help Australia?

In his New Year message at the beginning of 1942, Prime Minister Curtin told Australians:

> I make it quite clear that Australia looks to America, free of any pangs as to our traditional links or kinship with the United Kingdom [Britain].

When Singapore fell Curtin demanded that Australian troops should be sent back from the Middle East to defend Australia. Winston Churchill, Britain's prime minister, insisted that they should go to protect Burma. Burma was still a colony of Britain. But Curtin refused to send them. Over 46 000 soldiers returned to Australia. It was the first time that an Australian leader had disobeyed Britain in a time of crisis.

In March 1942 General Douglas MacArthur was put in charge of all Australian and United States troops in the south-west Pacific. The USA sent thousands of tonnes of guns and equipment. About 33 000 American soldiers arrived in Australia. There were almost half a million Australian soldiers—both conscripts and volunteers—ready to defend Australia.

Figure 5.28
Torn-up paper fell like snow as these troops were welcomed back from the Middle East. Why were they brought back to Australia?

Think *for yourself*

The cartoon (Figure 5.29) was published in an Australian newspaper at the end of 1941.

1 Who do the two people in the cartoon represent?
2 What does the picture on the wall show about the way Britain thought of Australia at the beginning of the war?
3 What did Curtin say in his speech that changed Britain's mind?
4 What were the 'Australian Pacific War Plans' that worried Britain?
5 How did Australia 'grow up' during the Second World War?

Figure 5.29
MANHOOD

The Kokoda Trail

Japan invaded Buna and Gona on the north coast of New Guinea in July 1942. The Japanese planned to move south along a track that passed through the village of Kokoda and then through the rugged Owen Stanley mountains to Port Moresby. Port Moresby is less than 500 kilometres from the north of Australia.

In August, Japanese troops captured Kokoda. Then they pushed further south. They were only 48 kilometres from Port Moresby when they were stopped by an Australian force. Slowly they pushed the Japanese back to Kokoda. At the beginning of November 1942, Kokoda was captured by the Australians. After a long struggle, the Australians were able to force the Japanese to leave New Guinea in 1944. The immediate danger was over.

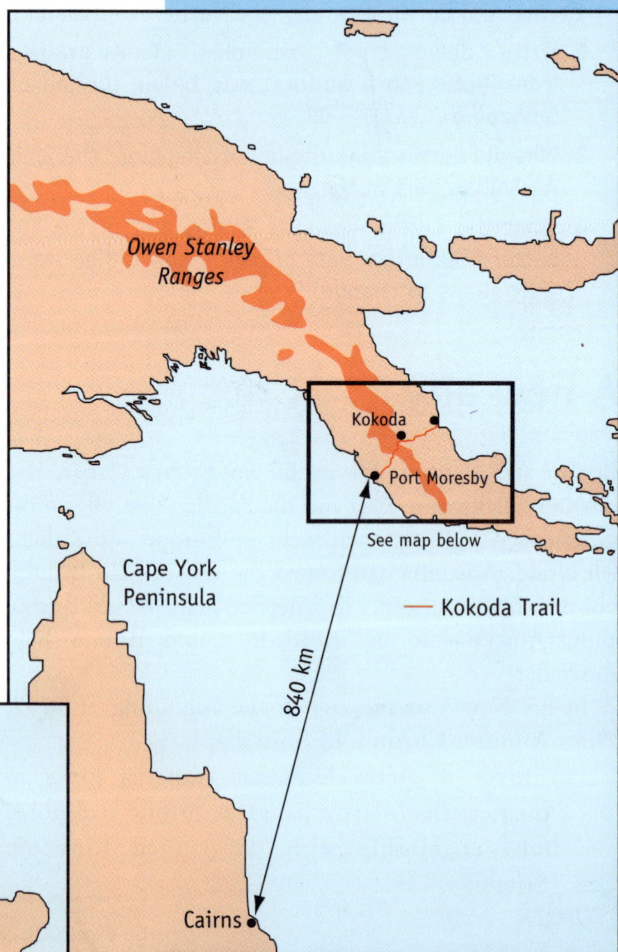

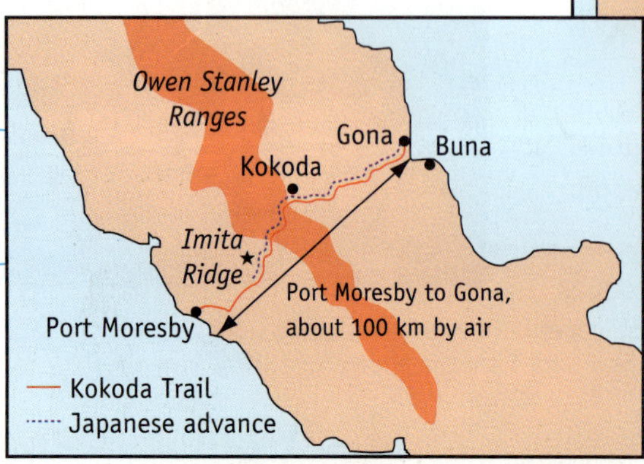

Figure 5.30
The Kokoda Trail

Jim Davis was not a real person but his story could have been told by many of the Australian soldiers who fought on the Kokoda Trail.

They brought us back from the Middle East to fight in New Guinea. I'd done some hard fighting over there, but I'd never seen anything like that jungle before. We had some conscripts with us. 'Chokkos' we called them—short for chocolate soldiers. But they did a good job, although they weren't as experienced as us AIF blokes. The natives did a good job too. They helped us with food and carried our supplies when they could. They took a lot of my wounded mates back to safety on stretchers. We called them the fuzzy wuzzy angels. I reckon they were too.

It was a terrible place to fight a war. It was always hot and almost always raining. We were always tramping through thick mud and swamps, fighting our way through the trees and vines. It took us hours just to go a couple of miles. Up one side of a mountain and down another. We had to build our own bridges across the rivers too.

Figure 5.31
We relied on the fuzzy wuzzy angels in New Guinea. Thousands were killed in the campaign.

Figure 5.33
We called this the Golden Staircase. There were more than 2000 steps cut into the mountain. We had to take our food and supplies with us to the top.

Figure 5.32
This painting shows a scene on the Kokoda trail. Describe what is happening in this scene.
William Dargie, 'Stretcher Bearers in the Owen Stanleys', oil on canvas, 143.2 x 234.4 cm, Australian War Memorial (26653)

Figure 5.34
Crossing rivers wasn't easy!

They treated us as heroes when we got home. I know how Dad felt now when he got home after the first war. They reckoned that we'd saved Australia. But the Japanese had a different idea. They called us 'The Mice of Moresby'. They said we spent all day in holes like the Rats of Tobruk.

Figure 5.35
When we got to Buna we had to find and clear out the Japanese bunkers. Some of them were cleverly hidden.

We had to carry all our supplies with us. There was only one proper airfield and that was at Kokoda. The Japs had that. Our planes dropped supplies and guns when they could, but we could never rely on it. We often had to live on our emergency rations for days. We even had to take our big guns to pieces and drag them with us along the track.

There seemed to be Japs everywhere sniping at us. They were so well camouflaged that it was almost impossible to see them. We wore our jungle gear too. The Japs were good fighters but we soon learnt to beat them at their own game. Sometimes we had all-out battles against the Japanese. We lost a lot of our men that way. But those terrible tropical diseases killed off a lot more of our boys. Malaria was the worst.

We got up to Kokoda in November. We killed about 600 Japanese in the battle there. Once we'd taken Kokoda, things got better. We got the airfield into working order again. From then on it was a lot easier to get our supplies in.

Then we pushed on to the north coast. There were 11 000 Japs waiting for us near Buna and Gona. Sometimes they were really hard to find. They'd dug bunkers in the ground and covered them with sheets of iron. The airforce helped us a lot by bombing Japanese ships in the harbour. That stopped them bringing more men in. But it took us two months to get rid of the Japanese. It was a great day at the end of January 1943 when the last of them left that part of New Guinea.

One of our boys wrote a poem about the war. Here's a bit of it:

Rats of old Tobruk
Or merely Moresby mice—
We've had our share of fighting
And of hardships once or twice …
We have toiled and we have sweated
In the humid, tropic heat
And we've longed for many comforts
And fresh food that we could eat.

CHECK the facts

Use the information about the Kokoda Trail and Jim Davis' story to answer these questions.

1 How long did it take the Japanese to move from the north coast of New Guinea to Kokoda?

2 What did the Japanese plan to do when they had captured Kokoda?

3 Why was this plan a threat to Australia?

4 How long did it take the Australians to capture Kokoda from the Japanese?

5 Why did the Australian volunteer soldiers call the conscripts 'chokkos'?

6 Why did they call the New Guinea natives 'fuzzy wuzzy angels'?

7 Why did Australian soldiers have to carry most of their supplies with them along the Kokoda Trail?

8 How did the airforce help the AIF at Buna and Gona?

9 Why did the people at home think that the soldiers who fought in New Guinea had saved Australia?

10 Read the story and the poem. Look at the pictures. Use them to make a list of the problems that the 'Moresby Mice' had to face.

War comes to Darwin

At half past nine on the morning of 19 February 1942 a missionary on Bathurst Island reported by radio telephone that planes were flying towards Darwin. Australian officials thought that they were United States planes and it was twenty minutes before anyone realised that they were Japanese bombers. The warning sirens had been going for less than a minute when the attack started.

For almost an hour that morning 188 bombers attacked Darwin. Eight ships in the harbour were sunk and 150 crewmen were killed. The town itself was badly damaged.

Just before midday there was another attack. This time fifty-four bombers shelled the airforce base. Twenty Australian planes were wrecked.

After the raids there was panic. War had come to Australia for the first time. The people of Darwin believed that Japanese troops were about to invade Australia. Many people fled into the bush. Others went south in cars, trucks or anything they could drive or ride in. Airmen, soldiers and civilians started looting shops. They stole everything they thought was valuable.

More than 240 people were killed in the Darwin bombings and 400 were hurt. But the rest of Australia did not learn what really happened. Newspapers reported that only seventeen had been killed and twenty-four wounded. The government was afraid that people would panic if they knew the truth. Newspapers were allowed to print only what the government wanted people to know. This **censorship** caused newspaper owners and many others to criticise the government during the war.

Figure 5.36
Black clouds of smoke rise over Darwin after the first Japanese attack

Figure 5.37
A painting of the Japanese attack on Darwin Harbour. What are the planes bombing in this picture?
Keith Swain, 'Japanese Air Attack on Darwin Harbour, 19th February 1942', 1975, tempera on canvas on plywood, 175.3 x 243.9 cm Australian War Memorial (28075)

War comes to Sydney

The war came to Sydney on the night of 31 May 1942. A Japanese submarine outside Sydney Harbour launched three midget submarines. Each of these midget submarines held two people. One submarine got caught in the boom nets that had been put at the entrance to Sydney Harbour. One was sunk by a navy patrol boat. The third fired torpedoes at a United States warship in the harbour. One torpedo hit a Sydney ferry that had been converted into a depot ship. Nineteen sailors were killed. The submarine then left the harbour.

A week later a submarine shelled Sydney's eastern suburbs. A block of flats and some houses were damaged. One person suffered a broken arm. Newcastle was also shelled, but there was not very much damage.

Figure 5.38
This ferry was sunk by one of the Japanese midget submarines in Sydney Harbour

More power to the government

During the Second World War the Australian government passed laws that gave it much greater control over the lives of its citizens. Figure 5.40 shows some of the ways in which the government controlled people's lives.

Conscription—again

In the Second World War conscription did not cause the bitterness that it had caused in the First World War. There were two kinds of Australian forces: **volunteers**, who could be sent to fight anywhere in the world and **conscripts**, who could only be used for home defence.

At the start of the war, soldiers in the CMF could only be used to defend Australia. This meant that they were allowed to fight in Australia and in the part of New Guinea that was ruled by Australia. But when Japan came into the war and quickly took over the Pacific Islands, it was clear that in order to defend Australia, soldiers in the CMF would have to be sent overseas. In February 1943 Curtin increased the area in which conscripts could serve. This area was bordered by what became known as the 'Curtin Line'. It included all of New Guinea, most of the East Indies (now Indonesia) and some of the Pacific Islands.

Figure 5.39
How the government became more powerful during the war

Think *for yourself*

1. In what ways was the attack on Darwin similar to the attack that the Japanese made on Pearl Harbor two months earlier?
2. After the Japanese attack on Darwin, Prime Minister Curtin told Australians: 'The government has told you the truth. Face it like Australians.' Did the government tell Australians the truth about the raid on Darwin? Why?
3. Why did the government want to take so much control over people's lives during the war?
4. Why do you think the government banned the Communist Party and the Fascist Party?
5. What sort of factories would do well in a war?
6. Do you think the government should be able to force people to do certain jobs in wartime? Why?
7. Why did John Curtin think it was necessary to allow conscripts to be sent overseas to fight after 1942?
8. Most Australians agreed with Curtin when he said that conscription for overseas was needed. Why do you think this was so?

The war at home

I joined the Women's Army Service in 1942 soon after it was formed. There were nearly 24 000 of us by the end of the war. About 500 went to New Guinea but most of us stayed in Australia. We did a lot of back-up work for the army. I was a plane spotter. Other women joined the navy or airforce. Of course there were many nurses who served with the forces as well.

I worked in a factory that made shells. They called us 'soldiers in overalls'. There were a lot of women in my factory because so many men had gone to the war. We worked as hard as the men in the factory but we didn't get anywhere near as much money. It was hard work, too, and very boring. We worked for long hours, and it was dirty and noisy. We were always tired.

Figure 5.40
The Women's Army Service

Figure 5.41
Women working in a munitions factory

Figure 5.42
The Land Army

I joined the Land Army. There were about 3000 of us working full time. We helped farmers with whatever work was needed. I worked on a sheep station. It took me a while to get used to it because I came from the city. But after a while I quite liked it, although I had to work harder than I'd ever done before.

Figure 5.44
Volunteer Defence Corps training on a Sydney golf course, 1943

I was in the Volunteer Defence Corps. I joined in 1940 when it was started. I'd served in the first war and wanted to do my bit to help in this one, too, even though I was too old to join up. I was a signaller. Some of my mates were factory guards. Others were coast watchers or air raid wardens.

Figure 5.43
Thousands of soldiers worked on farms during the war. Why?

I was a farmer. I worked flat out during the war. The government had arranged to grow food for the Americans as well as for our own people. They even let 20 000 men from the army come back to the farms to help. The Land Army girls did a great job too. But we didn't have the machines we needed to grow so much food and harvest it quickly. It was hard to get enough fertilisers too.

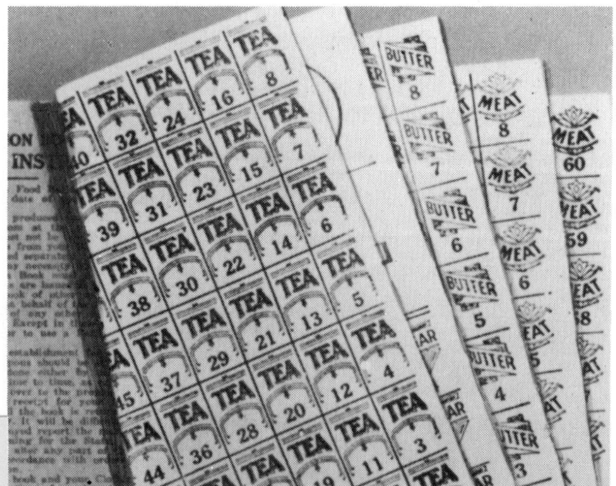

Figure 5.45
Householders had ration books. Food items were rationed so that there would be more for the troops.

I was a housewife. Things were tough during the war but they weren't as bad in Australia as they were in England. At least we didn't get bombed every night like they did in London. But it was hard getting enough food and clothes for my family. The government wanted to save as much as it could for the troops, so we had to go short. We all had a ration book and we could only buy as much as we had coupons for. It was hard to get eggs and butter and tea and beer and tinned food. But we usually had enough meat and fruit. Shopping was hard work, though. There were always queues because there wasn't much food about. Sometimes I even took my own wrapping paper to the shop—the government thought that paper was a luxury we could do without. Some people were able to get all sorts of things on the black market, especially cigarettes and alcohol. But you had to know the 'right' people to buy things you weren't supposed to.

I was lucky because my husband worked in the mines. He wasn't allowed to change his job but at least he was at home during the war to help with the kids. It was really hard on the mothers whose husbands were away fighting.

I was at school in the war. For a while things didn't change much. But after the Japanese came into the war there were quite a lot of changes. We had an air raid shelter in our school playground. There was one in the park too. At home we had special blinds that we had to keep closed at night so that planes wouldn't be able to see where the cities were. Even buses, cars and trucks were painted brown and green camouflage colours. At school we did air raid drill. We sewed and knitted and collected money for the soldiers. Mum said she did the same thing in the last war. We were supposed to save our money to buy savings stamps. It was a way of lending money to the government to help pay for the war. There were silly rhymes about them in one of our schoolbooks. This is one I remember:

Little Miss Muffet
Safe on a tuffet,
Counting her stamps one by one;
Saying, 'Each one I buy
Helps a bomber to fly
And this war simply has to be won.'

We didn't have many toys during the war. Everything was plain and practical. One year the shops weren't even allowed to have a Santa Claus in their toy department. Still, things could have been a lot worse I suppose.

Figure 5.46
Why are these children hiding under their desks?

THE HISTORIAN AT WORK

Working with pictorial sources

Figure 5.47

Figure 5.49

Figure 5.50
Artist unknown, 'Food is a munition of war!', 1942–1945, lithograph, 75.5 x 50.4 cm, Australian War Memorial (V161)

Figure 5.51
James Northfield, '"Doing a grand job!" Join the WAAAF', 1942 photo lithograph, 99.8 x 63.2 cm, Australian War Memorial (V5170)

Figure 5.48

Figure 5.52

Figure 5.53

Figure 5.54

1 What do the initials WAAF and AWAS stand for? From the evidence in these pictures and the information on pages 115–117, what kind of jobs did women in the armed services perform during the Second World War?

2 What organisation did the woman in Figure 5.48 belong to? What kind of work did these women do? Why was this organisation formed? Do you think this advertisement gives a very accurate picture of what life was really like for women in this organisation?

3 What evidence can you find in these pictures that some things were in short supply during the war years? Why were many products hard to get during the war years?

4 What is the 'coupon savers' picture encouraging people to do? What were coupons used for? Why would people want to save them?

5 Why, do you think, did the Australian government launch the Liberty Loans? How could people invest in them?

6 What was the purpose of the 'Food' poster in Figure 5.50? Who are the people in this poster? What kind of food is shown in the poster? Why is this food described as a 'munition of war'?

7 What is the 'Joy Toys' advertisement encouraging people to do? Why was this necessary during the war?

8 From what you have read earlier in this chapter, and from the evidence of these posters and advertisements, explain some of the ways in which women made important contributions to the war effort.

9 Even though they were not involved directly in fighting the war, many Australian women served overseas during the Second World War. Do some research to find out what they did.

The American invasion

They saved us from the Japs,
Perhaps;
But this place is at present too Yank-full
For us to be decently thankful.

Figure 5.55
What is this boy doing? Why was it useful during the war?

By September 1943 there were 120 000 American soldiers in Australia. Some were on leave. Others were stationed here. They used Australia as a base for attacks on the islands to the north.

The GIs, as they were called, looked smarter than the Australian soldiers. (GI stood for 'general issue', which was marked on the American soldiers' equipment.) They earned twice as much money and were prepared to spend it in having a good time. Australian girls fell for the glamorous soldiers who bought them nylon stockings, flowers, Coca Cola and chocolates. The Americans could afford black market beer and cigarettes too.

Australian men were angry and resentful when their girlfriends went out with the Americans. Australian soldiers on leave wondered why they had to fight so far away when the Americans seemed to be having such a good time in Australia. There were often fights and brawls, especially in Brisbane where most of the Americans were based.

One day in 1943 two trains pulled up alongside each other in Queensland. One train was full of Australian soldiers going north to join their ships to get to the war in the Pacific. The other train was full of American soldiers going south on leave. They started hurling friendly insults at each other. Things quickly got out of hand. Before long soldiers from both trains had swarmed on to the other one. There was a wild fight with fists, boots, bottles and belts.

Figure 5.56
These GIs have met some Australian service women

Figure 5.57
'Wot'll you do, Cabby, when the Yanks go?'
'Wot''ll YOU do, sister?'
Why were the Americans popular with taxi drivers?
Why were they popular with Australian girls?

Australian and American soldiers came to blows again in Brisbane at the end of November 1943. One night an Australian soldier was killed by an American army policeman. The next night Australian soldiers spent five hours beating up every GI they could find.

CHECK the facts

Are the statements below true or false?

1 Australia was well prepared for the Japanese attack on Darwin in February 1942.
2 Torpedoes were fired from three Japanese midget submarines in Sydney Harbour in May 1942.
3 In 1943 most Australians believed that conscripted soldiers should be sent overseas to fight.
4 Most of the women who joined the army spent the war years in Australia.
5 The women who joined the Land Army were called 'soldiers in overalls'.
6 In the 1940s Australian women workers did not get as much pay as men.
7 The Volunteer Defence Corps was formed in 1941.
8 Miners were not allowed to change their jobs during the Second World War.
9 People bought savings stamps when they wanted to post a letter.
10 Most of the fights between GIs and Australian soldiers were in Sydney.

Think *for yourself*

1 Ask your parents, grandparents, other relatives and older people you know, whether they remember the Second World War. Some of them may have served in the war. They could tell you a lot more about what it was like to fight in the war. Those who were in Australia during the war will be able to tell you about life at home. If your parents, relatives or friends lived in another country during the Second World War, they may be able to give you a lot of information about what that country was like during the war years.

Ask your parents, grandparents, other relatives and friends if they have any photos from the war years. Perhaps they have medals or other things that they have saved from the Second World War. You may be able to draw these in your book or use them to prepare a display about the Second World War.

2 The fight between the two trainloads of soldiers in Queensland in 1943 was not reported in the newspapers. Can you suggest why it was not reported?

3 Petrol was rationed in Australia after October 1940. Each car was allowed enough petrol to travel about 25 kilometres a week. Why did the government ration petrol? Petrol rationing did not affect as many people in the early 1940s as it would affect today. Why not?

Australia's wartime leaders

Robert Menzies

Prime minister from April 1939 to August 1941
Previous job: Lawyer
Party: United Australia Party
What he did: In September 1939 Menzies declared that Australia was at war with Germany. His government formed a war council to decide on war policy. In 1941 Menzies visited the troops and spoke with British and American leaders about Australia's part in the war. But he did not have the full support of his party and was forced to resign in August 1941. Three years later he formed the Liberal Party.

Figure 5.58
Menzies announces that Australia is at war in 1939

Figure 5.59
The strain of war affected Curtin's health. He died a few weeks before the war ended.

John Curtin

Prime minister from October 1941 to July 1945
Previous job: Journalist
Party: Labor Party
What he did: Curtin became prime minister two months before Japan entered the war. He led Australia through a time of danger and fear. Curtin increased the government's control over industry and farming. He brought Australian troops back from the Middle East to defend Australia. He turned to the USA for support when Australia was threatened. He put the whole country on to a war basis and expected all Australians to do their part to help win the war. The strain and pressure of his task weakened Curtin's health, and he died a few weeks before the war ended.

Joseph ('Ben') Chifley

Prime minister from July 1945 to December 1949
Previous job: Train driver
Party: Labor Party
What he did: Ben Chifley had been Curtin's treasurer. His main job when he became prime minister was to organise the peace after the war and get Australia back to normal.

Figure 5.60
Ben Chifley became Australia's prime minister just before the end of the Second World War.

The war ends in Europe

By 1942 it was clear that Germany and Italy would be defeated. The map (Figure 5.61) shows how they were beaten by the forces of Britain, USA and the USSR. You can see how important it was for the British and United States forces to win North Africa back from German and Italian troops. This allowed them to invade Italy. You can see, too, that Germany was caught between British and American soldiers attacking from the west and Soviet troops attacking from the east.

The war in Europe officially ended with the surrender of Germany on 8 May 1945.

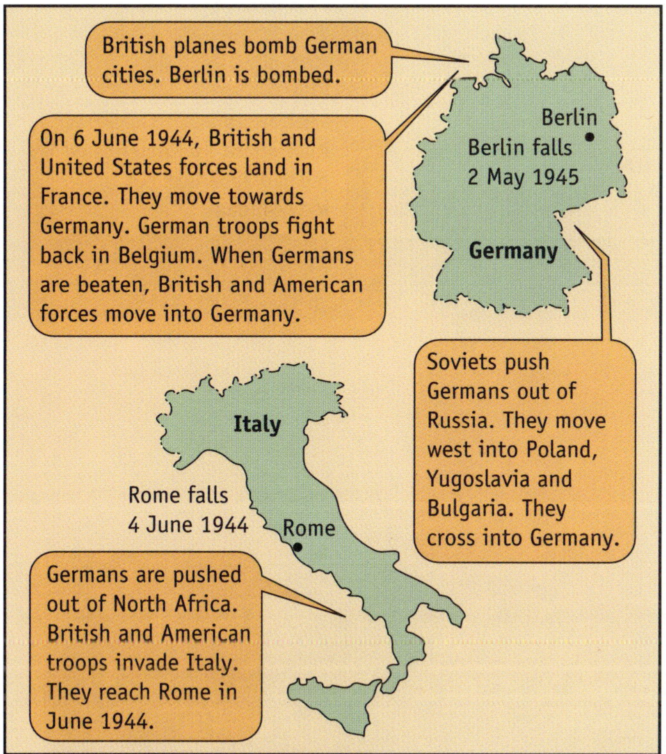

Figure 5.61
The war ends in Europe

The war ends in the Pacific

The map (Figure 5.62) shows how much land Japan controlled by May 1942. From that time on, Japanese troops were pushed back. British forces won back Burma. Two great naval battles in the Pacific—Coral Sea and Midway—stopped Japan from taking more territory. Australian soldiers regained New Guinea. General MacArthur moved north from island to island, fighting a series of fierce battles as he went.

By the beginning of 1945, it was obvious that Japan would be defeated. In March, United States forces captured the island of Iwo Jima, just 1200 kilometres from Tokyo. Three months later, they seized the Japanese island of Okinawa. Then the Americans started bombing islands even closer to Japan.

But Japan refused to surrender. The USA could have invaded Japan. Many thousands of American soldiers would have been killed before Japan gave in. Instead, President Truman decided to use a deadly new weapon that had been developed in the USA during the war.

The atomic age begins

On the morning of 6 August 1945 three United States bombers flew over the Japanese city of Hiroshima. One of them dropped the world's first atomic bomb. As the bomb exploded, 70 000 people were burned to death instantly. The city was flattened to rubble by the atomic blast. The mushroom cloud rose high in the sky, scattering deadly radioactive fallout over a large area. This killed many thousands more people.

Three days later a second atomic bomb was dropped on the city of Nagasaki. About 40 000 people were killed.

On 2 September 1945, Japan surrendered. The Second World War had ended. But the world had gained a frightening new weapon.

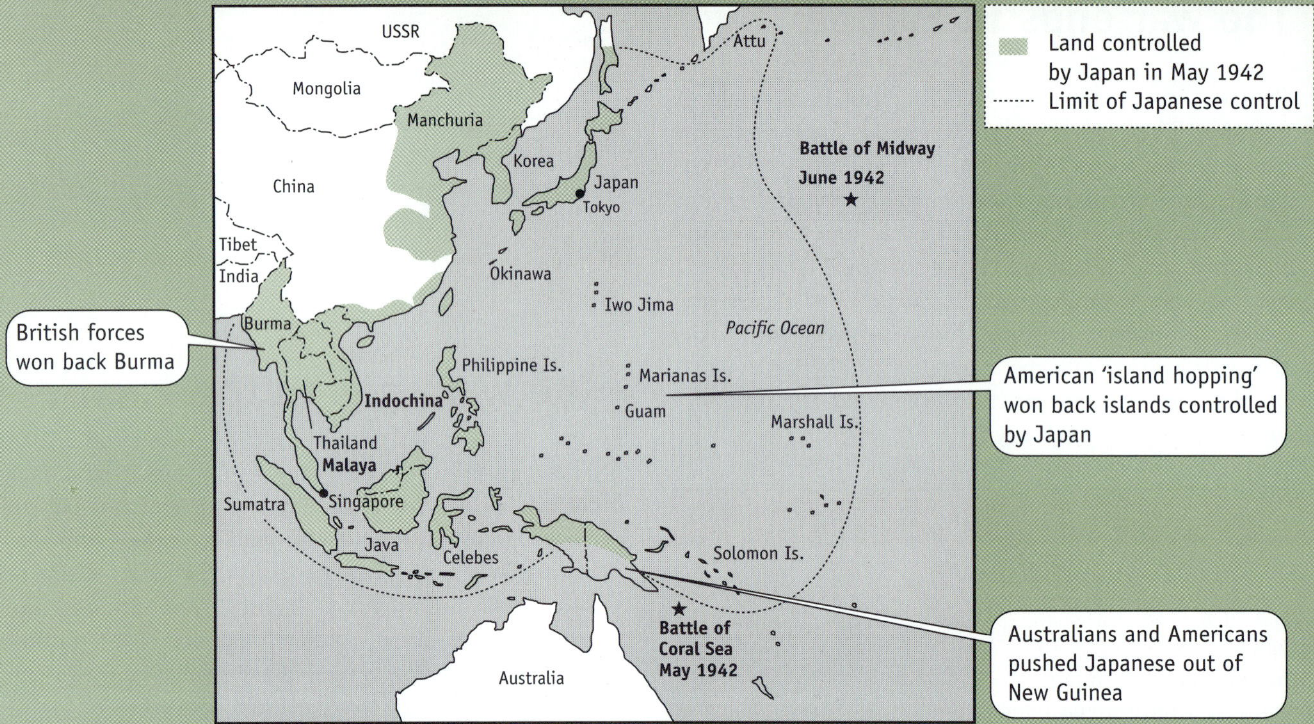

Figure 5.62
The war ends in the Pacific

Figure 5.63
The city of Nagasaki on 9 August 1945. Like Hiroshima, Nagasaki was destroyed by a single atomic bomb. Why did the USA decide to use atomic bombs on Japanese cities?

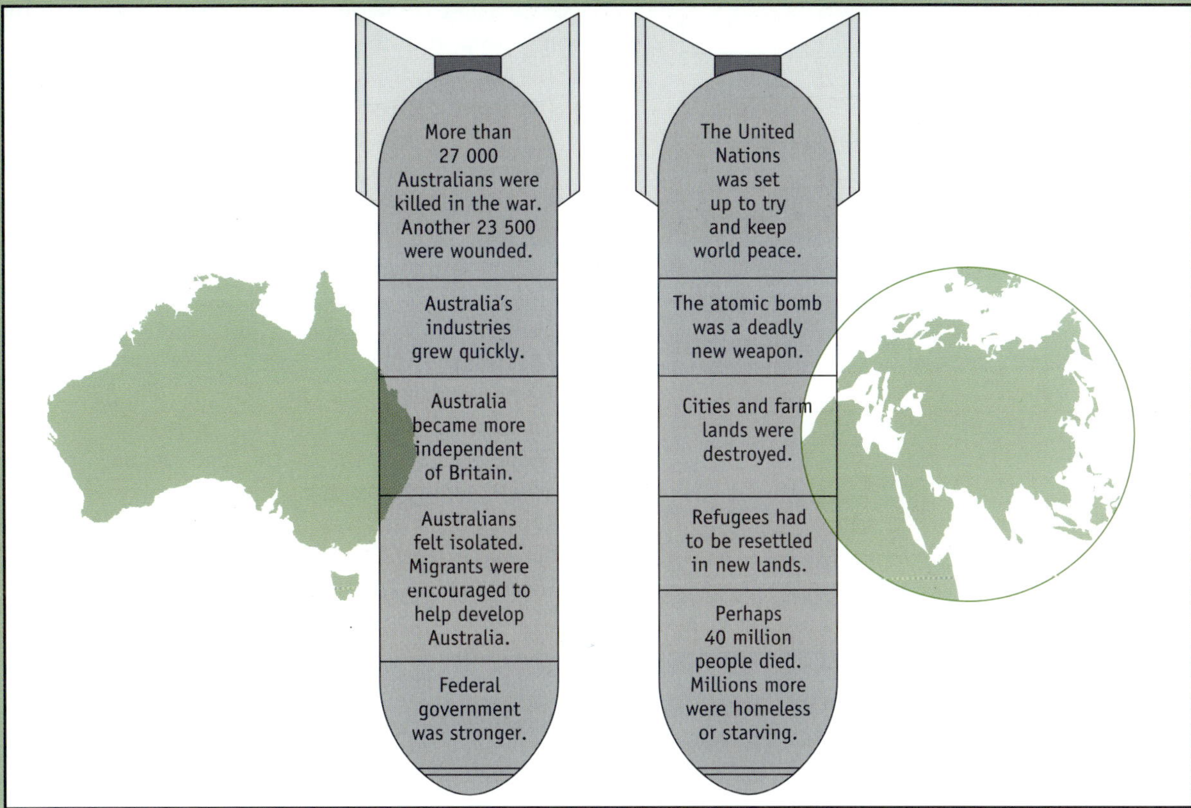

Figure 5.64
Some results of the Second World War

KNOW the chapter

1 Who was I?

- **a** I was a soldier in the First World War. I wrote a book called *Mein Kampf*.
- **b** I became the dictator of Italy in 1922. I wanted to make Italy a strong and powerful country.
- **c** I was the emperor of Japan in the 1930s. My country needed more land.
- **d** I sent my troops to attack Poland at the beginning of September 1939.
- **e** I was the prime minister of Australia when the Second World War started.
- **f** I was Britain's prime minister during the Second World War.
- **g** I was in charge of Australian and United States troops in the south-west Pacific after 1942. I pushed the Japanese back from island to island.
- **h** I was the Australian prime minister who extended the area in which conscripts could fight after February 1942.

2 Which country

- **a** left the League of Nations in 1933 and attacked China in 1937?
- **b** was invaded by German troops in October 1939?
- **c** surrendered to Germany in June 1940?
- **d** invaded the USSR in June 1941?
- **e** had its Pacific fleet destroyed on 7 December 1941?
- **f** was captured by Japan on 15 February 1942?
- **g** turned to the USA for help in January 1942?
- **h** surrendered on 8 May 1945?

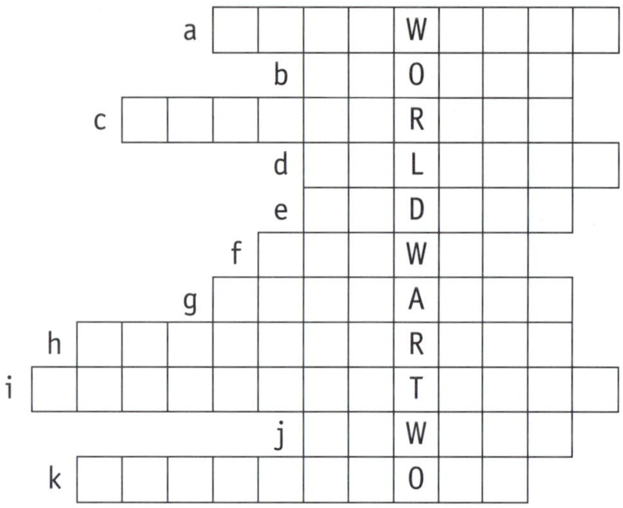

3 Use the clues below to fill in the word puzzle. All the words are in this chapter.

a The German airforce.
b The months after September 1939 were called the __________ war.
c German battle tactic.
d A tropical disease caught by soldiers in New Guinea.
e __________ submarines attacked Sydney.
f This Australian city was bombed.
g Women in this organisation worked on farms. (2 words)
h Where goods could be bought without ration coupons. (2 words)
i People bought these to lend money to the government. (2 words)
j Robert Menzies was a __________ before he became a politician.
k This new weapon forced Japan to surrender. (2 words)

THE HISTORIAN AT WORK

The bombing of Hiroshima and Nagasaki

Wilfred Burchett, an Australian journalist, visited Hiroshima just a month after the atomic bomb destroyed the city. This is what he wrote:

A Thirty days after the atomic bomb destroyed the city and shook the world, people are still dying mysteriously and horribly from its effects …

I saw people in hospitals who … are dying … from the effects of the bombing … They lost their appetites, their hair fell out … their flesh began rotting away from their bones …

The Japanese authorities thought that the (plane) which dropped the bomb was leading a normal attack. When the planes passed out of sight, thousands of people came out of shelters and watched the bomb descend by parachute. It exploded when nearly everyone in Hiroshima was in the streets. There is no trace of thousands who were near the centre of the explosion … They were burnt to ashes instantly by atomic heat.

Fifty years after the dropping of the atomic bombs on Hiroshima and Nagasaki, the *Weekend Australian* published the following recollections and opinions. This is how Tom Morris, an Australian solider who was a prisoner-of-war of the Japanese in August 1945, recalls what happened:

B For me, August 15, 1945 was just another weary day in my three-and-a-half years of Japanese captivity. My small group of Australians, British and Dutch, still slaving away in the jungles of Thailand, was totally unaware of the atomic devastation of Hiroshima and Nagasaki. Recurrent fever, dysentery and our starvation diet had taken its toll of me and my spirit was probably at its lowest ebb since becoming a prisoner.

Then, on August 16, quite unexpectedly, the Japanese issued the order: 'No worko. All men yasume.' Rest, or yasume days, had long been abolished for us, so we knew that something unusual had happened. The following day, trainloads of POWs, passed our camp heading south. Each was crowded with cheering, waving troops …

Finally our turn came and we, too, headed south. As dawn broke on August 20, we crossed over the wooden trestle bridge at Tamarkan, and then straightened up for the run past Kanchanaburi. There, a short distance ahead, was all the evidence we needed. Flying proudly at the mastheads were the flags of the USA, Holland, Great Britain and our own Blue Ensign. It was all over—I had made it safely through.

... Our ex-guards had been rounded up and at least one was held in custody pending war crimes charges ...

People, especially those who by age are so far removed from the event, talk disparagingly of the use of the atomic bombs on Japan. I make no apologies for the horrors of Hiroshima and Nagasaki. After all, Japan set the ground rules by its own barbaric behaviour.

The atomic bombings ended the war and prevented the potential for a much higher civilian death rate had the Japanese homeland been invaded by the Allies. For me, it saved my life. There is written evidence that all POWs were to be exterminated. The date set for those of us in Thailand was August 25, 1945.

I do not want, or expect, Japan to apologise for going to war in 1941. However, I do expect and want an apology for their barbaric and inhumane treatment of both POWs and civilians who had the misfortune to come under their ruthless rule.

When that apology is forthcoming, then I will endeavour to forgive. However, I will never forget. Nor will I ever trust the Japanese as a nation.

The following recollection is by the Australian scientist, Sir Mark Oliphant:

C When the war ended on August 15 my overwhelming feeling was one of sadness. I was sad that an area of physical science that sought to understand the ultimate structure of matter had become the source of nuclear weapons, a thousand times as effective at killing and destruction as the most powerful of existing chemical weapons.

I had been fortunate to work with [Sir Ernest] Rutherford in the Cavendish Laboratory, Cambridge. He had unravelled the complex series of changes which radium experienced as it transformed itself into lead.

Later, Rutherford's second-in-command discovered the neutron, a particle without electric charge, which Rutherford had described twenty years earlier.

This was the start of an exciting era in science known as particle physics. But by the end of the war this excitement had turned to dismay—the nuclear weapons dropped on Japanese cities were products of this growing knowledge of the internal structure of all matter.

Rutherford had been aware of the possibility of the release of enormous energy locked up in the nucleus of heavy atoms. In 1916, he gave a lecture in which he deplored the desire of some of his colleagues to be able to release this energy at will, saying that he hoped it would not happen in his lifetime 'or some silly fool might blow the world to pieces!'

The gentle Dane, Niels Bohr, who had made a reality of Rutherford's nuclear atom, was the most respected, and hence the leader of those among the developers of the nuclear weapon who endeavoured to persuade the President of the United States that it be used as a weapon of peace, not war.

Unfortunately, Roosevelt died before he could take action which would have ensured that this terrible new weapon was not dropped on the civilian inhabitants of a city.

So I remain sad, fifty years later, that the search for knowledge of the structure of matter, and hence of the universe, became the source of a killing agent which will threaten the whole world until it is banned universally, and the ban enforced.

1 From the evidence of what he wrote, would you say that Wilfred Burchett (document A) approved or disapproved of the bombing of Hiroshima and Nagasaki? Imagine that you were Wilfred Burchett in 1945. Write two or three sentences explaining your opinion about the dropping of the atomic bombs.

2 In what way was the bombing raid on Hiroshima on 6 August 1945 different from previous bombing raids on the city? Why did the people of the city come out of their shelters to watch the bomb descend?

3 Where was Tom Morris (document B) when the atomic bombs dropped on the two Japanese cities? What kind of work was he doing as a prisoner of the Japanese? Use the evidence of his description to give some impression of the conditions under which the prisoners were working.

4 According to Tom Morris (document B) the atomic bombings saved his life. Why does he think this? If you could talk to Tom Morris, are there any questions you would want to ask him before you were convinced that he was right about this?

5 In a few sentences sum up Tom Morris' (document B) reasons for approving of the atomic bombings. Is there any reason to think his opinions may be influenced by his experiences in the war?

6 Briefly summarise how Sir Mark Oliphant feels about the dropping of the atomic bombs (document C). Why does he feel that way? Do you think Tom Morris' arguments in favour of the bombings could cause Oliphant to change his mind? Why?

7 What kind of science was Oliphant (document C) involved in before and during the Second World War? Do some research and find out more about Oliphant's life and work. What other scientists are mentioned in Oliphant's article? Do some research to find out how their work contributed to the development of atomic weapons.

8 Who was Roosevelt? Find out when he died. Why does Oliphant think that he may have prevented the dropping of the atomic bombs (document C)? Do some research to find out who gave the order for the use of atomic weapons against Japan.

Fear *and* suspicion

In 1917 there was a violent revolution in Russia. A group of communists, led by Lenin, took control of the country. Five years later, in 1922, Joseph Stalin became the Russian leader. While Stalin was leader he made the Communist Party stronger and changed Russia from a backward farming country to a giant industrial state. Gradually, Russia gained power over nearby countries. Russia and the other countries that it ruled became known as the Union of Soviet Socialist Republics (USSR) or Soviet Union.

In the Second World War the USSR fought on the same side as the USA. Both countries wanted to stop Germany from taking over Europe. But the USA and the USSR did not really trust each other. The USA feared Russian communism. The USSR feared the power of the USA.

The beginning of the Cold War

After the Second World War the countries of Europe were divided into two groups. The western group of countries was supported by the USA. The eastern group was controlled by the USSR. In 1946 Winston Churchill, the British wartime leader, said that the countries of eastern Europe were behind an 'Iron Curtain'. This phrase was commonly used to describe those countries in eastern Europe that were under the control of the USSR.

Figure 6.1
This poster was published in Russia. It shows Lenin sweeping away kings, rich people and priests. They were the enemies of the communists.

Figure 6.2
How Europe was divided in 1949

The USA had exploded an atomic bomb in 1945. Four years later the USSR had developed a similar bomb. Each of these powers knew that it could destroy or be destroyed by the other. War did not break out between the USSR and the USA. But each power was doing its best to try to defeat the other. For many years the USSR and the USA used threats and bluffs against each other. This state of affairs became known as the Cold War.

The superpowers

The graphs in Figure 6.3 show some important facts about the USSR and the USA in the late 1980s, near the end of the Cold War.

Because of their size, wealth and population, the USA and the USSR were called 'superpowers'.

How the superpowers differ

The USSR and the USA were both large, wealthy countries with many millions of people. In these ways they were similar. But in many more important ways they were very different.

Yuri Kondrashin and Yvonne Kenny were not real people, but their comments indicate some of the most important differences between the USSR and the USA in the 1970s and 1980s.

Yuri Kondrashin

- It is 1980. I live in the USSR. The USSR is a **communist** country.
- I can elect any government I want by choosing people from only one party—the Communist Party.
- I cannot openly criticise the government if I disagree with what it does.
- I believe that the government should have a lot of control over people's lives to make things fairer and more equal for everyone.
- I live in a flat owned by the government. I can work in a factory or on a farm owned by the government.
- I buy what I need from a state-owned shop. There is not a wide range of things to choose from, but I can usually get what I need.
- I am not rich but I am not poor either. I am as well off as most of thc people around me.

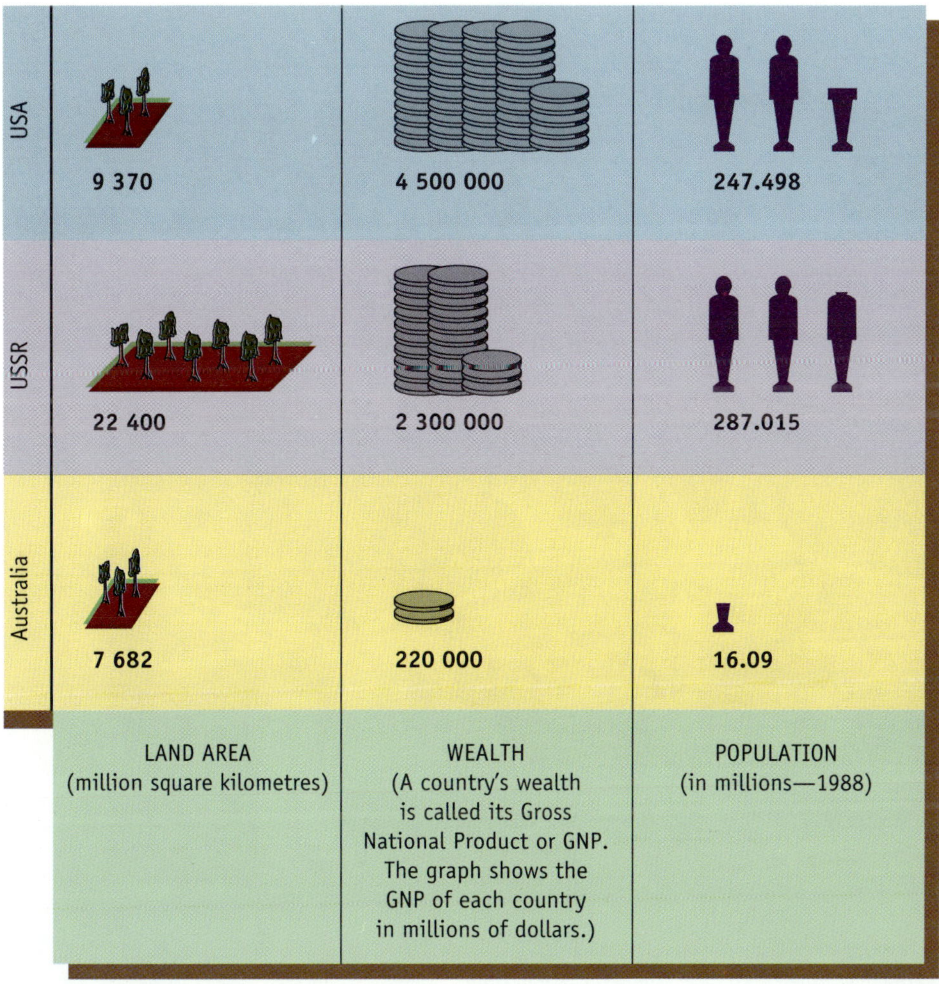

Figure 6.3
The USA, the USSR and Australia as they were in 1988

Yvonne Kenny

- It is 1980. I live in the USA. The USA is a **democratic capitalist** country.
- I can elect the government I want by choosing people from more than one political party.
- I can criticise the government if I disagree with what it does.
- I believe that people should have as much freedom as possible. The government should not interfere too much in people's lives.
- I can own my own house or farm or business.
- I can choose what I want to buy from a wide range of things made by different companies.
- I can become very rich. But I may be very poor.

The Cold War was the result of these differences between the superpowers. Each country believed that its own way of life was right. Each wanted to protect itself from attack by the other country. Each wanted to strengthen its own power.

Figure 6.4
The Kremlin in Moscow. This was the centre of Soviet government.

Figure 6.5
The Capitol in Washington. This is the centre of the United States government.

CHECK the facts

Write out these sentences. Use information from this section to complete them.

1 Russia became a communist country in __________
2 The USA and the USSR fought together in the Second World War because __________
3 The __________ was an invisible border between east and west Europe after the Second World War.
4 After the Second World War the USA and the USSR did not attack each other directly because __________
5 The USSR and the USA were called superpowers because __________

Think *for yourself*

1 The USA dropped atomic bombs in 1945. Where were these bombs dropped?
2 From what you have read about the differences between life in the USA and the USSR during the Cold War, make a list of the advantages and disadvantages of living in each country.

• Flashpoint! Berlin 1948–49

At the end of the Second World War, Germany was divided into four zones. The USSR controlled the eastern part. The western part was divided between Britain, France and the USA.

Berlin, Germany's capital, was in the Soviet zone. It too was divided into four areas. The western part of Berlin was like an island surrounded by Soviet-controlled Germany.

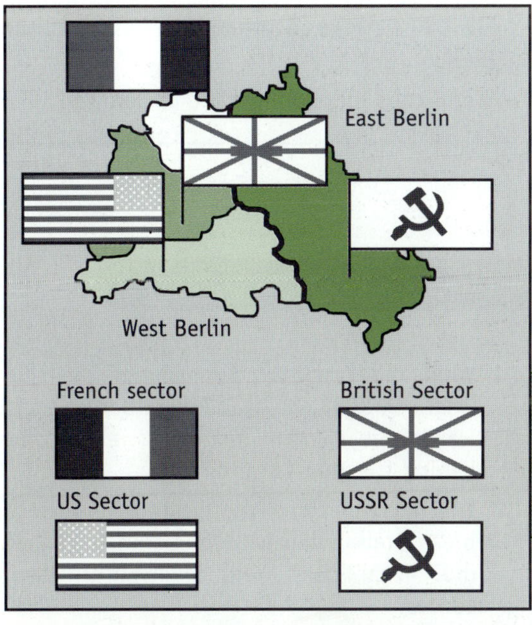

Figure 6.6a
How Berlin was divided

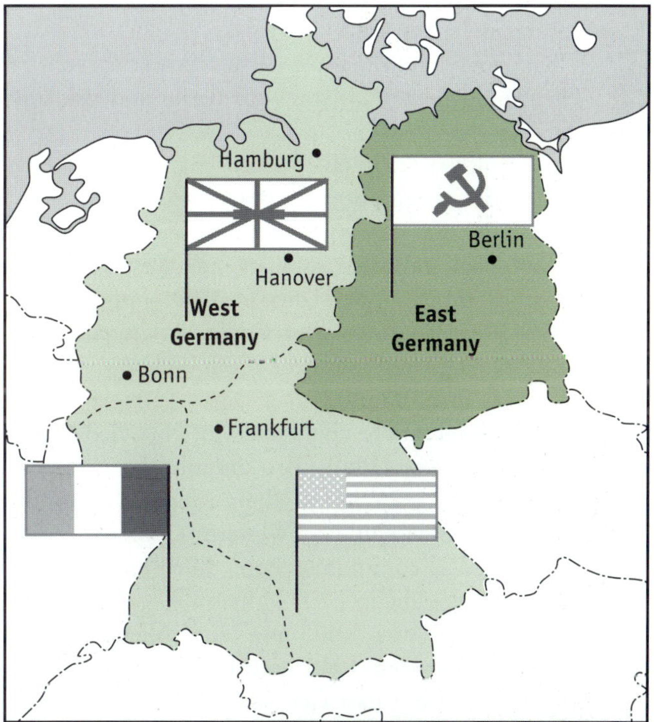

Figure 6.6b
How Germany was divided

Figure 6.7
Part of the Berlin Wall, built in 1961 to divide East and West Berlin. Why was the wall built? Why was barbed wire put at the top?

Joseph Stalin, the Soviet leader, wanted to gain control over the whole of Berlin. In May 1948 he blocked all the roads and railways out of Berlin. It was impossible to get to Berlin from the western part of Germany. Stalin hoped to starve the Berliners into accepting Soviet control.

What choices did the three western powers have?

- They could force their way into Berlin and risk full-scale war.
- They could let Stalin take Berlin.
- They could try and beat the blockade.

They chose the last way. A huge airlift was arranged to take food, coal and other supplies into West Berlin. In the months that followed almost 2000 supply planes landed at the airport in West Berlin. At its peak, the airlift supplied 13 000 tonnes of goods each day. A plane landed every three minutes.

Stalin realised that he could not win. He called off the blockade in March 1949. Two months later France, Britain and the USA joined their zones to form the German Federal Republic (Western Germany). The USSR created a communist state called the German Democratic Republic in East Germany.

West Berlin was still not controlled by the communists. Between 1949 and 1961 over 3 million people escaped from East Germany to freedom in West Berlin. To stop this, the East German government built a wall of concrete and barbed wire through Berlin in 1961. The Berlin wall was a reminder of the conflict between the communist and the non-communist countries.

CHECK the facts

Put these events in the right order. Start with the one that happened first.

— An airlift is arranged to take food and supplies into Berlin.

— Germany is divided into four zones.

— Two separate countries (West Germany and East Germany) are created.

— Stalin blocks all roads and railways into Berlin. The East German government builds a wall through Berlin.

— Stalin calls off the blockade of Berlin.

Think *for yourself*

1 What did President Kennedy of the USA mean when, in 1961, he called West Berlin 'an island of freedom in a communist sea ... a beacon of hope behind the Iron Curtain'?

2 Why do you think the western powers chose to break Stalin's blockade of Berlin in the way they did? What risks were involved in taking this course?

Fighting the Cold War

When Joseph Stalin blockaded Berlin in 1948, he directly threatened the power of the USA, which was the strongest of the three countries in the western part of Germany. This was really the beginning of the Cold War. During the Cold War, which lasted for more than forty years, the superpowers never actually fought each other. But, as we shall see later in this chapter, there were times when real war between them seemed to be very close. The two superpowers threatened each other in less direct ways. Figure 6.8 shows some of these ways.

Figure 6.8
Fighting the Cold War

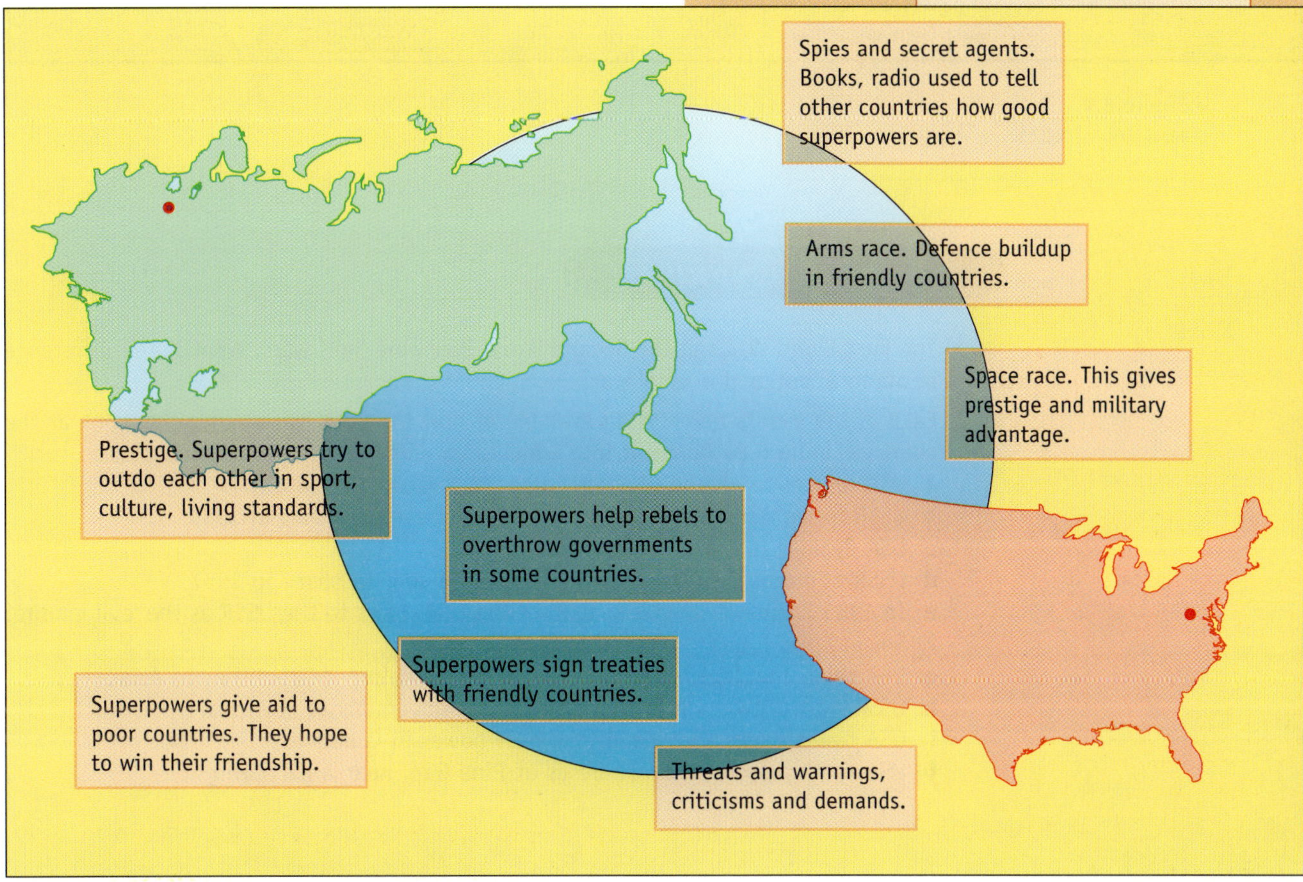

NATO and the Warsaw Pact

The two opposing sides in the Cold War formed military alliances. Because they feared invasion by the communist countries of eastern Europe, the countries of western Europe, as well as Turkey and Canada, wanted to protect themselves by becoming allied with the USA. This alliance, the North Atlantic Treaty Organisation, which is normally referred to as NATO, was formed in 1949. The members of NATO give over part of their armed forces. This is controlled as a single unit. It trains so that it will be ready to defend any NATO country that is attacked by another country.

In 1955, the communist countries of eastern Europe formed an alliance with the USSR. This alliance was known as the Warsaw Pact. Like the members of NATO, the Warsaw Pact countries put some of their army, navy and airforce into a joint force that could act for them all. Figure 6.9 shows the countries that made up NATO and the Warsaw Pact.

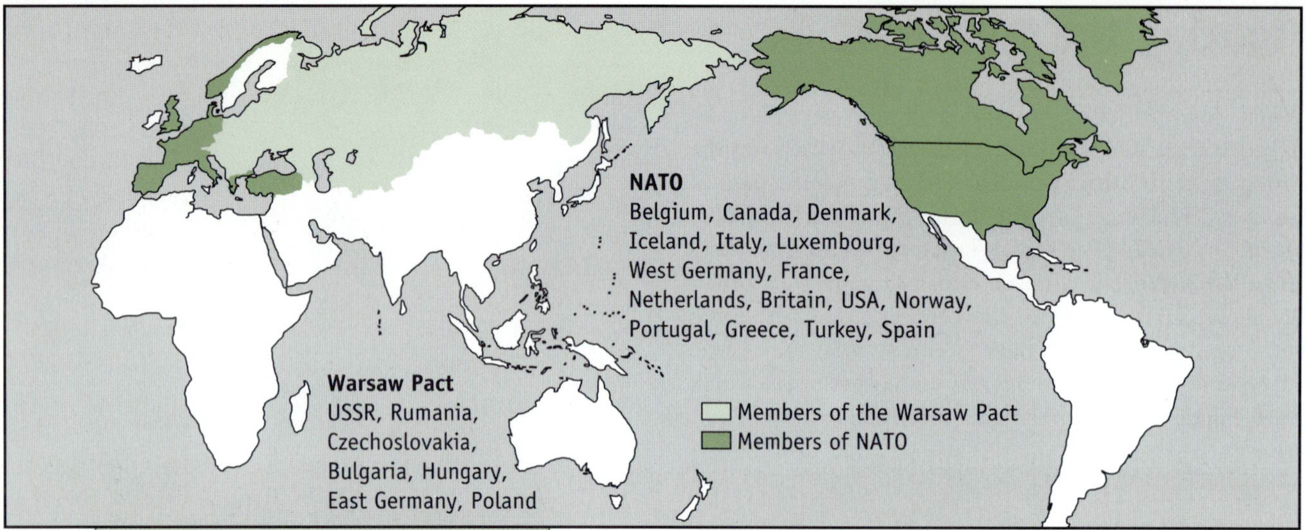

Figure 6.9
Members of NATO and the Warsaw Pact

Think *for yourself*

1 The First World War and the Second World War were 'hot' wars. What is the difference between a 'hot' and a 'cold' war?

2 Each of the events below is an example of how the Cold War was fought. Look at the chart in Figure 6.8. Work out into which area each of these events falls.
- **a** USA refuses to attend Olympic Games in Moscow in 1980.
- **b** USSR forms Warsaw Pact with eastern European countries in 1955.
- **c** USA decides to make neutron bombs in 1981.
- **d** USSR's Sputnik 1 is the first satellite to be sent to space in 1957.
- **e** In 1983 President Ronald Reagan of the USA refers to the USSR as the 'evil empire'.
- **f** Soviet spies found in Australia in 1954.
- **g** USA sends hundreds of millions of dollars to help poor countries in Asia.
- **h** USSR warns USA to stop supporting weak governments in Africa.
- **i** USA trains forces to try and take over power in Cuba.
- **j** USA sets up secret defence bases at Pine Gap, near Alice Springs.

• Flashpoint! Cuba 1962

Cuba is a small island about 150 kilometres from the coast of the USA. Between 1952 and 1959 Cuba was ruled by a dictator, General Batista. The USA supported Batista. Most of Cuba's banks, railways and sugar plantations were owned by American companies. Cuba was tied to the USA. It was a very corrupt country that gave protection to American gangsters, yet gave no justice to the Cuban poor.

In 1959 Fidel Castro defeated Batista and became Cuba's new dictator. Castro was determined to rid Cuba of the influence of the USA. He took over land and property that belonged to Americans and made it clear that the USA was no longer welcome in Cuba. Early in 1961 the USA stopped buying Cuban sugar. Castro agreed to sell the sugar to the USSR.

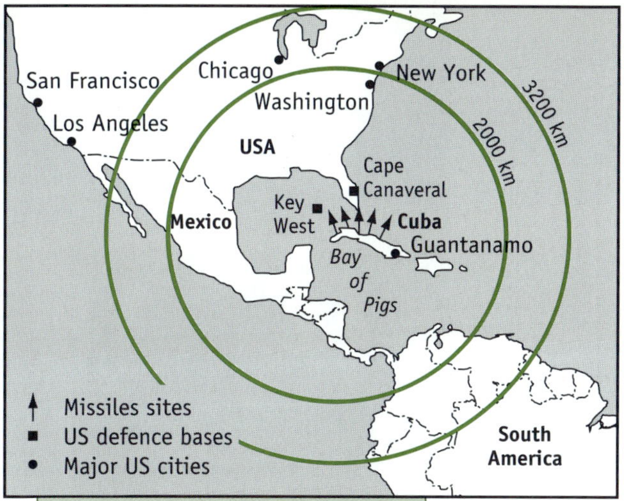

Figure 6.10
Cuba, 1962. You can see from the map that the Soviet missiles threatened several American cities and defence bases.

In April 1961, 1400 Cuban enemies of Castro tried to invade Cuba at the Bay of Pigs. They had been trained and armed by the USA. But they were quickly beaten by Castro's forces. The invasion was a complete failure.

After this attempted invasion at the Bay of Pigs, Cuba moved closer to the USSR. Trade between the two countries increased and the USSR gave Cuba money and equipment. In August 1962 Soviet missiles were sent to Cuba. They were placed where they could attack several large American cities.

The stage was now set for a crisis that brought the world to the brink of war. The crisis lasted for thirteen days.

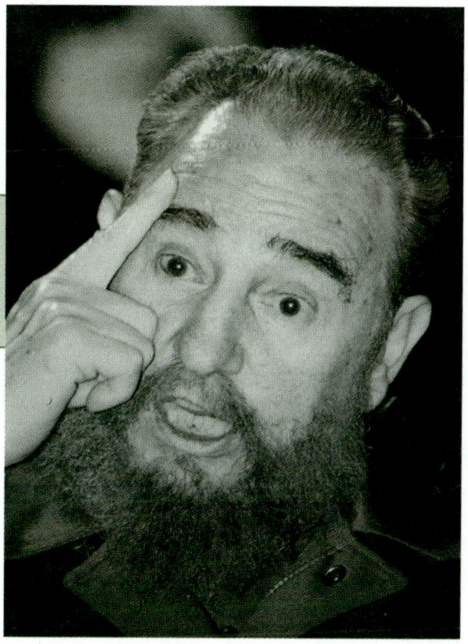

Figure 6.11
Fidel Castro entered Havana, the capital of Cuba, in January 1959

This is what happened in the month of October 1962.

October

16	President Kennedy of the USA is shown photographs of Cuba taken by United States spy planes. The photographs clearly show Soviet missile bases with missiles directed at the USA.
21	Kennedy and his advisers consider what they can do. • They can do nothing and allow the missile bases to stay. • They can order the United States Air Force to destroy the bases. • They can blockade Cuba and stop the USSR from sending any more missiles. They decide to blockade Cuba.
22	Kennedy tells the world that all ships carrying weapons to Cuba will be turned back. He calls on the leader of the USSR, Premier Khrushchev, to remove the missiles that are already in Cuba.
24	Ships of the United States navy surround Cuba. Kennedy orders them to turn back any ships bringing weapons to Cuba.
24–27	Letters and notes pass between Khrushchev and Kennedy.
27	Khrushchev offers to get rid of the USSR's missile bases in Cuba if Kennedy will get rid of the United States' missile bases in Turkey. Kennedy agrees.
28	Khrushchev orders that the missiles in Cuba should be taken down and sent back to the USSR.

The crisis was over. Within two months the missiles had been removed. Both countries realised how close they had been to full-scale war. As a result, a telephone link was built between Moscow and Washington. This was called the **hot-line**.

CHECK the facts

Put these events in the right order. Start with the one that happened first.

- The hot-line is built between Moscow and Washington.
- Fidel Castro becomes dictator of Cuba.
- Kennedy asks Khrushchev to remove missiles from Cuba.
- Khrushchev removes missiles from Cuba.
- Enemies of Castro try to invade Cuba but are beaten at the Bay of Pigs.
- Khrushchev agrees to remove missiles from Cuba if United States' missiles are removed from Turkey.
- United States ships surround Cuba to turn back ships carrying weapons.
- USSR sends missiles to Cuba.

Figure 6.12
John Kennedy, President, USA

Think *for yourself*

Read the following statements. Two of them were made by President Kennedy of the USA. Two of them were made by Premier Krushchev of the USSR. Which leader made each statement?

1. When we put our ballistic missiles in Cuba, we had no desire to start a war ... We were well aware that a war which started over Cuba would quickly expand into a world war.
2. Any vessel or craft which may be proceeding toward Cuba may be intercepted and may be directed to identify itself, its cargo, equipment and stores, and its ports of call.
3. The 1930s taught us a clear lesson: aggressive conduct, if allowed to go unchecked ... leads to war ... I call upon Chairman Krushchev to ... halt ... this threat to world peace.
4. You are worried by Cuba. You say it worries you because it is a distance of 90 miles [150 kilometres] ... from the coast of America. But Turkey is next to us. Our sentries walk up and down and look at each other.

Figure 6.13
Nikita Krushchev,
Premier, USSR

Communist China: a new world power

One out of every four people in the world is Chinese; but until 1949 China was like a sleeping giant. What happened inside China did not have much effect on the rest of the world. There had been many revolutions throughout China's long history. But China remained a poor country. Most of its people were peasant farmers.

A Communist Party grew up in China in the 1920s. Its leader was Mao Zedong, a librarian at the Beijing University. Mao believed that the Communist Party could win power in China if it was supported by the peasants. By 1929 he had gathered an army of over 11 000 peasants. This army was known as the Red Army.

In the 1940s Mao Zedong had more supporters than China's leader, Chiang Kai-shek. He had won the support of the peasants. Here are three reasons why.

1 'I supported Mao Zedong because he was prepared to go out and fight the Japanese, who had invaded our country in 1937. Chiang Kai-shek's government took a lot of money from the USA. The money was supposed to help the government fight the Japanese. But the government army spent more time attacking the communists than fighting the Japanese. Mao Zedong was a good leader. His Red Army was very loyal to him. Many peasants like me helped the Red Army. We fed the soldiers and hid them from the Japanese.'

2 'I supported Mao Zedong because he was honest. He wanted to improve our lives. The government was dishonest. It didn't seem to be interested in the Chinese people. Government officials just wanted to make themselves richer, and they didn't care how they did it.'

3 'I supported Mao Zedong because he promised to make my life better. He promised to share out the land more fairly. He promised to cut down our taxes and rents. He promised to set up new industries so that more people would have jobs. He promised to make China a great world power. Things were so bad under Chiang Kai-shek that I thought it was worth letting Mao have a go at making things better.'

After years of bitter fighting, Mao Zedong defeated Chiang Kai-shek in 1949. The People's Republic of China was born. Mao Zedong said:

> Our work will be written down in the history of mankind, and it will clearly demonstrate the fact that the Chinese … have from now on stood up … Our nation will from now on enter the large family of peace-loving and freedom-loving nations of the world … Our nation will never again be an insulted nation. We have stood up.

Near the end of the war in China, Chiang Kai-shek withdrew to the island of Taiwan, off the coast of mainland China. Here he set up a government which he claimed was the real government of China. Chiang Kai-shek became president of Taiwan, which became known officially as the Republic of China. Since 1949, there has been almost constant tension between Communist China and the government of Taiwan.

Figure 6.14
Mao Zedong talks with a few of his peasant supporters. Why did so many peasants support Mao?

CHECK the facts

Are the sentences below true or false?

1 Three-quarters of the world's people are Chinese.
2 The Communist Party grew up in China before the First World War.
3 The Red Army was the Japanese army that invaded China in 1937.
4 Many peasants supported Mao Zedong when he fought against the Japanese in the 1940s.
5 Most Chinese people were happy with the government of Chiang Kai-shek.
6 China became a communist country in 1949.

Think *for yourself*

1 In the early 1800s Napoleon said: 'Let China sleep. When she wakes, the world will be sorry.'
   a What did Napoleon mean by these words?
   b When did China 'wake up'?
   c Which of the words spoken by Mao Zedong show that he thought China had 'woken up'?

2 You have read some of the reasons why people in China supported Mao Zedong. What sort of people do you think would have been opposed to him? Why?

3 Mao Zedong died in 1976. Who is the present leader of China?

Guerilla warfare

Mao Zedong was a guerilla leader. His Red Army was a guerilla army. It was not the official army of China.

Guerilla armies are usually smaller than official armies. They cannot use large amounts of weapons and equipment. Instead, they must move fast and travel light. They hit and run. Guerilla armies try to avoid full-scale, open battles. They prefer to make small but constant attacks on their enemy. They ambush the enemy on roads, bridges and railway lines. They lay mines and booby traps. They snipe at enemy soldiers. They steal weapons and use them against the enemy.

Guerilla fighters must rely on the support of the local people. Peasants in China helped the soldiers of the Red Army by feeding and hiding them. Guerilla armies are often called 'people's armies'.

Guerilla tactics have become an important part of modern warfare. The Vietnam war provides a good example of how guerilla warfare worked. It shows how a determined 'people's army' was able to defeat a well-equipped, large official army.

Think *for yourself*

1 Mao Zedong said: 'Seem to come from the east, but attack from the west ... deliver a lightning blow, seek a lightning decision.'
   a What did Mao Zedong mean by this statement?
   b Read again what Hitler said about *blitzkrieg* (see page 101). In what ways are *blitzkrieg* and guerilla warfare alike? How are they different?

2 From what you have read about guerilla warfare, what advantages do you think guerilla fighters would have over official armies? What disadvantages would they face?

• Flashpoint! Vietnam 1954–75

The country of Vietnam has been invaded many times. In the nineteenth century it became part of France's empire in South-East Asia.

During the Second World War Vietnam was invaded by Japan. Ho Chi Minh, a Vietnamese leader, gathered a group of guerilla fighters to attack the Japanese. He was supported by many Vietnamese people who agreed with his demand for Vietnam to become independent.

In 1945, when Japan was defeated, Ho Chi Minh declared that Vietnam was an independent country. But France did not want to give up its colony. French soldiers returned and fought against Vietnamese guerillas. This war lasted for almost ten years. Finally, in 1954, the Vietnamese guerillas defeated the French troops at the battle of Dien Bien Phu.

After the French troops left, Vietnam was divided into two zones. Ho Chi Minh ruled the north from his capital, Hanoi. His communist government was supported by the USSR and China. In the south another Vietnamese government was set up. Its capital was Saigon.

Figure 6.15
Vietnam before 1975. Read the section about the Vietnam war. How would a map of Vietnam today differ from this map?

Figure 6.16
Helicopters landing Australian soldiers in a paddy field. Their task was to search for Vietcong bases and destroy them.

President Diem, the leader of South Vietnam, was afraid of the growing power of the north. Raids by North Vietnamese guerillas along the border made these fears even stronger. There were many Vietnamese who lived in South Vietnam but who supported the north. They were called Vietcong. Arms and equipment were sent to the Vietcong from North Vietnam. The Vietcong worked inside South Vietnam to try and defeat the government.

The USA had been sending money, equipment and advisers to South Vietnam since the mid-1950s. By 1961 there were 10 000 American soldiers in South Vietnam. But these soldiers were not officially fighting against North Vietnam. They were supposed to be teaching the South Vietnamese how to defend themselves. In 1962 Australia sent equipment and a group of thirty army instructors to Vietnam to support the Americans.

Figure 6.17
A North Vietnamese soldier. He is carrying a Soviet missile-launcher.

Figure 6.18
These North Vietnamese men are sheltering in one-person bomb shelters. Many thousands of these were built in the cities of North Vietnam. More bombs were dropped on North Vietnam than on Germany and Japan together in the Second World War.

In 1965 the USA sent troops to fight in Vietnam. In the next few days thousands of American soldiers were sent to Vietnam. Their helicopters bombed the cities of North Vietnam and their tanks and infantry tried to find and kill Vietcong in South Vietnam.

Australia, too, started sending troops to Vietnam in 1965. There were two main reasons for doing this. First, the government wanted to support its ally, the USA. Second, Australia wanted to stop the spread of communism in Asia. In 1966, conscripted soldiers were sent to fight in Vietnam. Two years later there were 8000 Australians fighting in Vietnam. More than 3000 of them were conscripts.

By 1970 it became clear that neither side would win in Vietnam unless nuclear weapons were used. The USA had more troops and better aircraft and guns. But many of the South Vietnamese supported the Vietcong. They worked against the Americans. The war had become very unpopular in the USA and in Australia.

After long peace talks, a ceasefire was arranged in 1973. The United States troops went home. Most of the Australians had already left. But fighting between the north and the south continued. In April 1975 North Vietnamese soldiers marched into Saigon, the capital of the south. South Vietnam surrendered. Vietnam was again united, this time under a communist government.

Over 1 800 000 people were killed in the Vietnam war, including 56 000 Americans.

Just over 50 000 Australians served in the Vietnam war. Almost 2500 Australians were wounded and 496 were killed in the war.

CHECK the facts

1 Make a time line to show the main events of the Vietnam war. Write these dates down the left-hand side of a page in your history book. Next to each date write an important event that happened in that year.
1945 1954 1962 1965 1973 1975

2 Choose the correct ending for each of the following sentences.
   a After Vietnam was divided in 1945 the north was ruled by
      — President Diem
      — Dien Bien Phu
      — Ho Chi Minh.
   b The Vietcong were supporters of
      — the USA
      — France
      — North Vietnam.
   c The capital of North Vietnam was
      — Dien Bien Phu
      — Hanoi
      — Saigon.
   d Australians fought in Vietnam because
      — we supported our ally the USA
      — we supported our ally France
      — we wanted to teach South Vietnam a lesson.
   e Vietnam is now controlled by
      — the USA
      — a communist government
      — communist China.

Fighting in Vietnam

The three people whose stories are told below were not real people but their experiences were similar to the experiences of many people who fought in the Vietnam war.

A North Vietnamese soldier

My name is Nguyen Viet Tu. I live in North Vietnam. In 1939 I joined the Vietminh. That was a guerilla group led by Ho Chi Minh. He was a communist but most of all he wanted Vietnam to be independent and not to be ruled by France. At first we fought against the French. Then, when the Japanese came in 1942, we attacked them, too. There were just a few of us at first, but by the end of the war, we had a lot of supporters.

When we had beaten the Japanese, the French came back again. We fought them until 1954. In that year we had a great victory at Dien Bien Phu. There were 11 000 French soldiers but we had 45 000 men. It was a long, hard battle—it took fifty-four days before the French surrendered. Our leader, General Giap, knew how to organise his army well.

The Americans started bombing Hanoi, our capital, and our other cities in 1966. Their giant bombers terrified us. When the bombs fell they left big craters in the ground.

Figure 6.19
A Vietcong soldier. He is carrying a Soviet gun. His sandals were probably made from an old truck tyre.

In the wet season these holes were filled with water. Then mosquitoes would breed there and spread malaria to our people. The Americans blew up our ports, too, and destroyed our ships. Many bombs hit schools and hospitals. They were trying to stop us from sending weapons to our friends in the south, the Vietcong.

We were determined not to give in. We were going to fight till the end. In 1972 we pushed our way well into the south. The Americans didn't want to use nuclear weapons to beat us. They were afraid that the USSR and China would join in. But they knew they couldn't beat us any other way. So they left our country in 1973.

Two years later I marched into Saigon with the North Vietnamese army. The South Vietnamese government wasn't strong enough to last by itself. Now we control the whole of Vietnam. We changed the name of Saigon to Ho Chi Minh City to remind everyone of our great leader.

A member of the Vietcong

My name is Phum Van Trung. I was born in a village in South Vietnam. The Americans came to our village when I was a teenager. They burned our houses and destroyed our crops. They forced us to move to a camp. They said it was for our safety, but we knew that it was so they could check on what we were doing.

I hated the Americans for this. So I joined the Vietcong. We lived in the south but we supported the north. The Americans never found me. I lived in a village so they didn't know that I was any different from any of the other villagers. There were a few other Vietcong in the village too. We made booby traps so that we could capture the Americans. We put land mines down, too, so that they would explode when their tanks went over them. Once I killed an important man in the government who was a friend of the Americans. At night we went out to do as much damage as we could to the Americans. It was dangerous work. Many of my friends were killed.

The Americans sprayed our land with chemicals and used bulldozers to pull down our villages. They said that they had to do this to find us Vietcong. But they killed many innocent people, too. That's why a lot of South Vietnamese people supported us.

The Americans had a lot more helicopters and planes and guns than us. But we knew our country well. We knew how to hide and fight in the jungle. We were prepared to die for Vietnam. That's why they couldn't beat us.

Figure 6.20
Traps like these had been used for hundreds of years to catch animals. The Vietcong used them to wound enemy soldiers. The spikes were made of bamboo. The pit was covered with twigs, leaves and grass. When a soldier stood on it, he fell into the trap. The spikes cut through his boot and wounded his foot.

An Australian conscript

I'm Pete Davis. I was born in 1947. The government had brought in conscription in 1964 to get more people into the army. It was a funny system really. All the days of the year were given a number. Then the numbers were drawn out of a barrel. All the twenty-year-old boys who had their birthday on that day had to join up for two years. My birthday came out of the barrel.

I didn't mind the training too much. But then the government decided to send us conscripts off to

Vietnam to fight the communists. I went in 1968, two years after the first lot went. They said that we had to beat the commies in South Vietnam or they'd be taking over all of Asia. The domino theory they called it, but I'm not sure why.

We were based in Phuoc Tuy province. It was a real eye-opener to me. Dad fought on the Kokoda Trail and he'd told me a bit about war in the jungle. But I wasn't really prepared for the endless rain, the heat, the swamps and all the insects. The mosquitoes could give you malaria.

We spent a lot of time on patrol duty. Bush-bashing we called it. Our job was to find and kill the Vietcong. But they were clever fighters. They hid during the day and came out to snipe at us when it was dark.

We often worked from helicopters. They were really useful in the kind of fighting we were doing. At first we felt pretty safe up there in those big choppers. But then the Vietcong got hold of some big Soviet anti-aircraft guns. That made things a lot harder for us.

I was in Vietnam for less than a year. When I got home I was surprised to see all the demonstrations and protests that were going on about the war. There were a lot of people who thought that Australia shouldn't interfere in another country's business.

Perhaps we *should* have left the Vietnamese alone. Australia sent about 50 000 soldiers to Vietnam. Almost one in every three of them was a conscript like me. We lost almost 500 Australians in that war and another 2500 or so were wounded. Many Australians who returned from the war suffered a great deal as a result of their experiences in Vietnam. Some of them found it impossible to return to normal life in Australia. But the communists took over South Vietnam in 1975. Laos and Cambodia became communist countries too. I wonder if it was worth it.

Figure 6.21
An Australian soldier. He is carrying a light machine gun.

Figure 6.22
Australian soldiers in Vietnam. What are the foot-soldiers doing? What do you think the tank will be used for?

Figure 6.23
As the Vietnam war dragged on and more Australians were sent to fight, many people at home felt that Australia should leave Vietnam. Demonstrations such as this one became common.

Think *for yourself*

1. Read what Phum Van Trung says about how they fought the Americans. Why do you think American soldiers found the Vietcong so hard to defeat?
2. Why did Pete Davis go to Vietnam? Do you think he really wanted to go?
3. Pete Davis is not sure what is meant by the 'domino theory'. Look at Figure 6.24. Write two or three sentences to explain what people who believed in the domino theory predicted would happen in Asia.
4. What were some of the things that Australian soldiers found hard to cope with in Vietnam? Had Australian soldiers ever before had to fight in the same kinds of conditions?
5. Pete Davis asks whether Australia should have left the Vietnamese alone. Read the three stories again. What do you think?

CHECK the facts

1. Who were the Vietminh? What were they fighting for?
2. Why did the Americans blow up ships in the ports of North Vietnam?
3. In 1975 the name of the old capital of South Vietnam was changed. What was its old name? What is its new name? Why was the name changed?
4. Why did American soldiers destroy villages in South Vietnam?
5. When were the first Australian conscripts sent to Vietnam?

Figure 6.24
The domino theory. If Vietnam falls, what will happen next?

THE HISTORIAN AT WORK

On 29 April the Australian prime minister, Sir Robert Menzies, made the following statement to the Australian parliament:

A The Australian Government is now in receipt of a request from the Government of South Vietnam for further military assistance. We have decided—and this has been after close consultation with the Government of the United States—to provide an infantry battalion for service in South Vietnam … There can be no doubt of the gravity of the situation in Vietnam. There is ample evidence to show that, with the support of the North Vietnamese regime and other Communist powers, the Vietcong has been preparing on a more substantial scale than hitherto insurgency action designed to destroy South Vietnamese Government control, and to disrupt by violence the life of the local people … We have not of course come to this decision without the closest attention to the question of defence priorities. We do not and must not overlook the point that our alliances, as well as providing guarantees and assurances for our security, make demands upon us … Assessing all this, it is our judgment that the decision to commit a battalion in South Vietnam represents the most useful additional contribution we can make to the defence of the region at this time. The takeover of South Vietnam would be a direct military threat to Australia and all countries of South and South-East Asia. It must be seen as part of a thrust by Communist China between the Indian and Pacific oceans … We and our allies are not seeking to take over North Vietnam. The North Vietnamese must not take over South Vietnam by armed force or subversion.

The next day, a number of Australian newspapers commented on the prime minister's statement:

B No Australian who is conscious of the dangerous position in which his country stands, and the crucial importance to it of the war in Vietnam, can doubt that this is a right and indeed inevitable decision. (*Sydney Morning Herald*)

An act of support for our American allies, limited though it is by our resources, is the far-sighted course to take at this critical stage. It may have grave consequences, but it deepens the friendship we need. (*[Melbourne] Herald*)

There are … sound reasons for an unambiguous expression of Australian solidarity with the United States in the bitter and tiring battle to prevent an apocalyptic disruption of the balance of power in Asia. (*Australian Financial Review*)

This is clearly a United States call to share, even in a small way, more of the burdens. In fact, we now stand in the company of thirty other countries, including important Asian friends and allies. There was no alternative but to respond as we have. (*[The Melbourne] Age*)

The Menzies Government has made a reckless decision on Vietnam which this nation may live to regret. It has decided to send Australian soldiers into a savage, revolutionary war in which the Americans are grievously involved—so that America may shelve a tiny part of her embarrassment.

Their decision is wrong, at this time, whichever way we look at it. It is wrong because Australia's contingent can have only insignificant military value, because it will be purely a political pawn in a situation for which Australia has no responsibility whatsoever.

It is wrong because it deliberately and coldly runs counter to the mounting wave of international anxiety about the shape of the Vietnam war and the justification and perils of America's military escalation.

It could be that our historians will recall this day with tears. (*Australian*)

Twenty years later, on 30 April 1985, the following report appeared in the *Sydney Morning Herald*:

C

Australians disown Ky, Holt, LBJ

Today, ten years after the fall of Saigon, Australians have disowned the Vietnam War.

A special *Herald* survey has found that two-thirds of voters think we were wrong to send troops to Vietnam and, in similar circumstances, should not do so again.

By a statistical irony, that is almost exactly the same proportion of people that, eighteen years ago, thought we were right to continue with our growing commitment to the war.

That poll … was carried out in June 1967. It was a turbulent time. Harold Holt had committed Australia 'All the way with LBJ'. The South Vietnamese Prime Minister, Air Vice-Marshal Ky, had been here saying the Vietcong could be pushed out of the South within three years. The Australian Army had not long sent 900 reinforcements plus a Civil Affairs Unit of 46. The RAN had just made its first deployment of the war.

Against this, most of the mainstream Protestant Churches were raising their 'cry of anguish' against the war, and the Catholic bishops were appealing for peace, especially in Vietnam.

The 'cry of anguish' fell on deaf ears. At least 59 per cent of Anglicans, Roman Catholics, Methodists and Presbyterians were prepared to support the war.

Since then, the mood of the people has changed dramatically. Here is a comparison between the polls of 1967 and 1985.

1967: Do you think we should continue to fight in Vietnam, or bring our forces back to Australia?

Continue, 62 per cent

Bring back, 24 per cent

Undecided, 14 per cent.

1985: Do you think Australia was right to send troops to fight in Vietnam?

No, 66 per cent

Yes, 27 per cent

Undecided, 7 per cent.

If a similar situation arose today, do you think, on balance, that Australia should again send troops, or not send troops, to a conflict in South-East Asia?

Send troops, 24 per cent

Not send troops, 67 per cent

No opinion, 9 per cent

The 1985 survey was carried out on the weekend of April 20 and 21 among people of voting age in all Federal electorates of NSW and Victoria. The size of the sample was 622.

The 1967 … survey … covered about 2000 people in Federal electorates across Australia.

1 Do some research to find out who Harold Holt and 'LBJ' were. What do you think the phrase 'All the way with LBJ' meant?

2 How can you tell from Robert Menzies' statement (document A) that Australia was already giving military aid to South Vietnam before 1965?

3 What does the word 'escalation' mean? In what way did Menzies' announcement (document A) mean that Australia was escalating its involvement in the Vietnam war? What other escalations of Australia's involvement are mentioned in the above documents?

4 What evidence can you find that Robert Menzies believed in the domino theory (document A)? Can you find any evidence that any of the newspaper editorial writers believed in the domino theory (document B)?

5 Why did people who believed in the domino theory think that Australia would be in danger if South Vietnam lost the war?

6 How important do you think Australia's alliance with the USA was in the government's decision to send troops to Vietnam? How many references to this alliance can you find in the above documents?

7 Why do you think many Australians may have changed their minds about the Vietnam war between 1967 and 1985? If the war had ended differently do you think people may have had different opinions in 1985?

8 Surveys such as the ones referred to in the 1985 *Sydney Morning Herald* article (document C) are being carried out all the time. They are often called 'opinion polls'. What kind of opinions do they investigate? Why do you think governments are interested in finding out what people think about various issues?

9 Are opinion polls such as the ones referred to in the 1985 *Sydney Morning Herald* article (document C) always accurate? Why? Do you think that the 1967 or the 1985 survey was likely to be more accurate? Why?

• Flashpoint!
The Falkland Islands 1982

The Falkland Islands is a group of two large islands and about 200 very small ones. They are situated in the South Atlantic Ocean near the west coast of South America.

Even though these islands, which had a population of less than 2000 people, had been a colony of Britain for 150 years, the South American country Argentina had never recognised Britain's right to rule the Falklands. On 2 April 1982 troops from Argentina invaded the islands and claimed them for Argentina.

British troops were immediately sent to the Falklands and by 14 June had recaptured them. More than 1000 people were killed in the Falklands war. About 750 of them were Argentinians. Many of the deaths occurred when the British sank the *Belgrano*, an Argentine battleship.

Although the war was a short one there were fears that the British government might decide to use nuclear weapons against Argentina and create a much wider conflict.

Figure 6.25
Argentina and the Falkland Islands. The two main islands of the Falklands group, East Falkland and West Falkland, are the largest of about 200 islands that make up the group. The capital is Stanley.

Terrorism

Headlines like those in Figure 6.26 are quite common. We often read about hijacking, assassination, kidnapping and bombing. These acts are described as **terrorist** attacks.

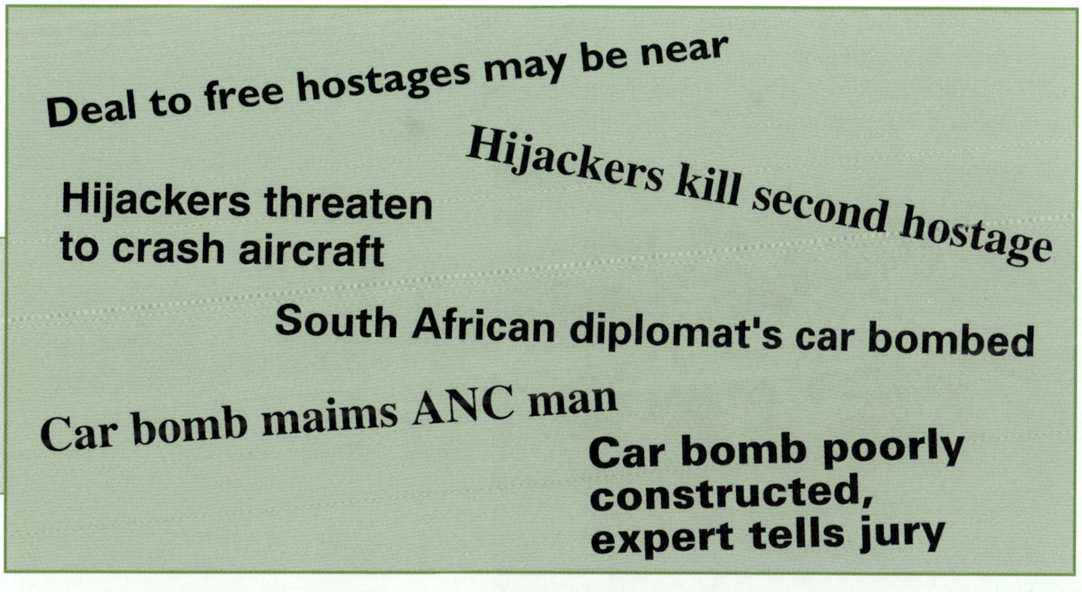

Figure 6.26
Headlines like these can be read in the newspaper almost every day

Terrorists believe very strongly in the cause they are fighting for. They want to make other people aware of what they want. They believe that they will get nowhere unless they use violence. Terrorists sometimes try to get what they want by frightening their enemies. Of course, they also want to kill their opponents.

Terrorists have developed many ways of working. Sometimes they send bombs in parcels or in letters. They may put a bomb in a car engine so that it will explode when the car starts. At other times they blow up shops, railway stations, pubs or other public places. Often, innocent people are killed. Sometimes terrorists hijack planes. They force the pilot to take the plane to a certain place. Then they refuse to free the passengers until their demands have been met. Terrorists also kill or threaten world leaders. They kidnap well-known people and use them as hostages.

One of the most common forms of terrorism, especially in recent times, is the use of car bombs. Bombs, set to explode at a particular time, are left in parked cars in public places. When they go off, they often kill many people in the nearby area and create a great deal of fear. One of the most famous terrorist car bomb attacks occurred in New York in February 1993, when a car bomb exploded in the basement of New York's giant World Trade Centre building. It killed five people and injured more than 1000 others. It also started many fires and severely damaged the lower floors of the building.

In October 1995, an Egyptian terrorist and nine other Middle Eastern men were convicted in New York of being involved in the bombing of the World Trade Centre and of plotting to blow up a number of other buildings including bridges and road tunnels.

A terrible air disaster occurred on 21 December 1988 when a bomb exploded on a United States airliner on a flight from London to New York. The plane crashed on the small Scottish town of Lockerbie, killing all 259 people on board and eleven people on the ground. The mystery of his bombing has not been completely solved, but a Middle Eastern terrorist group from Iran has claimed that it was responsible.

Figure 6.27
Part of the town of Lockerbie in Scotland was destroyed when a United States airliner crashed here in December 1981

Conflict in the Middle East

The Middle East is a name that is given to a number of countries around the eastern end of the Mediterranean Sea. If you look at a map of the world, you will see that the Middle East is the place where the continents of Europe, Asia and Africa meet.

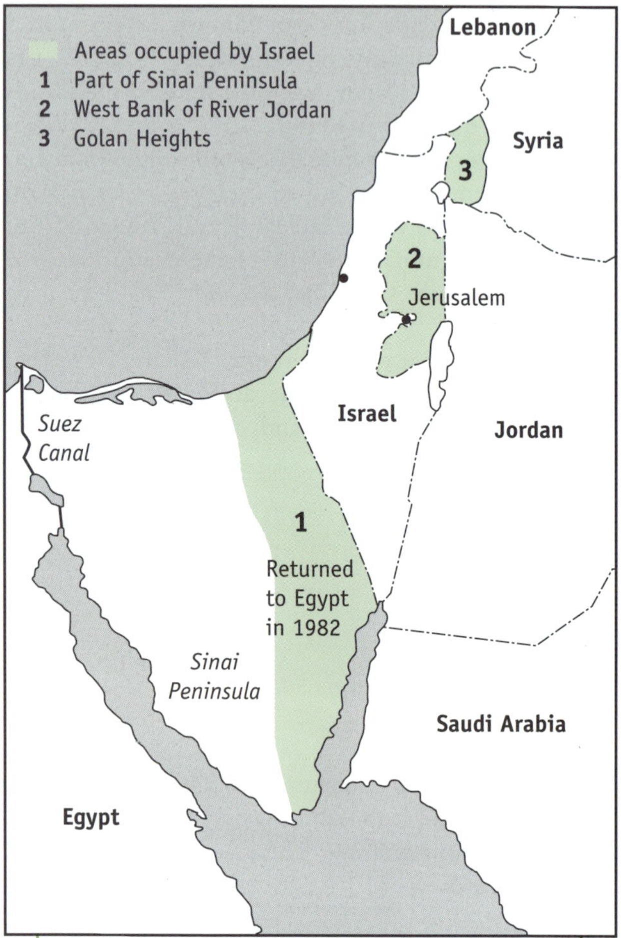

Figure 6.28
Israel and neighbouring countries. The shaded sections show areas that have been occupied by Israel. This land is still the cause of conflict between Israel and its Arab neighbours.

Figure 6.29
Israeli army troops pass a truck of Egyptian prisoners in the desert. This photo was taken during the Six Day War in 1967. Israel attacked and defeated Egypt, Syria and Jordan. Israel captured the Sinai Peninsula from Egypt, the Golan Heights from Syria, and land on the West Bank of the Jordan River from Jordan.

For almost fifty years the Middle East has been one of the world's most troubled areas.

The main cause of this trouble was the creation of a new country, Israel, in 1948. Because Jews have been persecuted throughout history, Israel was created to provide a homeland where Jews from all over the world could come and live together.

Israel was formed out of the small country called Palestine. Palestine had been captured by Britain during the First World War. Britain promised to create a Jewish state in Palestine, and in the years between the First World War and the Second World War, many Jews went to settle in Palestine. The Arabs who lived in Palestine were angry about the new Jewish settlers. These Arabs were afraid that they would be forced to leave their own country. There was a lot of tension and many violent clashes occurred.

In 1947 Britain handed control of Palestine to the United Nations. In 1948 Palestine was **partitioned**, or divided up. A part of Palestine became the new nation of Israel. The rest of it was divided between the neighbouring Arab countries.

From then until now there has been conflict between Israel and the Arab countries nearby.

War

Full-scale war between Israel and Arab countries has broken out four times since 1948.

- In 1948, on the very day when Israel became a country.
- In 1956, when Israel and Egypt became part of an international crisis over who should control the Suez Canal.
- In 1967, when Israel's army defeated the troops of several Arab countries in the Six Day War.
- In 1973, when Egypt and Syria launched a surprise attack on Israel. This became known as the Yom Kippur war because the attack took place on the sacred Jewish feast day of Yom Kippur, or the Day of Atonement. United Nations troops were sent to the Middle East to try to keep the peace between Israel and the neighbouring Arab countries.

Figure 6.30
History was made in 1974 when Yasir Arafat, the leader of the PLO, addressed the United Nations. This showed how powerful the Palestine Liberation Organisation had become.

Figure 6.31
President Sadat, President Carter and Prime Minister Begin join hands after signing the Egypt–Israel peace treaty. President Sadat was assassinated in 1981.

A number of other conflicts have broken out between Israel and its neighbours. In June 1982, for example, Israel invaded Lebanon, the small country to its north. Israel's leaders believed that Arab organisations were using Lebanon as a base from which to launch attacks on northern Israel. It was not until 1985 that Israel began to withdraw its soldiers from Lebanon. A special United Nations force was sent to Lebanon to help keep peace between the Arabs and Israelis. Some Australian soldiers were part of this 'peacekeeping' force.

Since 1985, Israel has carried out a number of air raids against targets in Lebanon and has several times sent troops across the border to attack groups that were considered to pose a danger to Israel.

Iran and Iraq

Between 1980 and 1988 two other Middle East countries, Iran and Iraq, waged a bitter war against each other. This conflict was mainly about which country would have control over the waters of the Persian Gulf. It was a highly dangerous dispute which very nearly involved other nations. Because the dispute threatened oil supplies to the West, the USA sent warships to the Persian Gulf. In 1987 the situation became extremely tense when a United States helicopter opened fire on an Iranian ship, killing several of its crew. In July 1988 tensions rose even higher when a United States cruiser mistook an Iranian passenger airliner for a fighter plane and shot it down, killing the 286 people on board.

Figure 6.32
Since 1980, the Persian Gulf has been an area of dangerous conflict in the Middle East

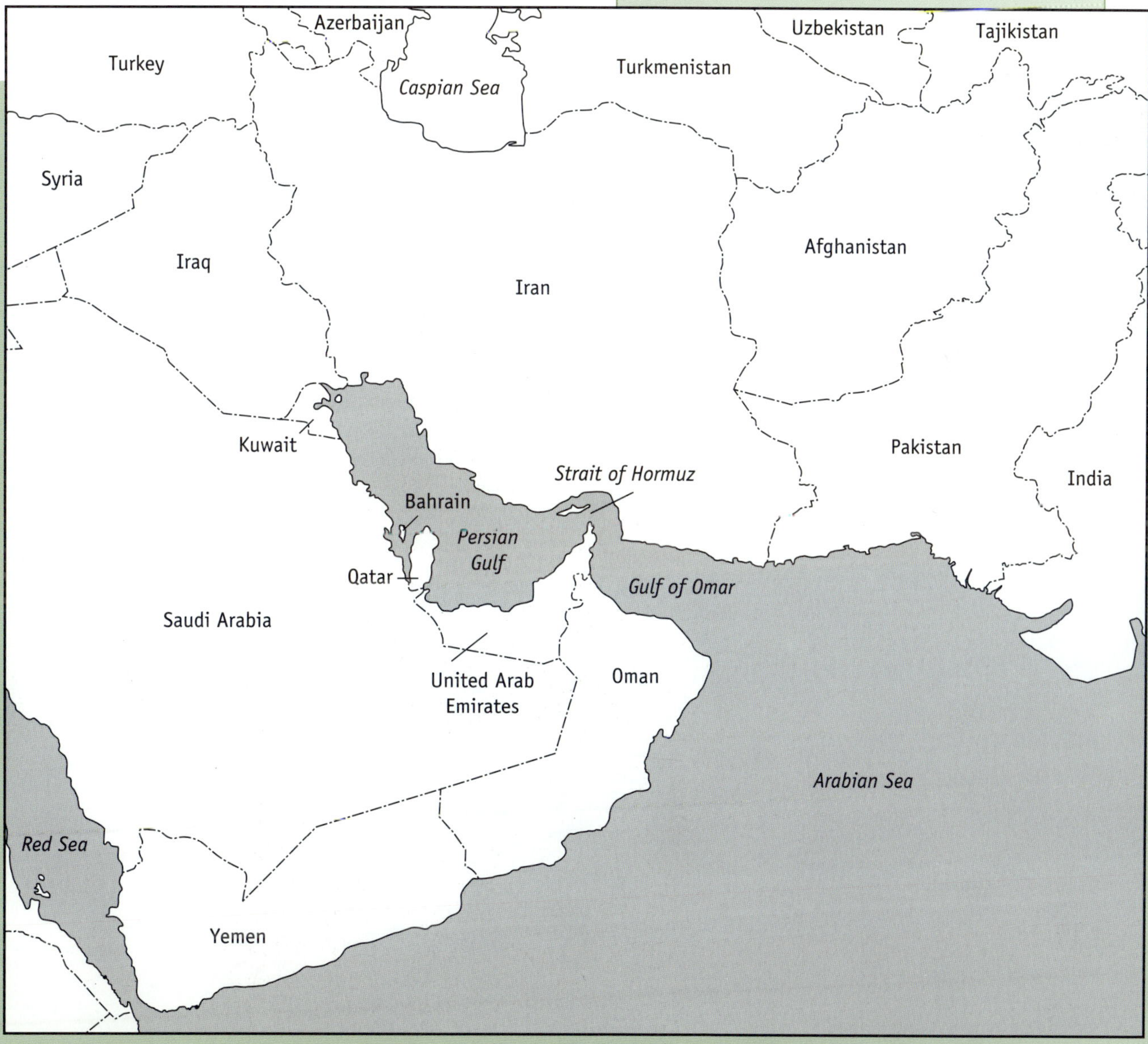

Iraq invades Kuwait

On 2 August 1990, world attention was again drawn to the Persian Gulf, when forces from Iraq crossed the border and invaded the kingdom of Kuwait. Although Kuwait was a tiny country with a population of just over 1.5 million people, it was a major source of Western oil supplies. The USA and European countries demanded that Iraq withdraw its forces, but the Iraqi leader, President Saddam Hussein, refused. In February 1991, a United Nations force, commanded by the USA, drove the Iraqis out of Kuwait. Several Australian warships were sent to the Gulf as part of the United Nations force. No Australians were killed or wounded in this war, which became known as the Gulf War.

The Gulf War was very short, but it was dangerous and brutal. As the United States-led troops attacked, the Iraqis fired long-range missiles towards Israel. Several of these landed on buildings in Tel Aviv and Jerusalem, killing and wounding a number of people. Saddam Hussein called on other Arab countries to join him in a *jihad*—this meant a 'holy war' of Islamic countries against Western countries. United States planes bombed targets in Baghdad, the capital of Iraq, in an attempt to force Saddam Hussein from power. Some of these bombs hit apartment blocks and killed many civilians. As the Iraqi forces retreated from Kuwait, they set fire to oil storage tanks. As a result vast quantities of oil spilt into the Persian Gulf, causing enormous damage to the environment.

In mid-1996, Saddam Hussein was still the president of Iraq. He was regarded as a dangerous force in the Middle East.

Terrorism and violence

Terrorism and violence have played an important part in the conflict in the Middle East. Here are some examples of events that have kept world attention focused on the Middle East.

- In 1972 eight terrorists of the Palestinian Black September Movement invaded the Olympic village that had been built in Munich for the Olympic Games. They seized eleven Israeli athletes and held them hostage. When the police tried to free the hostages, seventeen people (including all the hostages) were killed.
- In 1976 Israeli troops freed more than 100 hostages from a hijacked plane at Entebbe airport in Uganda. The plane had been hijacked by Palestinian terrorists almost a week earlier.
- In 1978 terrorists belonging to the Palestinian Liberation Organisation (PLO) hijacked two buses of tourists in Israel. They set fire to one of the buses and about forty people were killed.
- In 1982 President Bashir Gemayel of Lebanon, who was a Christian, was murdered. Two days later more than 2000 Palestinians in two camps in Beirut, the capital of Lebanon, were massacred by Lebanese Christians. Many people blamed Israel for this terrorist action because the two camps were supposed to be protected by Israeli soldiers.
- In August 1984 at least eighty-five people were killed and more than 200 were wounded when cars loaded with bombs exploded in Beirut. This kind of terrorism has been very common in Lebanon where there is great enmity between Christians and Moslems. The population is divided fairly evenly between these two religious groups.

Figure 6.33
This is what United Nations troops found in Kuwait in February 1991, after the Iraqis had retreated. In your own words, describe what is happening in this scene.

- In December 1987 riots by Palestinian residents of the Gaza Strip marked the beginning of a prolonged uprising by Palestinians against Israeli soldiers and civilians in the areas occupied by Israel (see map on page 00). This uprising was known as the *intifada*. Palestinians, including children, often used sticks, stones and any other weapons they could find to attack Israeli cars, buses and military vehicles.
- In 1994 an Israeli settler on the West Bank shot dead twenty-nine Arabs as they were praying in a mosque in the town of Hebron.
- In 1994 and 1995 a series of bombs exploded in buses in the Israeli cities of Tel Aviv and Jerusalem. These bombs killed more than 100 Israeli citizens and wounded many others.

The superpowers in the Middle East

For many years the Middle East was rather like the Balkans before the First World War. It was a 'powder keg', an area that could very easily become the starting place for another world war. Even today, many people believe that conflicts in the Middle East could threaten world peace. What happens in the Middle East is vital for another reason, as well. It supplies most of the world's oil. Trouble in the Middle East threatens this supply of oil.

For these reasons, the superpowers often became very involved in the conflict between Israel and the Arab world, as well as in the many other conflicts in the Middle East. The USA generally supported Israel, while the USSR was on the side of the Arab nations. Tension between the superpowers became very intense during the Yom Kippur war in 1973. The USSR airlifted weapons to Egypt and Syria, while at the same time the USA sent planeloads of arms and ammunition to Israel.

Peace?

In 1978 President Carter of the USA invited President Sadat of Egypt and Prime Minister Begin of Israel to meet at Camp David in the USA. At this meeting both Middle East leaders decided to work towards peace. In 1979 a peace treaty was signed between Israel and Egypt. In this treaty Israel and Egypt recognised 'each other's right to live in peace'.

Also as part of the treaty, Israel agreed to withdraw from the part of the Sinai Peninsula that it had occupied since the 1967 war. This withdrawal began in May 1979 and was completed by April 1982. Israel continued to control the area known as the Gaza Strip.

In spite of this treaty, many Arab countries still regard Israel as an enemy.

Peace with the Palestinians

As we have seen, the Palestinians who were forced out of their homeland when the state of Israel was created have been fierce enemies of Israel. Their hatred of Israel became even stronger after the 1967 war, when Israel took control of even more Arab territories. Tensions in these occupied areas have been constantly high and have often erupted into violence, especially as Israel established many Jewish settlements in these Arab areas.

After years of fighting each other, the Israeli government and the Palestinian Liberation Organisation held talks to try to bring about peace. In September 1993, the Israeli prime minister Yitzhak Rabin and the Palestinian leader Yasir Arafat met in Washington in the USA and signed a historic agreement. The two sides agreed that both Israel and the PLO had a right to exist and that they would work towards peace. Israel also agreed to give control of the Gaza Strip back to the Palestinians. Two years later, in October 1995, the two leaders met again in Washington with President Clinton of the USA and the leaders of Jordan and Egypt and signed another 'accord'. This time Israel agreed to begin withdrawing from the West Bank of the Jordan and to start transferring control of the occupied areas to the Palestinians.

In spite of these moves towards peace, many Israeli and Palestinian people are strongly opposed to any agreement between Israel and the Palestinian Liberation Organisation.

Figure 6.34
Historic scene in Washington, USA, September 1993. Can you identify the people in this picture? Why could this scene be called 'historic'?

CHECK the facts

Put these events in the correct order. Start with the one that happened first.

— Palestinian terrorists kidnap Israeli athletes at Munich Olympic Games.
— Israel invades Lebanon.
— Arab residents in areas occupied by Israel begin the *intifada*.
— Begin and Sadat sign a peace treaty.
— More than 2000 Palestinians are massacred in Beirut.
— Iraq invades Kuwait.
— Israel becomes a country.
— Britain hands Palestine over to the United Nations.
— War breaks out between Iran and Iraq.
— Arafat and Rabin meet and come to an agreement.
— Israel defeats Arab countries in the Six Day War.
— Leaders of Israel and Egypt meet at Camp David.
— Israel and Egypt are involved in crisis over the Suez Canal.
— Israel withdraws its soldiers from Lebanon.

Think *for yourself*

1 Why are so many outside countries involved in what happens in the Middle East?

2 Why is the supply of oil so important to many countries?

3 Why are some Arabs called Palestinians? Why do some Palestinians carry out terrorist attacks in Israel?

4 In 1978 President Sadat and Prime Minister Begin shared the Nobel Prize for their work towards peace. Why were they given this prize?

5 After signing a peace agreement with Israel in 1979 Egypt was suspended from an organisation called the League of Arab States. Why do you think some other Arab countries no longer wanted Egypt as a member?

THE HISTORIAN AT WORK

The following passages are extracts from articles published in *The New Internationalist* magazine in August 1994. Read them carefully and then answer the questions that follow.

A Miriam was sixteen years old when her home was razed to the ground in 1976. Many of her neighbours and friends were slaughtered and she herself was injured. Her family survived but had no food, water or shelter. They were moved to a house which had been shelled and had no doors or windows. They ... made the place their home for six years, until advancing Israeli tanks and shells forced them to flee once more ...

Miriam's crime? She is a Palestinian in Beirut ... Today she lives in Shatila, in the camp where a ... massacre occurred in 1982 ... under cover of invading Israeli troops.

Today, at last, the war has ended. The militias are disarmed, the Israelis have withdrawn—at least from Beirut and its environs—and Palestinians in Gaza and Jericho have autonomy. Palestinians in Beirut should finally be safe ...

But the government of Lebanon has other plans. Palestinians are no longer welcome in the new-style Beirut. Lebanon's Foreign Minister ... has made it plain that Lebanon wants its Palestinian refugees to leave.

This is easier said than done. Palestinians have been in Lebanon since 1948, when the creation of the state of Israel forced them to flee north ... The refugees were given tents and later were allowed to build camps on the outskirts of the major Lebanese towns. Registered refugees were entitled to education, health and other benefits—though the unregistered refugees who came after the lists were closed in the early 1950s have always been non-statistics, making it very difficult to know exactly how many Palestinians there are in Lebanon.

Over half the registered Palestinians still live in such camps, in crowded and often unsanitary conditions, vulnerable to any opponent … Shatila and Shaba … have been shelled and then rebuilt more times than most people can count …

Palestinians I met were extremely concerned about … the precariousness of their situation in Lebanon … They are also feeling the pinch economically. As Miriam put it: ‘Even the war was better than this. A bomb can kill someone but if we have no money and no food lots of people with die.’ She has her bags already packed in case the family has to leave once more.

B Umm Rajab is one of many Palestinians in Beirut who have no near family. A son somewhere in Eastern Europe is ‘good’ (in camp language this means that he occasionally sends his mother money). She has two married daughters in Jordan but hasn’t been able to see them for twenty-four years. Hunched by rheumatism, wounded during the Amal sieges between 1985 and 1987, Umm Rajab moves around the four square metres of her home by holding on to bits of furniture. Like other Palestinian women of her generation, she has had a life full of loss and hardship. She was widowed at the age of thirty and three out of her four sons are now dead. Besides rheumatism she has heart problems. Neighbours do her shopping. Abu Muhammad, a neighbouring shopkeeper, brings her a couple of gallons of water from a street tap.

The doorway is the only source of light. Public electricity hasn’t been restored to Shatila camp since the battles of the mid-1980s. The people of Shatila say that the government is withholding electricity because ‘to give light to the camp would be to approve of its existence’ …

Umm Rajab talks readily about her life before 1948. She lived in a village near Jaffa, inside the current borders of Israel. Village women worked hard inside and outside the house. But she remembers with great pleasure outings to Jaffa and picnics by the sea. She gives me a list of recipes of special foods village women used to cook for Ramadan. In 1948 war drove her family to a refugee camp on the West Bank and then in 1970 to Lebanon. She has been at Shatila ever since …

Palestinians in Lebanon face an unknown future as pressures on them to migrate increase. As someone who entered the country after the official refugee registrations in the early 1950s, Umm Rajab doesn’t have resident rights in Lebanon. She hopes to be reunited with her children either in Gaza/Jericho or in Jordan, but if and when depends on how a final settlement works out. Others here, the exiles of 1948, who have never known any ‘home’ but Lebanon, face an even greater degree of uncertainty. They have no papers to leave the country—even if they have the money to do so—and nowhere to live but the camps. With no clear provisions for Palestinians in exile the current precarious agreement between Israel and the PLO has intensified their insecurity.

1. What does the term ‘refugee’ mean? Are Miriam and Umm Rajab refugees? Why?
2. Why is the place where Miriam and Umm Rajab live referred to as a ‘camp’? What is the difference between a camp and a village or a town?
3. Both of the above articles deal with the ‘plight’ of Palestinian refugees. In a few sentences, describe the plight of Palestinian refugees who are living in Lebanon.
4. In what ways did the formation of the state of Israel affect Umm Rajab’s life?
5. What is the attitude of the Lebanese government towards the people who live in Shatila and other refugee camps? Why does the government of Lebanon have this attitude?
6. What do you think is the difference between ‘registered’ refugees and ‘unregistered’ refugees? Why do you think the government of Lebanon ‘closed the lists’ in the early 1950s?
7. What evidence can you find that these articles were written after September 1993?
8. Do you think that the people who wrote these articles have been to the camp at Shatila and have met the people they are writing about? Why?
9. What do you think the writer of the second article is referring to when she talks of ‘the current precarious agreement between Israel and the PLO’?

Figure 6.35
These boys are at the Shatila refugee camp in Beirut. What does this picture tell you about the life at Shatila?

The balance of fear

If two trucks loaded with dynamite meet on a very narrow road, one of them has to give way. If they both go forward and crash, they will both be destroyed. In some ways the USA and the USSR during the Cold War were like two trucks loaded with dynamite travelling in opposite directions on a very narrow road. Whenever they met head-on, one of them had to give way. If they clashed, neither of them could be a winner.

Compared with the bombs that exist today, the ones that were dropped on Hiroshima and Nagasaki were mere firecrackers. Today's bombs are thousands of times more powerful. Most of these bombs were made by the USA and the USSR, but Britain, France, China and India have also made their own nuclear bombs. It seems likely, too, that some other countries, including Israel and possibly South Africa, have also developed nuclear weapons.

The bombs that fell on Hiroshima and Nagasaki were dropped from an aeroplane. Modern nuclear weapons would be sent to their target by missiles. The American Cruise missile, for example, can be launched by land, sea or plane. It can fly so low that it is not picked up by enemy radar screens. It can fly for 3000 kilometres and deliver a bomb to within 10 metres of a target.

Figure 6.36
A nuclear-powered cruiser launches a series of highly accurate 'Tomahawk' cruise missiles

Détente

The superpowers agreed that nuclear warfare would be a disaster for both of them. They also knew that nuclear accidents could kill thousands, or even millions, of people. They were both concerned about the huge cost of developing nuclear weapons.

During the 1970s there was a relaxation of the tension that existed in the 1950s and 1960s between the superpowers. The USA and the USSR developed a much more friendly attitude towards each other and there were a number of special meetings, called 'summit' meetings, between the leaders of the two countries. The situation became known as *détente*, which is a French word meaning 'relaxation'.

As a result of *détente*, important talks took place between the two superpowers during the 1970s in order to limit the kind and number of weapons that were being produced. The most important of these were the Strategic Arms Limitation Talks (SALT). The first SALT agreement was signed in 1972 and another was signed in 1979.

During the early 1980s, however, and especially after Ronald Reagan became president of the USA in 1981, relationships between the USA and USSR grew worse. Once again, it seemed, there was fear and suspicion on both sides, and the Cold War was back again. The USA began to create new and deadly weapons. It looked as though a new 'arms race' was about to begin. President Reagan planned to develop a system, called the 'Strategic Defence Initiative' (SDI). This was designed to provide a defensive shield over the whole USA against nuclear attack. Most people referred to this scheme as 'Star Wars'. The scheme, however, never went ahead. Many experts did not believe it could ever be made to work.

The situation improved again in the late 1980s. In 1985, Mikhail Gorbachev became the new Soviet leader. Gorbachev was a new style of Soviet leader. He wanted to make the USSR more democratic and he wanted to end the Cold War and stop the arms race. In December 1987, Reagan and Gorbachev signed a treaty, known as the 'Intermediate and Shorter-range Nuclear Forces' treaty, generally known as INF. For the first time in the history of the Cold War both sides agreed to dismantle a large number of their nuclear weapons. A year later, Gorbachev addressed the United Nations and surprised the world by announcing that the USSR was going to withdraw large numbers of its troops and tanks from the countries of eastern Europe. He wanted, he said, to create a 'new world order'.

The Cold War ends

During the late 1980s two Russian words became famous throughout the world. *Glasnost*, which means 'openness', and *perestroika*, which means 'restructuring', were the two terms that Mikhail Gorbachev used to describe his plans for changing the USSR. He wanted the USSR to be a more open society, with fewer secrets from the rest of the world and he wanted to change some of the things about Soviet life that you read about on page 131. He wanted people to be freer to make choices, to be able to own property and even to run businesses as in Western countries. He even wanted to allow people to form new political parties that would compete in elections with the Communist Party.

Figure 6.37
Young East Berliners attack the Berlin Wall in November 1989

There was also a new feeling throughout much of eastern Europe. New political parties were formed and there were many protests and demonstrations against communist rulers. In September 1989, a non-communist government was established in Poland. The next month the communist government in Hungary resigned. By the end of 1989 there was a non-communist government in Czechoslovakia and there were protests and violent demonstrations in Bulgaria, Romania and East Germany.

On 7 November 1989 the communist government of East Germany resigned, and two days later, at midnight on 9 November, the authorities opened the Berlin Wall. As East German soldiers looked on, crowds of East Germans streamed through the checkpoints and were greeted by huge crowds on the western side. Many people attacked the wall with picks and axes, trying to destroy what had been for almost thirty years the most powerful symbol of the Cold War.

In December 1989, President George Bush of the USA met Mikhail Gorbachev in Malta. They agreed to continue to reduce the number of nuclear and other weapons and declared the end of the Cold War.

Figure 6.38
President Reagan and General Secretary Gorbachev pose for the press at a summit meeting to discuss the limitation of nuclear arms

The end of the USSR

During the years of the Cold War, it was common for people to refer to the USSR simply as Russia. But this was not strictly correct. Russia certainly dominated the USSR—it occupied three-quarters of the area of the country and had more than half the total population. But the USSR really consisted of fifteen separate countries, or 'republics'. Each one had its own culture and traditions and its own language. Most of these republics had become part of the USSR in the early 1920s. Three of them—the so-called 'Baltic' states of Lithuania, Estonia and Latvia—became part of the USSR when Soviet troops occupied them early in the Second World War.

The changes that were taking place in eastern Europe at the end of the 1980s also affected the people of the Soviet republics. Many of these people did not like being dominated by Russia. There were protests and demonstrations in many of these areas as people demanded that they be given their independence. In 1991 a group of communist officials, including some army officers, who were unhappy about the changes that were taking place in the USSR tried to seize power from Gorbachev. There were huge demonstrations in Moscow and other cities. The leaders of this 'coup' were arrested and all Communist Party activities were banned.

In December 1991 all the republics of the USSR became independent states and the USSR no longer existed. After the unsuccessful coup, Boris Yeltsin, a popular leader who was president of the Russian republic, emerged as the most powerful figure in the new country.

KNOW the chapter

1 In which country is each of these places: Bay of Pigs, Berlin, Camp David, Dien Bien Phu, Beirut, Washington, Entebbe, Hanoi, Munich, Beijing, Warsaw, Moscow?

2 Match each of the names in column A with a suitable description in column B.

A	B
Fidel Castro	became Soviet leader in 1985
Winston Churchill	ordered the blockade of Berlin in 1948
Ho Chi Minh	was the first eastern European country to elect a non-communist government in 1989
Premier Krushchev	became the first leader of communist China in 1948
Poland	became the ruler of North Vietnam in 1954
Mao Zedong	became the dictator of Cuba in 1959
Yasir Arafat	agreed to remove Soviet missiles from Cuba in 1962
Mikhail Gorbachev	signed a peace treaty with Israel in 1979
Joseph Stalin	said that eastern Europe was behind an Iron Curtain
President Sadat	signed an agreement with Prime Minister Rabin in 1993

3 a Each of these scrambled words has been used in this chapter. Unscramble each one.

L	E	G	I	A	R	L	U
	1	*	2	*		3	4

(page 140)

R	E	L	I	S	A
*	*	5	6		*

(page 151)

M	O	C	S	T	I	N	U	M
7		*			8		*	

(page 131)

S	T	E	W
9	10	*	

(page 134)

b Rearrange the numbered letters in the words you have formed to complete the following sentence:

One of the world's main problems during the Cold War was the threat of

c Rearrange the starred letters to complete the following sentence:

As time went on, this threat became more serious because the superpowers kept developing more powerful and accurate

7 Conflict *and* co-operation

When the Cold War ended many people thought that the world was entering a new period of peace. But watch the television news or read the daily newspapers and you will soon realise that in many parts of the world savage wars are still raging. Some of these conflicts have arisen since the end of the Cold War. Others are old conflicts that have been going on for many years—or even decades—and still show no sign of coming to an end.

There is, however, another side to the story. Countries often co-operate and help each other. Co-operation does not get as many headlines as the threat of war. But countries work together in many ways. They may support large international organisations such as the United Nations or join smaller groups such as ASEAN or the League of Arab States. They trade with each other and many rich countries give aid to poorer ones.

In this chapter we shall look at examples both of conflict and co-operation between nations in the post-Cold War world.

World order or disorder?

As we saw in the last chapter, the Soviet leader, Mikhail Gorbachev, looked forward to a 'new world order' in 1987. The spirit of co-operation between the USA and the USSR would, he thought, result in a more peaceful world. It is probably true that the threat of a nuclear war is not as great now as it was during the Cold War, but the end of the Cold War has certainly not meant an end of all wars.

In fact, the Cold War had hardly been declared over before a new war started in Europe. It would prove to be the longest and most destructive war to break out in Europe since the end of the Second World War.

The break up of Yugoslavia

At the beginning of chapter 2 you read about the Balkan states of Bosnia and Serbia. What happened in Sarajevo, the capital of Bosnia, in 1914 was really the beginning of the First World War. At the end of that war, in 1918, Bosnia (which is now referred to as Bosnia-Herzegovina), Serbia and the neighbouring republics of Croatia and Slovenia were joined together to form a new country, which was controlled by Serbia. This country was called the Kingdom of Serbs, Croats and Slovenes. In 1929 the king of Serbia, Alexander, changed the name to Yugoslavia.

In 1945, at the end of the Second World War, Yugoslavia became a communist country ruled by Josip Tito. Tito was a strong and often ruthless leader. Although he was a communist, he refused to allow the USSR to dominate Yugoslavia as it did the rest of eastern Europe. After Tito died in 1980, the nation of Yugoslavia remained united for another eleven years, although many people in the non-Serbian parts of the country wanted their areas to become independent nations.

Eventually, in June 1991, Croatia and Slovenia declared their independence from Yugoslavia, followed in December 1991 by Bosnia-Herzegovina. In 1992, Macedonia, which had once been part of Serbia, also declared its independence. Almost immediately a vicious war broke out in Croatia and then in Bosnia-Herzegovina as Serbian troops, supported by large numbers of Serbs who lived in the newly independent states, tried to prevent the break up of Yugoslavia. Tens of thousands of people were killed, civilians as well as soldiers, many of them in brutal massacres. Cities have been destroyed and vast numbers of people have been forced from their homes and become refugees. The war in Croatia, where 12 per cent of the population are Serbs, lasted until January 1992, although fighting has broken out again several times since then. In Bosnia-Herzegovina, where one-third of the population is Serb and about 44 per cent are Bosnian Muslims, the war continued for several more years. In October 1995 the Bosnian government and Serb forces agreed to a ceasefire. At this stage about half of Bosnia-Herzegovina was under the control of Serb forces.

Figure 7.1
The country that was Yugoslavia is now a number of separate republics

Figure 7.2
Forty-three people were killed when Serb soldiers shelled this market place in Sarajevo in September 1995. Which country is Sarajevo in?

Think *for yourself*

1 Why do you think Serbia was so strongly opposed to Croatia's and Bosnia-Herzegovina's declaration of independence?

2 Look at the map in Figure 7.1. How many separate countries has the former Yugoslavia been divided into? List these countries.

3 Can you suggest why the war in Bosnia has taken much longer to resolve than the war in Croatia?

4 Some people have claimed that the end of the Cold War was at least partly to blame for the war in Croatia and Bosnia-Herzegovina. Can you suggest some reasons for this opinion?

THE HISTORIAN AT WORK

Figure 7.3
The world's trouble spots, 1994. Some of these conflicts have been going on for many years.
The numbers below show the total number of people who had been killed in each of these conflicts by 1994.

Country	Deaths		
Afghanistan	14 000	Iraq	Unknown
Algeria	10 000–25 000	Israel	12 500
Angola	122 000	Liberia	20 000
Azerbaijan	10 000	Peru	28 000
Bangladesh	3 000–35 000	Philippines	21 000–25 000
Bosnia-Herzegovina	20 000–50 000	Rwanda	5 500
Cambodia	25 500	Somalia	Unknown
Colombia	30 000	Sri Lanka	27 000
Georgia	25 000	*Sudan	37 000–40 000
Guatemala	463 000	Tajikistan	20 000–50 000
India (Kashmir)	9 000	Turkey	13 000
*Indonesia (East Timor)	15 000–16 000	Yemen	1 500–7 000
Iran	Unknown	*Military deaths	

The following is an extract from an article that appeared in *Time* magazine in October 1995.

The forgotten wars

The last India–Pakistan war ended in 1971, but in one barren corner of Kashmir the killing has not stopped. On the 6100 m high Siachen Glacier, which sits in a no-man's-land claimed by both nations, soldiers still exchange artillery barrages—when they can dig out from the deep snow …

Then there are the Kurds, whose suffering so touched the world's heart in 1991 when TV pictured them starving and dying on mountain tops in Iraq. They have long since found refuge in what amounts to their own autonomous zone in northern Iraq, protected by allied air power from Saddam Hussein's armies. Under that shield, however, the Kurds for the past fifteen months have been busily killing one another in a civil war to decide which of two factions will control their supposed haven …

These are only [two] of dozens of … conflicts around the world that grind on year after year. Last week, as usual, the press was focused on the Balkans, where hopes of peace rose when representatives of the three warring factions tentatively accepted a framework in which they would share power in a Bosnian government. But … a Bosnian peace will be devilishly difficult to achieve and maintain, if the history of other ethnic battles is any guide. There are many smaller-scale Bosnias, and most show no signs of resolution. In fact these endless wars are all but forgotten by almost everyone except the participants …

Savagery is all too typical of the forgotten wars. Many are small-scale and fought with relatively primitive weapons in sparsely populated areas … The causes of the wars vary widely. Many conflicts are fuelled by ethnic or religious hatreds … Others begin as personal struggles among rivals for power in an area without any strong central authority …

In some cases, it seems only outside pressure can end these interminable carnivals of destruction. But the major powers are increasingly reluctant to intervene. The end of the Cold War has ended any chance that the outcome of a conflict in a corner of Asia, Africa or Latin America could tilt the world balance of power. And many long-running wars are fought in areas where the major powers have no economic or strategic interests.

Besides, the history of what efforts the big powers have made to intervene is discouraging. Diplomacy has had some successes, but is difficult in situations where hated rivals have for decades talked only with guns. Often, too, there are more than two sides to bring together. The Sudanese war began as a rebellion of black Christians and animists in the south against a government dominated by Muslims of Arab descent in the north, but the rebels have since splintered into seven factions that fight one another as well as the government. Jimmy Carter [a previous United States president] did persuade all parties to agree to successive cease-fires that lasted from March through July [1995], but warfare promptly resumed at the beginning of August. No surprise. Sally Burnheim, spokeswoman for a United Nations relief operation in Sudan, notes that the combatants have often used cease-fires to regroup and prepare for new offensives.

Intervention by armed peacekeepers has usually been futile or worse … Perhaps the worst failure was the attempt of the Indian government to end the struggle between majority Sinhalese and minority Tamils in Sri Lanka. After four years of war, India in 1987 brokered an agreement under which the Sri Lankan government granted some autonomy [right to self-government] to the Tamils in the northeast, and [India] sent a peacekeeping force to disarm the [Tamils]. The Indians found themselves fighting a full-scale war against the [Tamils], but that did not win the hearts and minds of the Sinhalese. In fact, a Sinhalese rebellion broke out against the [Sri Lankan] government, which the rebels contended had no business inviting Indian troops onto the island for any purpose. The Indians pulled out in March 1990, and the war goes on.

There is one exception—sort of—to this sorry record … [Russia] has at least damped down, if not exactly ended, nearly all the wars in the Soviet republics that declared themselves independent nations upon the dissolution of the USSR in 1991. Its method: dispatch huge forces to turbulent areas; have the troops fight more or less openly on whichever side is most favourable to [Russia] … then virtually dictate the terms of a cease-fire and enforce it brutally.

Even this approach has not succeeded entirely. In the central Asian republic of Tajikistan, the 8500-man Russian 201st Motorised Rifle Division polices a cease-fire, while 17 000 Russian border guards stand watch over the frontiers. Nonetheless, Muslim fundamentalists and other anti-government forces driven into exile in Afghanistan and Pakistan regularly stage cross-border raids, capturing Tajik villages and sometimes whole districts until forced out again. Guerilla war continues deep inside Tajikistan too …

Figure 7.4
Kurdish fighters in northern Iraq. Who are these men fighting against?

Figure 7.5
This Tamil woman is a guerilla fighter. Who is she fighting against? In which country was this picture taken?

1. How many of the conflicts shown on the map in Figure 7.3 are mentioned in the article? How many deaths had each of these conflicts caused by 1994?
2. Why is the number of people killed in some conflicts either unknown or uncertain? Is there any reason to believe that the number of people killed in Sudan and East Timor is greater than the numbers given above?
3. One trouble spot that is very close to Australia is not mentioned in the article. Where is it? Do some research to find out what caused the conflict in this place. Is it still a trouble spot?
4. Name the three 'warring factions' in the Balkans war. The conflict in the Balkans is described in the article as an 'ethnic battle'. What does 'ethnic' mean? Which other conflicts mentioned in the article could be described as 'ethnic' conflicts?
5. Religion played a part in a number of the conflicts mentioned in the article. Which ones?

6 Why do you think many of the wars around the world could be described as 'forgotten'? Why are some wars widely reported in newspapers and on TV?

7 Who are the Kurds? Do some research to find out where Kurds live, apart from northern Iraq.

8 What problems did the Kurds in northern Iraq face in 1991? Why do you think they were reported so widely on TV? (Clue: reread page 154 in the previous chapter.) What has happened to the Kurds since 1991?

9 In the article, 'diplomacy' and 'intervention' are named as two ways of trying to end conflicts. Explain what each of these words means. Why did diplomacy not succeed in ending the war in Sudan? Can you think of any cases where diplomacy did help to solve a conflict? (Clue: see the previous chapter.)

10 Why did Indian intervention in Sri Lanka fail to end the war there? What other examples of intervention are mentioned in the article? Were they successful or unsuccessful?

11 The article refers to wars in former Soviet republics. Three of these trouble spots are marked on the map in Figure 7.3. Where are they?

The United Nations

When the Second World War broke out, it was clear that the League of Nations had failed. But during the Second World War, plans were made for a new organisation to replace the League. In June 1945 representatives from fifty countries signed a charter that set out the aims of the new United Nations Organisation. On 24 October 1945 the organisation came into being. Since then, 24 October has been celebrated round the world as United Nations Day.

Figure 7.6
The symbol of the United Nations. Can you work out what it represents?

The United Nations was set up to do three things:

1 to prevent wars and keep the peace
2 to overcome poverty and bring about progress
3 to protect human rights and freedoms.

In 1995 there were 185 countries in the United Nations. Each member country must obey the rules of the organisation. The most important rules are:

1 respect other countries and their people
2 settle disputes and arguments peacefully
3 help the United Nations when aid is needed.

The headquarters of the United Nations is in New York. The United Nations is a huge organisation. At its centre is the General Assembly. The General Assembly is a forum in which member countries can discuss world problems. You can see from Figure 7.7 that there are five other sections of the United Nations.

Keeping the peace

Keeping the peace is the most important job of the United Nations.

Keeping the peace includes trying to stop

- wars from starting
- small wars from growing into larger wars
- countries from building up huge supplies of weapons.

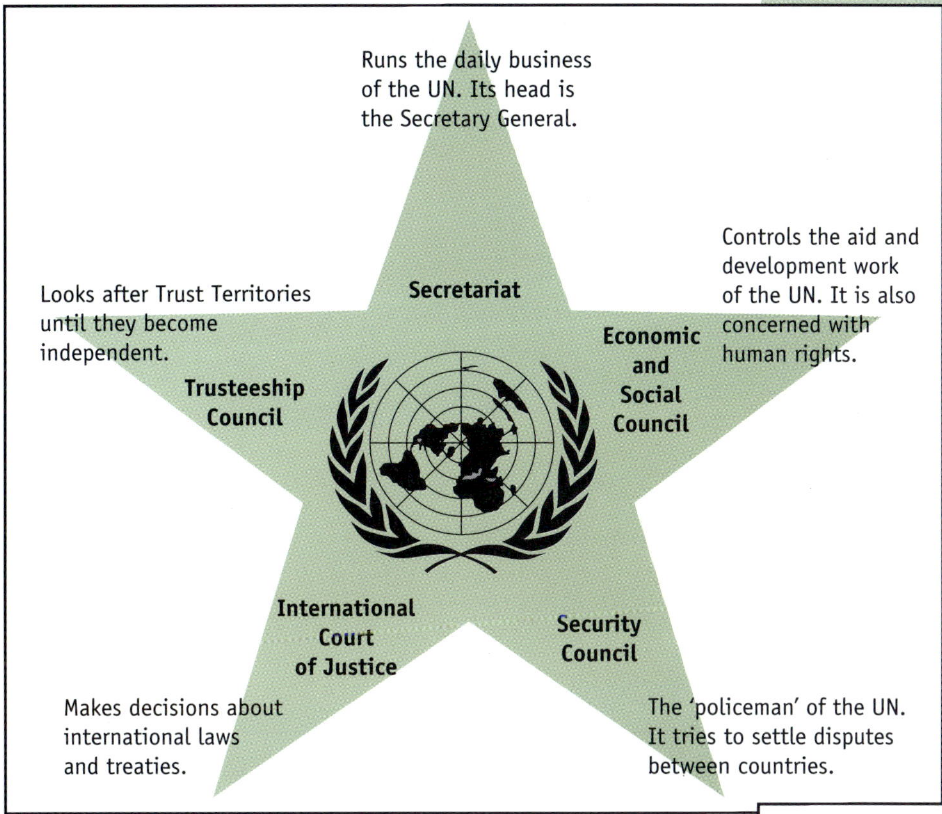

Figure 7.7
How the United Nations is organised

Figure 7.8
Keeping the peace is the most important job of the United Nations

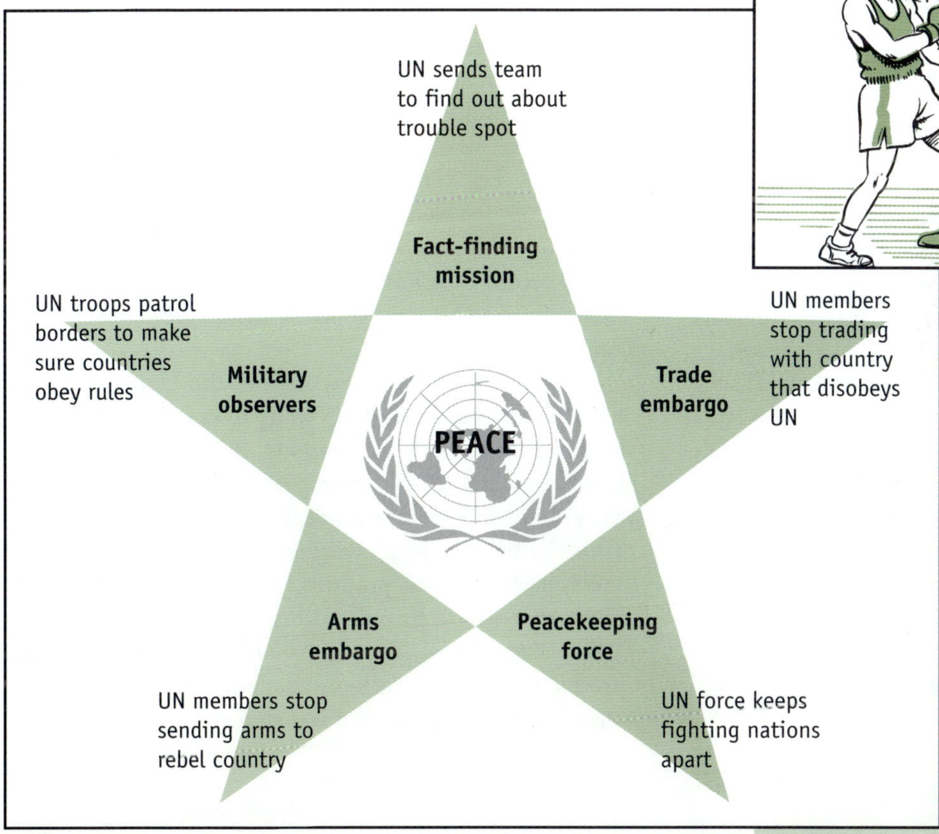

Figure 7.9
How the United Nations tries to keep the peace

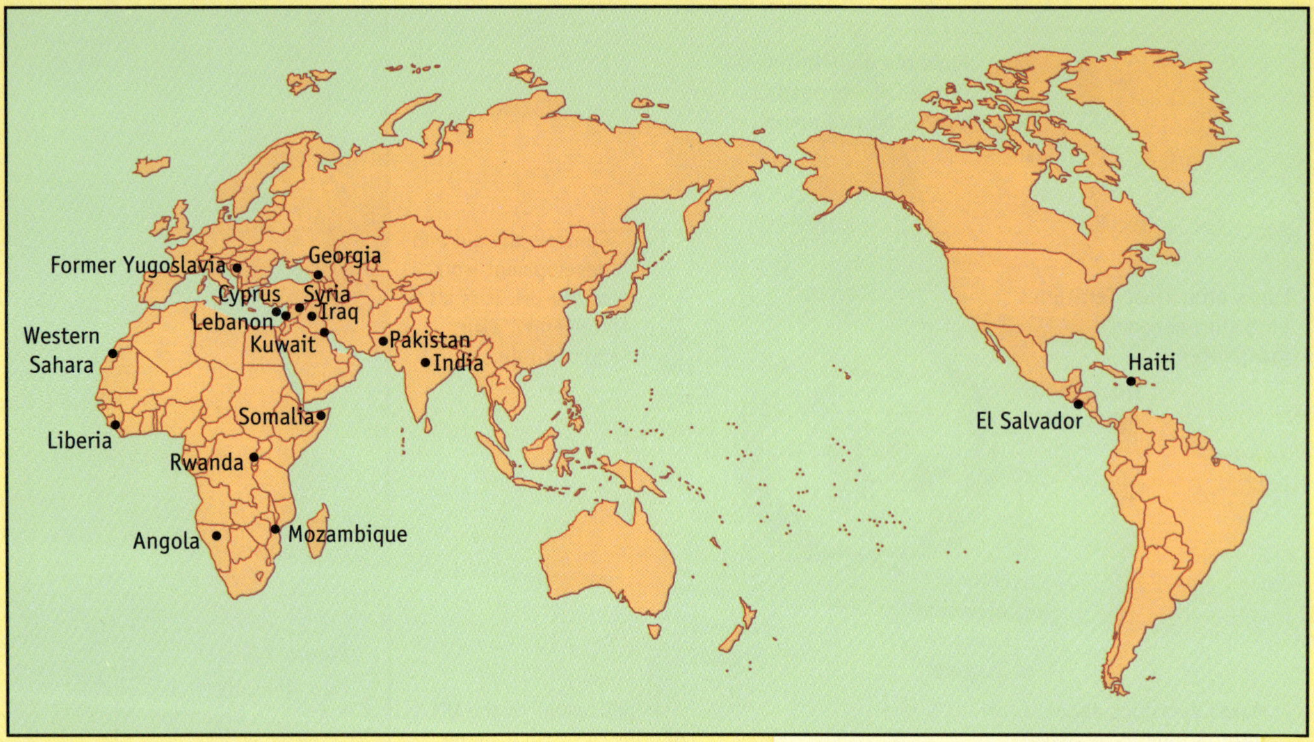

Figure 7.10
Places where United Nations peacekeeping forces were stationed during 1994

These are difficult tasks. Figure 7.9 on page 169 shows the main ways by which the United Nations tries to keep the peace.

Since it was formed in 1945, the United Nations has been involved in well over 100 disputes between countries all around the world. In almost forty of these disputes, the United Nations has sent soldiers to try to prevent wars from breaking out again. The map in Figure 7.10 shows the places where United Nations peacekeeping forces were still operating in 1994. These peacekeeping forces had been in some places for many years.

In more than fifty years since it was formed, the United Nations has helped solve many of the world's conflicts. But it has not always been successful in its role as peacekeeper. In recent years, especially, it has been criticised for failing to stop a number of disputes. In early 1995, for example, United Nations troops were forced to leave the African nation of Somalia where, after two years, they were unable to stop the civil war there. In Bosnia-Herzegovina, as well, many people blamed United Nations forces for failing to protect Bosnian civilians against attacks by Serb forces.

What some people who are critical of the United Nations do not realise is that since the end of the Cold War the number of peacekeeping operations has increased greatly. Between 1945 and 1988 United Nations peacekeeping forces were sent to thirteen places around the world. Between 1988 and 1995 United Nations forces were involved in twenty-five disputes.

Another problem is that the United Nations often finds it difficult to find enough soldiers for its peacekeeping missions. Many countries will not allow their troops to be sent to places which they consider too dangerous.

As part of its job as peacemaker, the United Nations has arranged many meetings to try to stop countries from building up supplies of weapons. In 1963 a Partial Test Ban Treaty banned the testing of nuclear weapons above the ground and under the sea. The Outer Space Treaty of 1967 banned nuclear weapons from outer space. In 1995, it seemed that progress was being made towards a treaty that would ban all testing of nuclear weapons. In 1993, a Chemical Weapons Convention, banning the production of chemical weapons, was finally agreed upon after twenty-five years of discussion.

Despite the work of the United Nations, it is hard to know how effective these treaties and agreements really are. Many countries refuse to sign these treaties, and the ones that do sign do not always obey them. As we saw in the last chapter, a number of countries have nuclear weapons. Iraq and some other countries, too, are suspected of having large numbers of chemical weapons which they could use against other countries.

Fighting poverty

The map in Figure 7.13 shows the rich and poor countries of the world. The poor countries are often called the **developing** countries. Another name for the developing countries is the **Third World**. The rich countries are called the **developed** countries.

Developing countries share these problems:

- too many people
- not enough food
- little industry
- poor farming methods
- low level of education
- unsafe water supply which spreads disease.

The United Nations is trying to solve these problems. It is a huge task. More than half the people in the world are badly fed and almost 800 million never have as much as they need to eat. It is estimated that every year 12 million people throughout the world die of hunger.

Figure 7.12
City slums in Bangladesh. How could the United Nations help people who live here?

Problems like these do not disappear overnight. But the United Nations has set up special agencies to try and solve them. The table on page 172 lists some of these agencies. There are many others. This kind of work needs a great deal of money. Some comes from the funds of the United Nations. The rest comes from gifts from richer members of the United Nations.

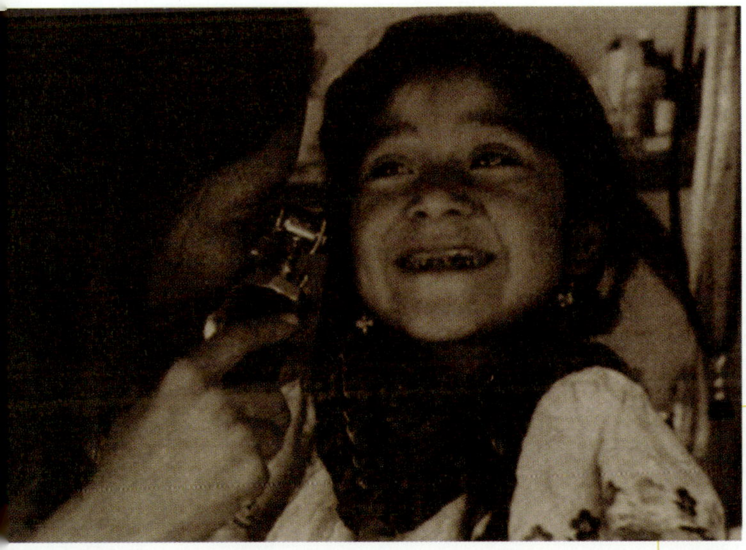

Figure 7.11
The United Nations tries to overcome poverty in the world. Here, a Mexican Indian girl is having a medical examination through a health care program supported by UNICEF.

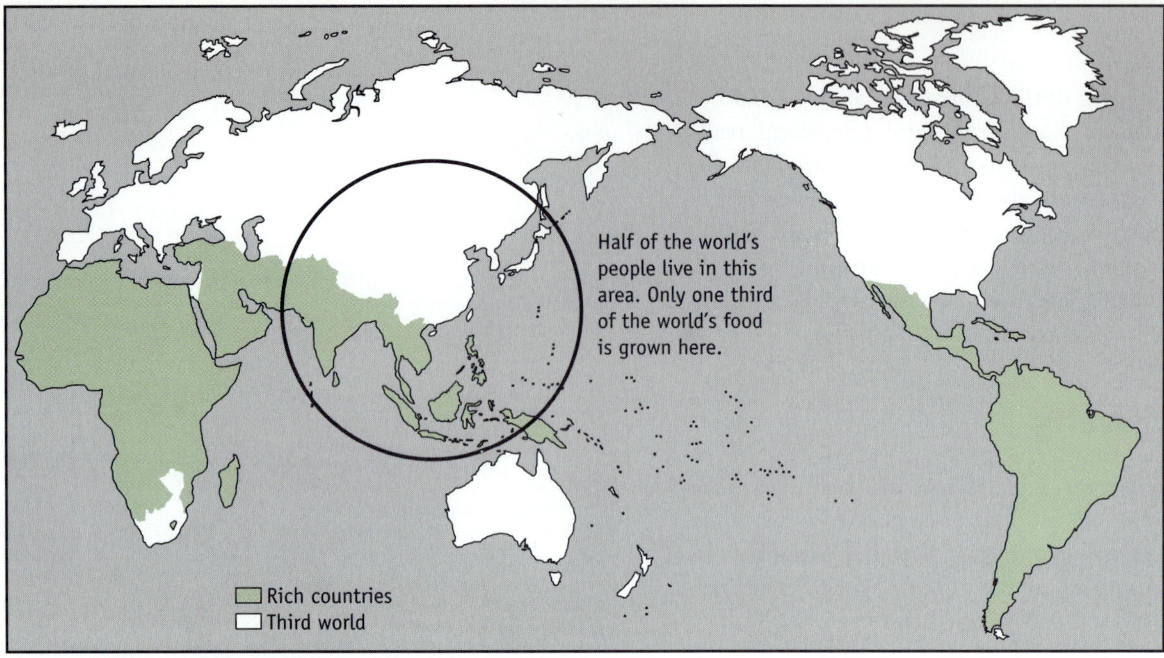

Figure 7.13 Rich and poor countries. In which continents are most of the Third World countries?

Special agencies of the United Nations

Agency	Aim	Examples of its work
World Health Organisation WHO	To improve health around the world	Helps governments to improve health services; builds hospitals; runs campaigns against diseases like TB, malaria and smallpox; provides doctors and nurses for developing countries
United Nations Educational, Scientific and Cultural Organisation (UNESCO)	To develop education, scientific co-operation and the arts	Improves basic education in developing countries; encourages sharing of books, films and music
Food and Agriculture Organisation (FAO)	To increase food supplies and prevent hunger	Develops better farming methods and advises farmers which crops to grow and how to grow them; improves irrigation, fertilisers; conducts experiments on pest control
International Labor Organisation (ILO)	To improve working conditions	Has set up guidelines on working conditions; arranges meetings of trade union leaders
United Nations Children's Fund (UNICEF)	To help all children who are in need	Arranges programs for mother and child care; gives emergency relief when needed

Peacekeeping at work: the United Nations in Korea, 1950–53

Korea is a peninsula jutting out from China. In 1910 it was taken over by Japan. In 1945, at the end of the Second World War, North Korea was occupied by the USSR. South Korea was occupied by the USA. Each country set up a government. There was a communist government in North Korea and a government that supported the USA in South Korea.

In June 1950 the North Korean army, trained by the USSR, invaded South Korea. The United Nations decided to help South Korea. It was able to do this because the Soviet representatives had walked out of the Security Council. If they had been at the meeting, they would have been able to use their vote to stop the United Nations from interfering in Korea. This is known as the right of 'veto'. A United Nations force was gathered together. Sixteen countries sent troops. Australia was one of them. The force was led by General Douglas MacArthur, who had been in Australia during the Second World War.

Figure 7.15
These Chinese communists were some of the many thousands who were captured by the United Nations forces in Korea. They are waiting for a meal outside a prisoner-of-war camp in South Korea.

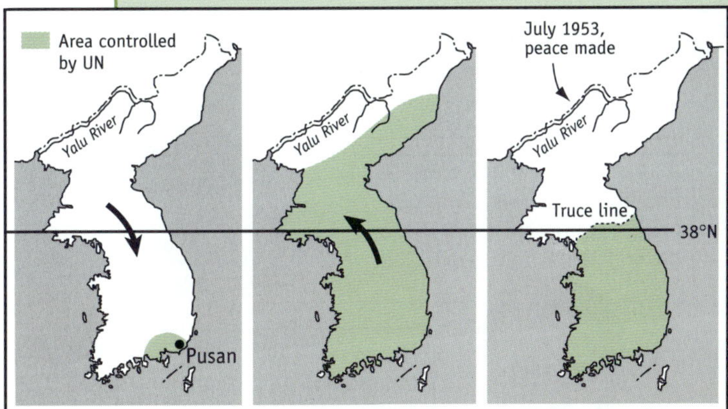

Figure 7.14
The Korean War, 1950–53

After three months' fighting, the United Nations force pushed the North Koreans back to the border. MacArthur decided to push into North Korea to try to take over the whole of Korea. His forces almost reached the Chinese border. Many thousands of Chinese soldiers came into the war. Fighting was heavy. By 1953 the North Koreans and Chinese had pushed the United Nations forces back to near the original border between North and South Korea.

A truce was signed in July 1953. Korea was divided into two separate countries. They are still not united.

Protecting human rights

> I live in Tibet. My country is controlled by China. My father is in prison because he demonstrated against the Chinese authorities.
>
> I live in Singapore. I can be imprisoned without trial if the police suspect me of a crime.
>
> I am a woman from the Philippines. I work as a maid in Saudi Arabia. My employer sometimes does not pay me and often beats me. I cannot afford to leave my job. If I defend myself I may be put in prison.
>
> I am an Australian Aborigine. I was born in 1953. When I was a child, I was taken from my parents and forced to live with a white family.

All these people are alike in one important way. They have all been denied their human rights. The United Nations believes that all human beings have certain rights that are worth fighting for.

In 1948 the United Nations adopted the Universal Declaration of Human Rights. This document sets out the basic rights that all human beings should have. It states that all people are born free and equal and that they should be able to live and work as they want to. In 1976, members of the United Nations agreed to protect human rights. But, despite agreements like this, it is clear that in many parts of the world human rights are being ignored. Organisations such as Amnesty International have been set up because the United Nations alone cannot protect human rights.

Australia and the United Nations

Australia was one of the fifty countries that signed the Charter to form the United Nations in 1945. Australia's representative was Dr Hubert Vere Evatt, the foreign minister. Dr Evatt helped to draw up the United Nations Charter. He wanted the new organisation to be a place where small countries could make their ideas known. In 1948 he was elected as president of the General Assembly. Because of the work and influence of Dr Evatt, Australia became known as a strong supporter of the United Nations.

The United Nations was important to Australia in another way, too. At the end of the First World War, Australia had been given control of the German colony in New Guinea. The League of Nations supervised Australia's control under a system called a **mandate**. After the Second World War, the system changed. Australia still controlled New Guinea, but now Australia acted as a **trustee** for the United Nations. It was now Australia's responsibility to prepare New Guinea for independence. Because of this responsibility, Australia was a member of the United Nations Trusteeship Council until 1975, when New Guinea became independent.

Australia has sent troops to trouble spots where United Nations forces have been fighting or working to keep the peace. Australians have served as part of the United Nations forces in Palestine, in Kashmir, in Korea and in Cyprus. In 1995, Australia contributed almost $68 million towards the United Nations' peacekeeping operations.

As well as providing soldiers, Australia has given the United Nations many millions of dollars to help pay for projects to help people in the Third World. In 1995, $85 million of the $275 million that Australia contributed to international aid organisations went to United Nations agencies. Most of this ($50 million) was given to the United Nations World Food Program.

Aboriginal Australians have used the United Nations as a way of telling the world about their problems and about the discrimination they find in Australia.

Figure 7.16
Some opinions on the United Nations

CHECK the facts

Choose the right ending for each of the following sentences.

1 The headquarters of the United Nations is in
- **a** London
- **b** New Delhi
- **c** Melbourne
- **d** New York.

2 The Secretary General of the United Nations is head of the
- **a** World Health Organisation
- **b** Security Council
- **c** Secretariat
- **d** General Assembly.

3 Between 1950 and 1963 United Nations forces were sent to
- **a** Suez Canal
- **b** Vietnam
- **c** Cyprus
- **d** Korea.

4 The Partial Test Ban Treaty in 1963 banned
- **a** testing of nuclear weapons above the ground and under the sea
- **b** use of poisonous gas in war
- **c** sending nuclear weapons into space
- **d** testing of all nuclear weapons.

5 The Third World is another name for
- **a** the rich countries
- **b** Asia
- **c** the developing countries
- **d** Africa.

6 The United Nations agency that helps children is
- **a** WHO
- **b** UNESCO
- **c** ILO
- **d** UNICEF.

7 The Universal Declaration of Human Rights states that
- **a** people should be able to express their opinions
- **b** nuclear weapons should be banned
- **c** all countries should be democratic
- **d** no one should be sent to prison.

Think *for yourself*

1 The developing countries are sometimes called the Third World. Can you suggest why they have been given this name?

2 Which of the United Nations special agencies would be most likely to help in each of these cases:
- **a** building a school or a village in Bangladesh
- **b** teaching nurses in India how to immunise children against cholera
- **c** arranging a meeting of trade union leaders from many countries
- **d** setting up a new irrigation works in Pakistan.

3 From what you have read, how true do you think the comments in Figure 7.16 are? Do you think the United Nations is worth keeping?

Figure 7.17
This cartoon appeared in an Australian newspaper in 1995. Why does the cartoon show a birthday cake? What point is the cartoon making about the United Nations?

The Commonwealth of Nations

From Empire to Commonwealth

At the beginning of the nineteenth century, the British Empire was a large group of colonies ruled by Britain. These countries were forced to accept the British king or queen as their head of state.

Things changed after the First World War. By then Canada, Australia, New Zealand and South Africa had become independent. They had their own governments. In 1931 the Statute of Westminster gave these countries a new position in the Empire. They were 'equal in status' with each other and with Britain. The name 'British Empire' was changed to 'British Commonwealth of Nations'. Independent countries now belonged to it because they wanted to, not because they were forced to.

There were many other colonies in Africa and Asia that were still controlled by Britain. After the Second World War their position changed as well. One by one they became independent. First India and Pakistan, then Ceylon (Sri Lanka), China, Malaya, Nigeria, Cyprus, Jamaica, Kenya, Zambia, Rhodesia (Zimbabwe) and many others became independent countries.

Most of these countries decided to remain members of the British Commonwealth. But many of them did not want to have the king or queen of Britain as the head of their government. So the rules were changed once again. Today members of the Commonwealth accept the queen as the head of the Commonwealth but less than half of them accept her as the head of their own government. Australia is one Commonwealth country that still accepts the queen as head of state. Other countries such as India have a president as head of state. These countries are called **republics**.

After the Second World War, the word 'British' was dropped; the name was changed to the Commonwealth of Nations. The new members were not as closely linked with Britain as the old ones had been. They did not see Britain as the head of the Commonwealth. They did not want to be reminded of the days when they were colonies of Britain. Today, the Commonwealth of Nations is very different from the British Empire of the early nineteenth century.

Figure 7.18
India's independence in 1949 was largely due to the work of Mahatma Gandhi. In this picture, Gandhi is working at a spinning wheel. He believed that Indians should develop their own ways of making things such as cloth.

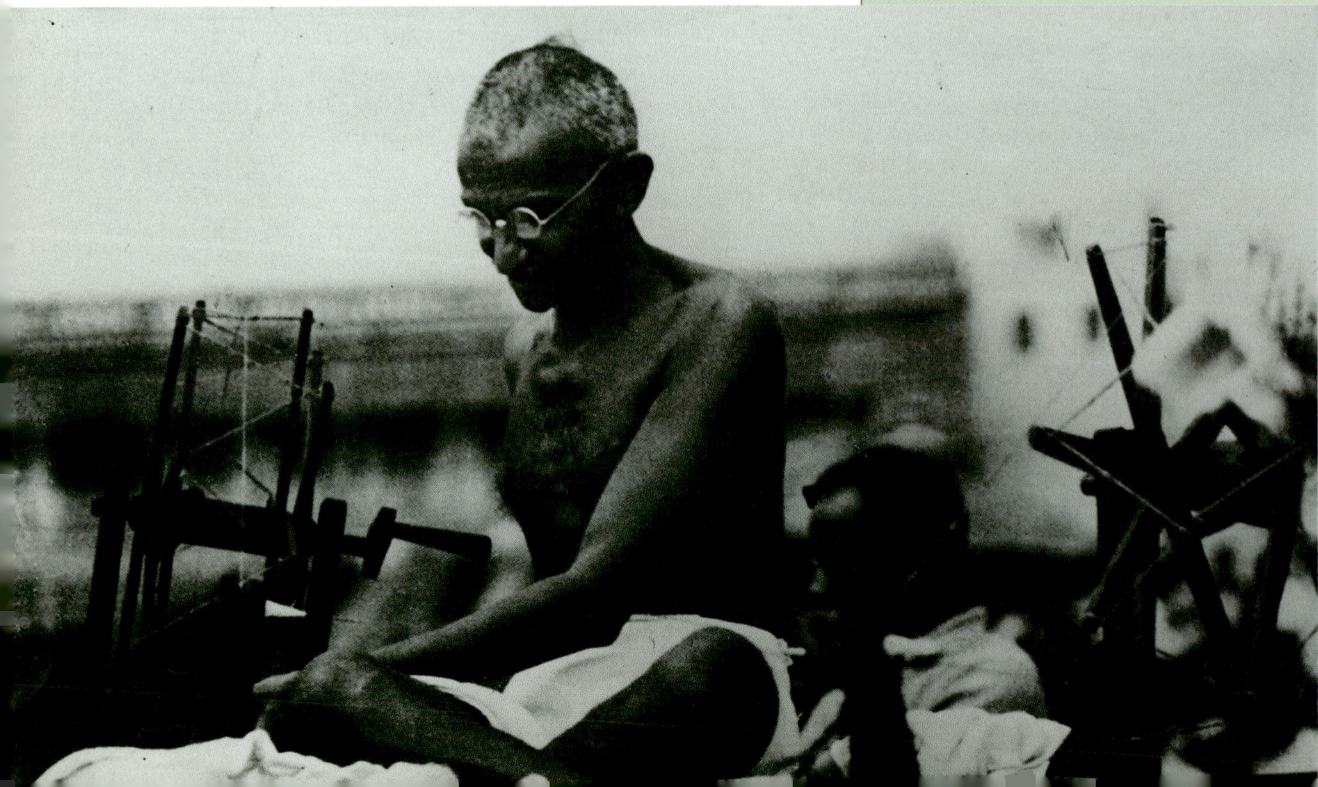

The Commonwealth today

The Commonwealth of Nations is made up of fifty-one independent countries which together contain about a quarter of the world's people. There are, as well, a few small places that are still controlled by another country because they are too small to become independent. These countries are called **dependencies**. Australia's dependencies include Christmas Island, Norfolk Island and the Australian Antarctic Territory. Britain's dependencies include the Falkland Islands and Gibraltar.

Unlike the United Nations, the Commonwealth does not have a strict set of rules. Members do not have to support each other in times of war. They are free to join other organisations and to sign treaties with countries that do not belong to the Commonwealth.

Every two years the heads of government of Commonwealth countries meet to discuss problems and important world issues. They work out ways of strengthening co-operation between members. The last Commonwealth Heads of Government Meeting (CHOGM) to be held in Australia was the 1981 meeting which was held in Melbourne.

Members of the Commonwealth co-operate in many ways. Figure 7.19 shows some of them.

South Africa

What happened in South Africa is a good example of how Commonwealth countries can co-operate with each other to help bring about change. In 1961 South Africa left the Commonwealth. Most other Commonwealth countries strongly criticised South Africa for its policy of *apartheid*. This meant that the black Africans, who made up most of the population, were ruled and dominated by the white population, who were in a minority. Black people were not entitled to vote, or to take part in the government and were forced to live in separate areas. Black leaders who tried to change this policy were imprisoned by the government. When black people demonstrated against the government white soldiers sometimes used violence to crush the demonstrations.

During the 1970s and 1980s the Commonwealth countries took steps to try to force South Africa to abandon its apartheid policy. In 1978 they agreed to ban sporting contacts with South Africa. In the mid-1980s the countries of the Commonwealth, as well as some other countries, introduced 'economic sanctions' against South Africa. This meant that they restricted their trade with South Africa. South Africa became more and more isolated from the rest of the world, and especially from nations with which it had been friendly.

Figure 7.19
The links between members of the Commonwealth of Nations

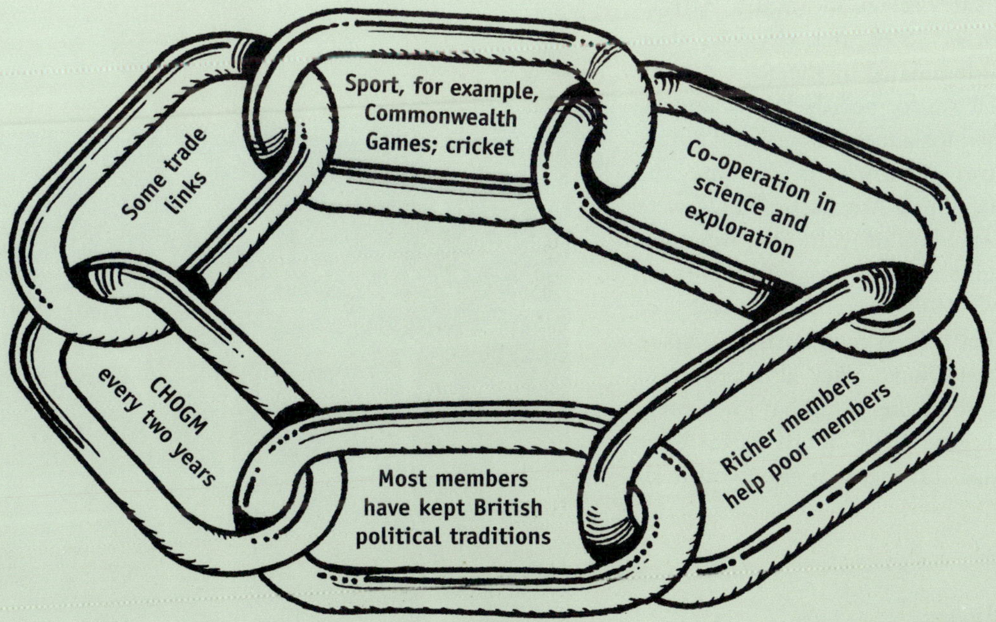

Figure 7.20
The 1993 Commonwealth Heads of Government meeting was held in Cyprus. Can you find the Australian prime minister in this photograph?

Figure 7.21
Nelson Mandela who became president of South Africa in 1994

These measures helped weaken the South African government. Eventually, in 1994, free elections were held and a government, dominated by the black African National Council (ANC) was formed. Nelson Mandela, who had been imprisoned for almost twenty-eight years by white South African governments, became the country's new president. South Africa's problems were certainly not over, but the days of white rule were and South Africa had a genuine democratic government.

During the early 1990s, representatives of Commonwealth countries helped South Africa prepare for its first democratic elections. They also helped to supervise the elections to make sure that they were conducted fairly. On 1 June 1994 South Africa once again became a member of the Commonwealth of Nations.

Problems in the Commonwealth

Some people consider that in the world of the 1990s countries receive very little benefit from belonging to the Commonwealth of Nations. They feel that the countries of the Commonwealth no longer have very much in common. There is no doubt that the Commonwealth of Nations has changed a great deal over the years.

In the 1930s Commonwealth countries worked out a way of making trade with each other easier. Today that agreement no longer works. Commonwealth countries still trade with each other, but they trade with countries outside the Commonwealth as well.

In 1973, Britain joined the European Economic Community, which is now known as the European Community, or EC. By joining the EC, Britain had to give up its special trade links with Australia and other Commonwealth countries. Until then Australia had sold most of its wool, wheat, meat and dairy products to Britain. Since the 1970s Australians have found new markets for these and other products.

Because the Commonwealth is not a military group, members often have treaties with countries outside the Commonwealth. In 1951 Australia signed the ANZUS treaty with New Zealand (a Commonwealth country) and the USA (not a Commonwealth country). In the 1960s India and Pakistan went to war because both countries claimed Kashmir as their own. Partly as a result of this clash, Pakistan left the Commonwealth in 1972. It once again became a member in 1989.

In 1987 Fiji left the Commonwealth after a military officer, Colonel Rabuka, seized control of the nation from the elected government and declared the country a republic. Fiji has not rejoined the Commonwealth.

Australia and the Commonwealth

Australia's links with Britain are no longer as strong as they were when the Commonwealth was formed before the Second World War. In those days almost all of Australia's population had descended from people in the British Isles and Australia depended on Britain for its defence. Most of Australia's trade was also with Britain. All these things have now changed.

But Australia still supports the Commonwealth. It accepts the principles on which the Commonwealth is based and sees the CHOGM meetings every two years as a valuable opportunity for leaders from different parts of the world to discuss important world issues.

Empire Day was once an important event in Australia. We still have a Commonwealth Day. It is celebrated in Australia and other Commonwealth countries on the second Monday in March. This day was chosen because it is a school day in every Commonwealth country. Some schools organise special Commonwealth activities on this day. Does yours?

Figure 7.22
Britain applied to join the Common Market in 1961. This photograph, taken in 1962, shows that not all British people supported the idea. Why did this man think that the Common Market would mean the end of the Commonwealth?

CHECK the facts

1 Are the statements below true or false?
  a Independent members of the Commonwealth are not allowed to leave the Commonwealth.
  b The Statute of Westminster made India an independent country in 1931.
  c All countries in the Commonwealth accept the British king or queen as head of their government.
  d A dependency is a country that is controlled by another country.
  e Commonwealth countries compete with each other at sport.
  f The last Commonwealth Heads of Government Meeting was held in Australia.

2 Identify the countries described below.
  a It went to war with another Commonwealth country, left the Commonwealth in 1972, but joined it again in 1989.
  b This country joined the European Community in 1973.
  c It signed a treaty with Australia and the USA in 1951.
  d Due to criticism of its apartheid policy from other Commonwealth countries, this nation left the Commonwealth in 1961. It joined the Commonwealth again in 1994.
  e This is one of the dependencies of Britain in the southern Atlantic ocean.
  f A Pacific nation which left the Commonwealth in 1987.

Some regional groups

The United Nations and the Commonwealth of Nations are large organisations which have members in all parts of the world. There are, as well, many smaller organisations. Some of these were formed to help countries to trade with each other more easily. Others are military alliances. They were set up to protect their members against attack from other countries.

The European Economic Community

The European Economic Community was formed in 1957 when six European countries agreed to trade freely with each other. This group was originally called the European Economic Community. The 'Six', as they were referred to, were Belgium, Luxembourg, France, Italy, the Netherlands and West Germany. They felt that their economies would be stronger and their people more prosperous if they co-operated with each other. Britain applied to join in 1961, but it did not become a member until 1973. In the same year Denmark and Ireland also became members. During the 1980s Greece, Spain and Portugal joined the community. At the beginning of 1995 Austria, Finland and Sweden were admitted, bringing the number of members to fifteen. When East and West Germany became one country in 1990, West Germany's membership was transferred to the new united Germany.

Think *for yourself*

1 The Commonwealth of Nations has been called 'a loose association of countries'. What does this mean? From what you have read in this section, give three examples to show how the Commonwealth is a loose association.

2 Figure 7.19 shows some of the ways in which Commonwealth countries help each other. Read the section about problems in the Commonwealth again. Draw a diagram to illustrate these problems.

3 Think of some ways in which your school or your history class could celebrate Commonwealth Day.

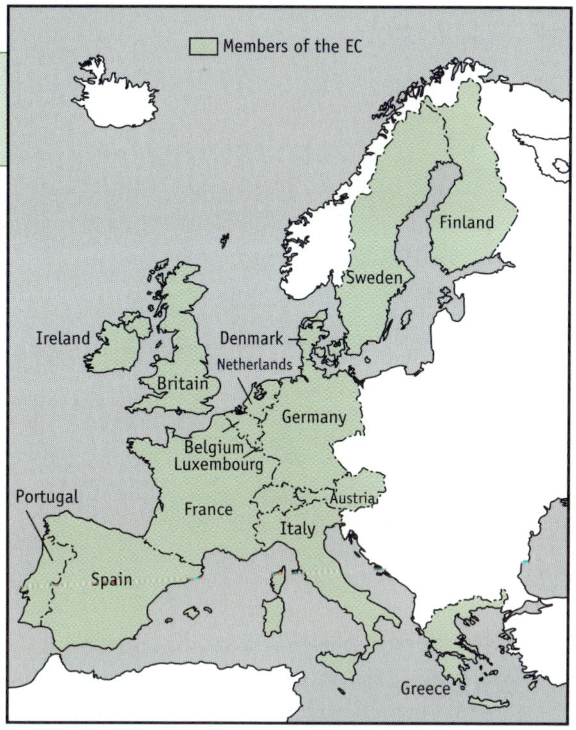

Figure 7.23
Members of the EC

ASEAN

The Association of South-East Asian Nations (ASEAN) was formed in 1967. Its members are Indonesia, Malaysia, the Philippines, Singapore, Thailand and Brunei. ASEAN hopes to speed up progress in its region and to make it a 'zone of peace'. The member countries have strong trade links with each other. Australia, too, has strong links with the ASEAN countries. In 1994 Australia provided aid worth $250 million to the ASEAN countries. As a group, the members of ASEAN are Australia's fourth largest trading partner.

Figure 7.24
Members of ASEAN

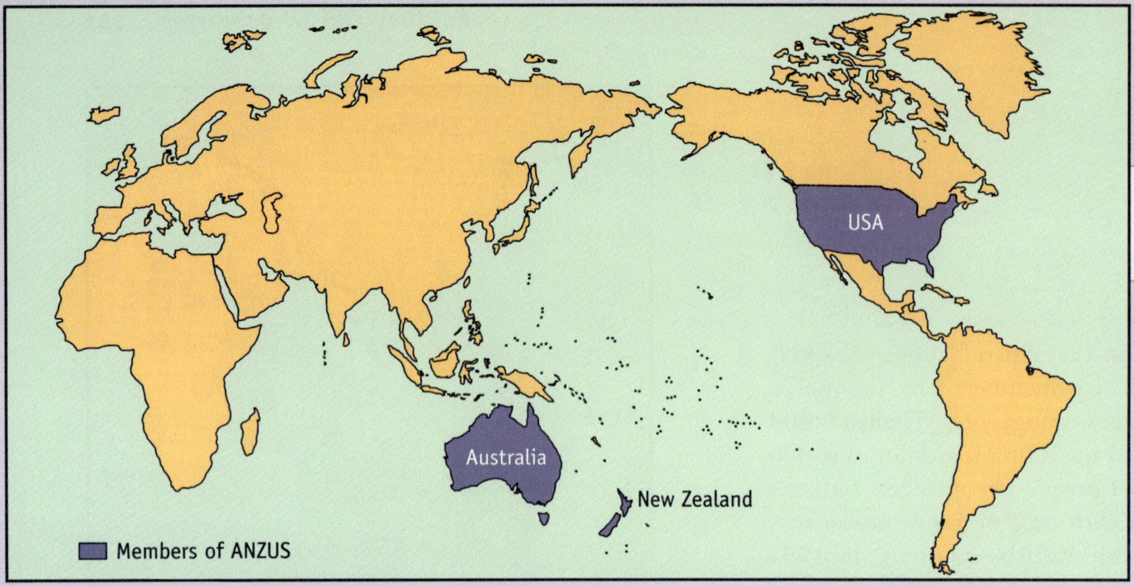

Figure 7.25
Members of ANZUS

ANZUS

The ANZUS treaty between Australia, New Zealand and the USA was signed in 1951. Under this treaty each of the three countries agreed to consult the others if any one of them was attacked and to help defend that country if asked to do so.

ANZUS was important to Australia. It was the first defence treaty that Australia signed without Britain. The ANZUS treaty made it clear that Australia considered the USA to be more important than Britain as an ally.

In 1986 the USA cancelled its obligations to New Zealand under the ANZUS treaty after the New Zealand government refused to allow any United States ships that might be carrying nuclear weapons to enter New Zealand ports. The ANZUS treaty still exists, but it is now really two separate treaties: one between Australia and New Zealand, and another between Australia and the USA.

APEC

In 1989 Australia suggested that nations in the region should join a group whose leaders could meet regularly to find ways of making trade between them easier. This organisation was named Asia-Pacific Economic Co-operation (APEC). The original members were Australia, New Zealand, the ASEAN countries, South Korea, Japan, the USA and Canada. In 1991 Taiwan, China and Hong Kong joined this group. Mexico and Papua New Guinea were admitted in 1993 and Chile became a member in 1994. The first meeting of APEC leaders was held in Seattle in the USA in 1993.

APEC is very important to Australia. Three-quarters of Australia's exports go to other member countries. Two-thirds of Australia's imports come from APEC countries.

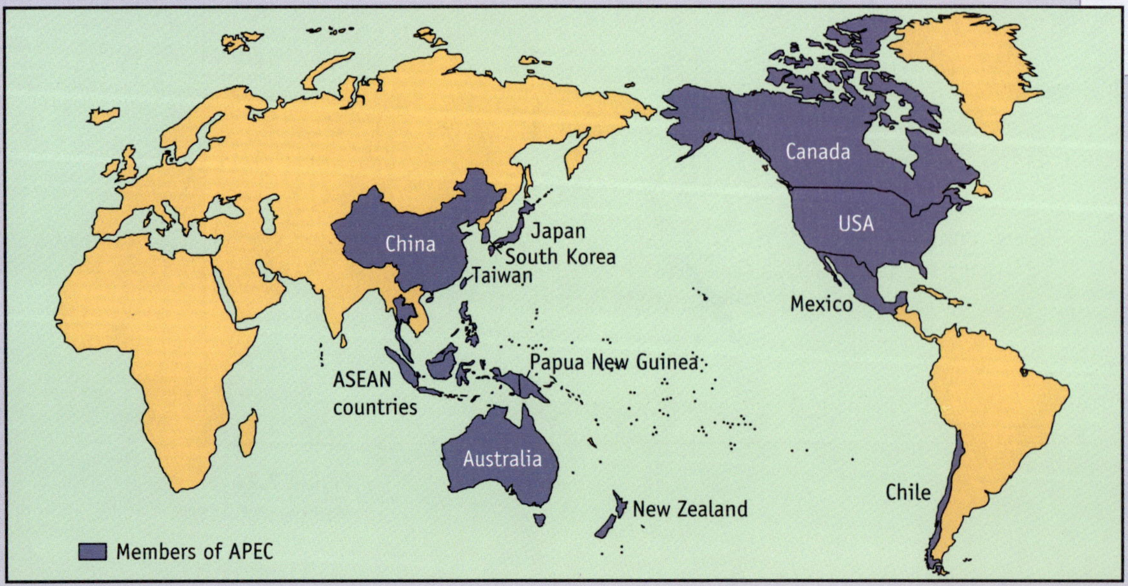

Figure 7.26
Members of APEC

Trade and aid

Trade

Countries buy goods they need and sell goods that other countries need. Trade depends on co-operation between countries. We have seen that groups such as the EC and ASEAN have been formed to make trade easier between countries.

Australia has made trade agreements with many countries. Before the Second World War, most of Australia's trade was with Britain. In the 1950s, Australia started trading with Japan. Japan bought a lot of Australia's meat, wool, wheat, sugar, coal and minerals. In return, Japan sold cameras, cars and electrical goods to Australia.

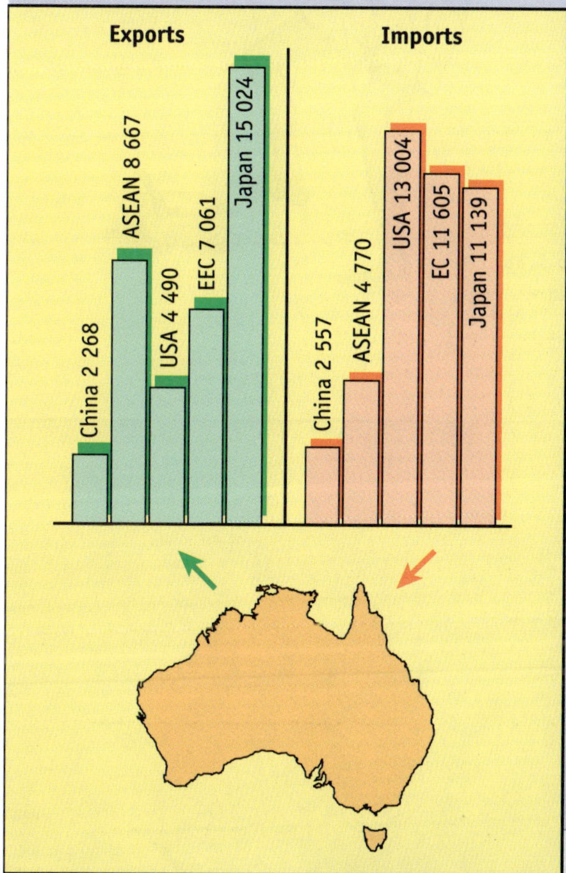

Figure 7.27
Australia's trade, 1992–93 (in $000 000)

Think *for yourself*

The graph in Figure 7.27 shows Australia's imports and exports in 1992–93. Study it carefully and answer the questions below.

1. If exports and imports are added together, which country is Australia's main trading partner?
2. This country was not an important trading partner in the 1940s. Why?
3. How many countries were there in the EC in 1993? What are they? How many countries have joined since? What are they?
4. Why are the EC countries grouped together in this graph?
5. What is Australia's second largest trading partner?
6. Which countries belong to ASEAN?
7. Find out what the terms 'trade surplus', 'trade deficit' and 'balance of trade' mean. With which country or group of countries did Australia have the largest trade surplus in 1992–93? With which country or group of countries did Australia have the largest trade deficit in 1992–93? How would you describe the balance of trade between Australia and China in 1992–93?
8. 'Australia will be rich only if Japan is rich.' Why would someone say this? Do you think it is true?

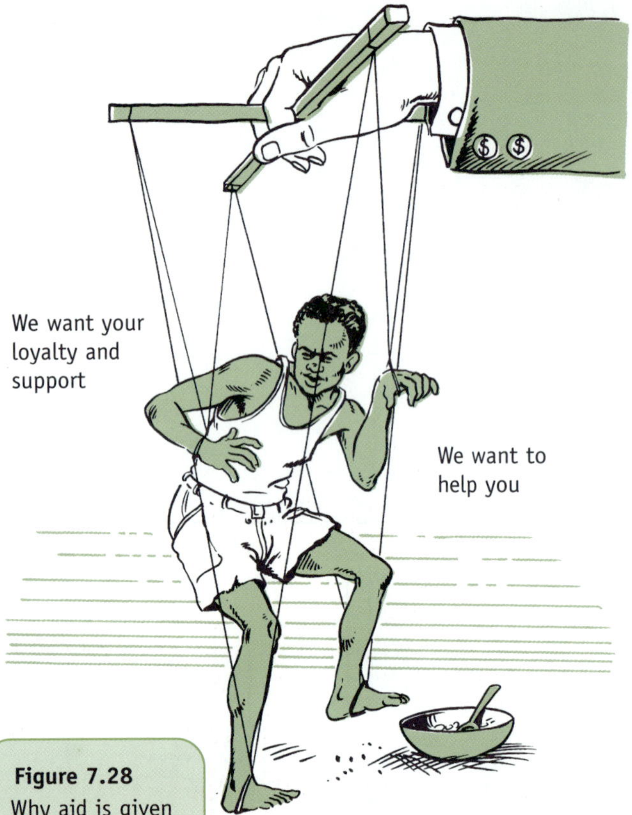

Figure 7.28
Why aid is given

Overseas aid

Trade is a two-way process. A country sells something and buys other things in return.

But sometimes a rich country gives money, food or equipment to a poor country without seeming to get anything in return. This is called **aid**. In 1993–94 Australia gave aid worth $1400 million dollars. Other rich countries do the same. Giving aid is one of the ways by which richer countries compete with each other. Each country tries to win friends by giving something away.

Most of Australia's aid is given directly to the governments of other countries. Sometimes this aid is 'untied'. That means that the country that receives the aid can use it for any purposes that it wishes. Sometimes the aid is 'tied'. That means it must be used for particular purposes, such as health or education, or for specific programs, such as building bridges or factories. The map in Figure 7.29 shows the countries to which Australia sent most aid in 1993–94.

As you read on page 174, Australia also gives aid to United Nations aid agencies and other international aid organisations. This money is then redirected to fund projects in poor countries in all parts of the world.

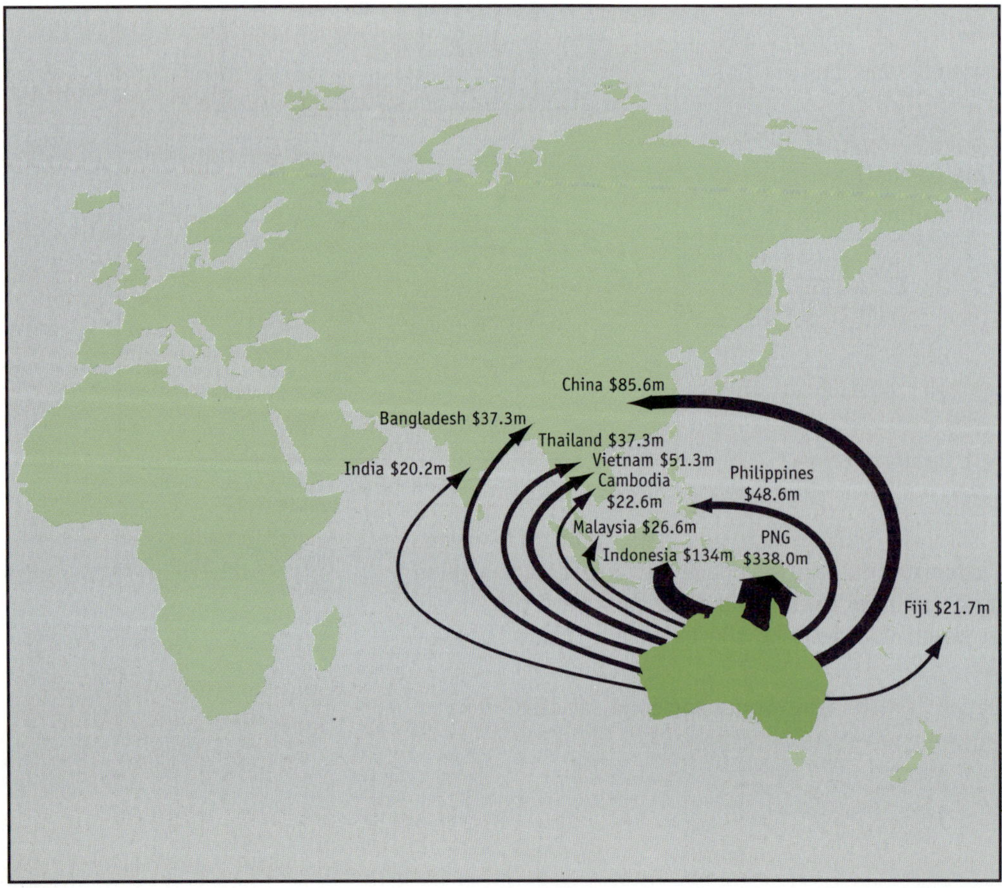

Figure 7.29
Countries which received the largest amounts of direct aid from Australia in 1993–94

Figure 7.30
The Australian government provided funds and staff to build this hangar in Dacca. Which country is Dacca in?

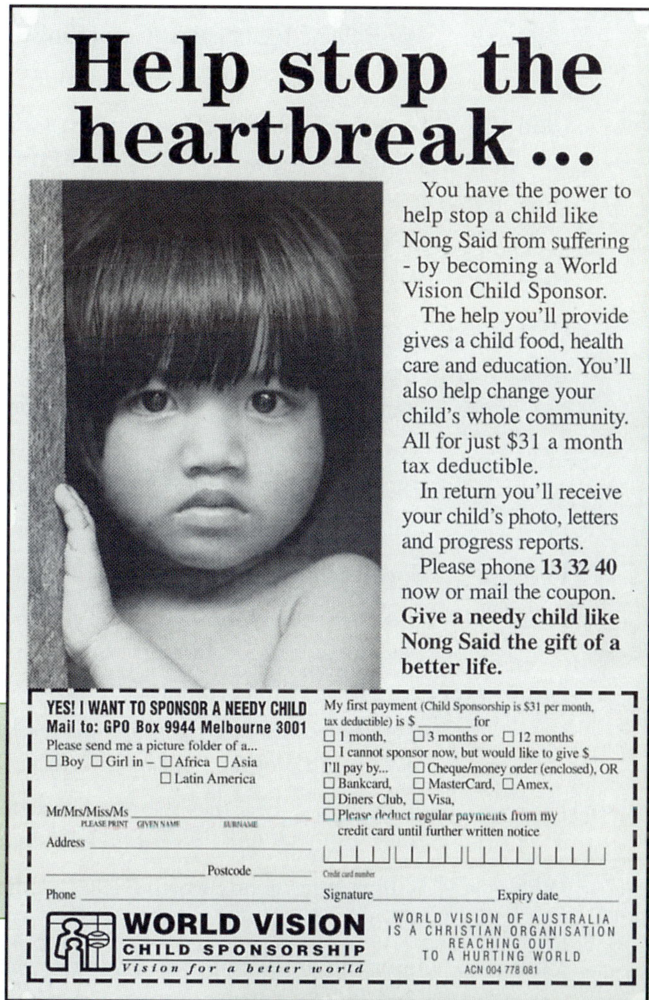

Figure 7.31
An advertisement used by a voluntary organisation to raise money

Voluntary aid

You have probably seen advertisements like the one in Figure 7.31 in the newspaper. There are many voluntary organisations in Australia that help people in other countries. Some of these organisations are Austcare, Community Aid Abroad, World Vision and Foster Parents Plan. They rely on donations from individuals to raise the money they need.

Think *for yourself*

1 How effective do you think the advertisement in Figure 7.31 is in persuading well-off people to donate money? Why do advertisements such as this so often feature children?

2 Which country receives most aid from Australia? Suggest some reasons why this country receives so much aid. (Clue: look back to page 174.)

3 In which part of the world are the countries that receive most aid from Australia? Why do you think Australia gives most of its aid to this part of the world?

4 Do you think that any aid from Australia in 1993–94 could have reached countries in Africa or South America? How?

Communist China: friend or foe?

You read in the last chapter about the end of the Cold War and the collapse of communist governments in Europe. There are, however, several Asian countries which still have communist governments. China, which has the largest population of any country on earth, is the most important and influential of these countries. Here are some facts about China and its relationship with Australia and some other countries since 1949.

1949 Communists win power in China. Australia, the USA and other Western countries refuse to accept Mao Zedong's government, even though it controls more than 600 million people. Instead, they recognise Chiang Kai-shek's government on Taiwan, even though it controls less than 20 million people.

1950–53 Australians fight against Communist Chinese forces in Korea as part of a United Nations force.

1953 An invasion of Taiwan by Communist China is prevented by United States warships.

1960 A serious split develops between Communist China and the USSR. There are clashes between troops along the border between the two countries.

1961 China buys 1 million tonnes of wheat, 320 000 tonnes of barley and 40 000 tonnes of flour from Australia. Other large sales made during the rest of the 1960s.

1964 China explodes its first atomic bomb.

1971 Communist China is allowed to join the United Nations. Taiwan is forced to leave the United Nations.

1972 United States president Richard Nixon visits China and has talks with Mao Zedong. The two leaders agree to work together to improve their relationship. Australia recognises Communist China.

1973 Gough Whitlam visits China. He is the first Australian prime minister to do so. An Australian ambassador is sent to China. A new trade agreement is signed.

1974 Malcolm Fraser, the Australian leader of the opposition (and soon to be prime minister) visits China.

1979 Fighting breaks out between China and Vietnam, both communist countries.

1979 China and the USA establish 'full diplomatic relations'. The USA no longer recognises the government of Taiwan as the government of all China.

Early 1980s Much of China's industry is modernised as new machines and other technology are imported from Western countries. Laws are changed to allow some degree of 'private enterprise'. People are allowed to own some property and open businesses.

1984 Bob Hawke becomes the third Australian prime minister to visit China. He signs an agreement that the two countries will co-operate in their iron and steel industries.

1985 China buys goods worth $1062 million from Australia. Australia buys goods worth $375 million from China.

1989 Students in Beijing hold huge demonstrations calling for greater democracy in China. On the night of 3–4 June, Chinese army tanks move into Tianenmen Square in Beijing, mowing down the demonstrators, killing hundreds and wounding thousands.

June 1989 Australian prime minister, Bob Hawke cancels a goodwill visit to China by an Australian navy ship. Leaders around the world condemn the 'Tianenmen Square massacre', as it becomes known.

Early 1990s Relations between China and Western countries get worse. China's 'human rights record' is widely criticised.

1994 Chinese leaders tell visiting United States politicians that China will improve its human rights record.

1995 China conducts a series of nuclear bomb tests, in spite of strong objections from Australia, the USA and many other countries.

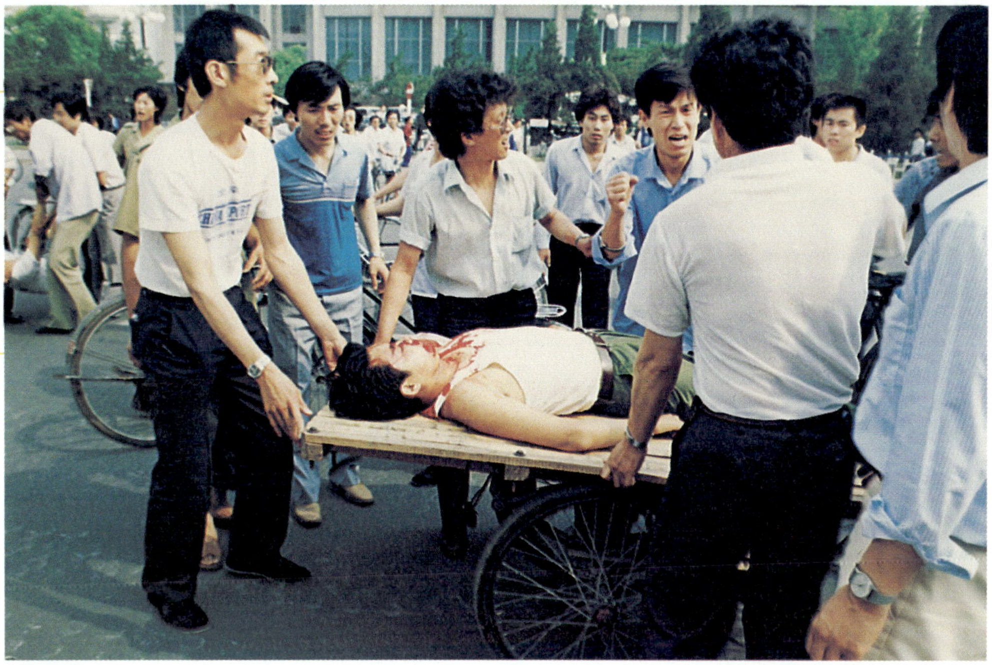

Figure 7.32
These students are rescuing another student who has been injured in the fighting in Tianenmen Square, Beijing. When was this photograph taken?

Figure 7.33
A cartoon published in an Australian magazine in 1954

Figure 7.34
During the 1980s many people from Western countries visited China. Fewer visitors came in the early 1990s. Can you suggest why?

Figure 7.35
Mao Zedong and Gough Whitlam meet in China in 1973

Think *for yourself*

1. Why do you think the governments of Australia and the USA did not recognise the communist government of China for so long?
2. Can you find any reasons why Australia recognised China in 1972?
3. Can you suggest some reasons why Australia started selling large amounts of food to China in 1961?
4. What happened between China and the USSR during the 1960s? Do you think this could have influenced the attitude of the USA towards China? Why?
5. Why do you think Communist China wanted to invade Taiwan in 1953?
6. Can you suggest why Taiwan was forced to leave the United Nations in 1971?
7. What does 'full diplomatic relations' mean? Which country was the first to establish full diplomatic relations with China—Australia or the USA?
8. How would you describe the balance of payments between Australia and China in 1985? How does this compare with the balance of payments between the two countries in 1992–93? (See page 183.) How can you explain the change?
9. The events of June 1989 came as a surprise to most people in Australia. Why do you think they surprised Australians?
10. Why did people in Western countries become more concerned about China's human rights record in the 1990s?

KNOW the chapter

1 The answer to each of these questions is either a date or a number.

a When was the United Nations formed?
b How many countries were in the United Nations in 1995?
c When did the United Nations adopt the Universal Declaration of Human Rights?
d When did Papua New Guinea become an independent country?
e When was the Statute of Westminster passed?
f How many independent countries are in the Commonwealth of Nations?
g When did the war in Korea end?
h When did China join the United Nations?
i When did Yugoslavia break up into separate countries?
j When did the massacre in Tianenmen Square take place?

2 These sets of initials are abbreviations for organisations or events. What are they short for?

ANZUS
ASEAN
CHOGM
EC
FAO
APEC
UNO
WHO

3 Choose a word or phrase from the list below to fit each explanation.

aid
mandate
apartheid
republic
dependencies
Third World

a countries that are ruled by another country
b a country ruled by a president
c the name of the poor or developing countries
d a policy of separating white people from black people and giving more privileges to white people
e help given by rich countries to poor countries
f system under which Australia controlled New Guinea after the First World War.

4 Use the clues below to fill in the word puzzle. All the words are names of countries. They are all in this chapter.

a Its soldiers fought against the United Nations force in Korea between 1950 and 1951. It bought many thousands of tonnes of grain from Australia in the 1960s.
b It juts out from mainland China. Since 1953 it has been a divided country.
c It was part of Yugoslavia until 1991 and is now a separate country.
d It is Australia's most important trading partner.
e It is a European country which joined the Common Market in 1981.
f An island in the Mediterranean Sea. United Nations troops were sent to this country in 1964 to stop the fighting between two groups of people.
g It once had the largest empire in the world. Now it controls only a few small dependencies.
h An Asian country which left the Commonwealth of Nations in 1972 but rejoined it in 1989.
I Its elected government was overthrown by the military in 1987.
j A member of ASEAN. Its capital city is Jakarta.
k A Third World country and a republic. It was the first colony of Britain to become independent after the Second World War.

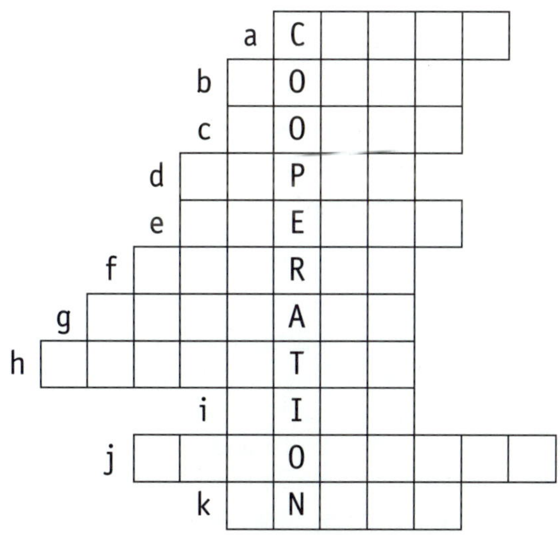

THE HISTORIAN AT WORK

The following is an extract from an article by Pilita Clark that appeared in the *Sydney Morning Herald* in mid-1990. Read it carefully and answer the questions that follow.

China and the US—the new Cold War

Barely six years have passed since the Western world began celebrating the fall of the Berlin Wall and the end of the Cold War.

But in Washington, talk has already turned to a new Cold War, this time with an enemy of far greater importance to Australia than the Soviet Union ever was: China.

The long weeks of the northern hemisphere summer have been punctuated by ... warnings of an inevitable clash between the USA and China ...

To sample but a fraction of the debate, the former US Secretary of State Henry Kissinger, has ... declared the two nations 'are on a collision course'. In the State Department, diplomats privately whisper that US–Sino relations have sunk to their lowest level since the Korean War ...

Through all this the Australian Government managed to remain almost mute, though the prospect of a US–China Cold War is of far greater importance than ... any of the other foreign policy issues preoccupying Canberra of late.

Should such a clash ever come close to being realised, the [Australian] Government's chief foreign policy goals—closer ties with East Asia via a strengthened Asia-Pacific Economic Co-operation group—would be the first casualties. Australia would be forced to choose between its traditional security allies in Washington and the trade bonanza it has assiduously worked for in China in recent years ...

Outwardly, at least, the spark for the dive in relations between two of APEC's biggest members was the [United States] decision to grant a visa to Taiwan's President Lee Teng-hui for a 'private' visit ... last June ...

Taiwan, as far as Beijing is concerned, is still a renegade province, not an independent country, and the ... decision to grant President Lee a visa was, Beijing claimed, a clear breach of Washington's promise to uphold a one-China policy ...

[China] cancelled planned military meetings with the Pentagon [United States defence authorities]. It withdrew its ambassador from Washington ... It blithely tested nuclear bombs, despite worldwide outrage over France's decision to resume testing.

Most worryingly, it started a series of blatantly intimidatory missile tests, aiming the weapons straight across the East China Sea at Taiwan.

Suddenly, Washington's mutterings about a new Cold War become more a roar ...

Talk of a new Cold War may fade in the coming months as ... President Jiang Zemin meets President Clinton and China stops rattling its missile sabres so loudly.

But after this summer, few would dare predict that such talk will never rise again.

1. When was this article written? How can you tell?
2. What war, apart from the Cold War is mentioned in this article? When did this war occur? Why were relations between China and the USA so bad at that time?
3. According to the writer of the article, how would Australia be affected if a new Cold War developed between the USA and China? What would happen if Australia took China's side? What would happen if Australia sided with the USA? Which of the two countries do you think Australia would support? Why?
4. When this article was written who was:
   - **a** the president of China
   - **b** the president of Taiwan
   - **c** the president of the USA?

   Do some research to find out the names of the people who occupy these positions now.
5. What trade organisation is mentioned in the article? When was it formed and what are its aims? If China and the USA became serious enemies, could this organisation survive? Why? Do some research to find out if this organisation still exists?
6. What, according to the writer, did the USA do to annoy China? Why were the Chinese so angry about this? How did they react?
7. What does the expression 'renegade province' mean? Why does China consider Taiwan to be a renegade province? (Clue: reread page 139.)
8. What do you think the writer means when she writes of a 'one-China policy'? Why did China think that what the USA did was 'a clear breach' of this policy?
9. Some of the statements made in this article are **opinions**. They state what the writer thinks could happen. Some statements in the article are **facts** about what actually did happen. Find two statements in the article that you would consider to be opinions. List at least four facts that are mentioned in the article.
10. What European country is mentioned in this article? At the time the article was written, why was this country unpopular with many other countries?

A *changing* **Australia** *1945–95*

In the fifty years after the end of the Second World War, two political parties and five or six strong personalities dominated the government of Australia. When the war ended the Labor Party was in government. During the 1950s and 1960s the Liberal Party, under Sir Robert Menzies, held government for a record term of twenty-three years. In the last twenty-five years, the Labor Party has held power for most of the time.

In this chapter we follow the fortunes of the major political parties and their leaders and look at the many other changes that have reshaped Australian society in the second half of the twentieth century.

The Labor Party government of Ben Chifley

Australia's wartime leader, John Curtin, died in July 1945, just six weeks before the end of the Second World War.

Ben Chifley was Australia's prime minister for the next four years. Chifley was the leader of the Labor Party. He believed that the government should be involved in many projects. The government should own airlines and banks. It should help those who were poor, sick or old. You can see from Figure 8.1 that Chifley's government was very active in the four years it was in power. Many of the projects it started were carried on by the next government.

Many Australians were concerned about how powerful the government was becoming. They had been prepared to accept a powerful government during the war years, but now that the war was over, they wanted the government to play a smaller part in their lives. Australians were also concerned about the strikes that were common in many industries. They thought that the communists had too much power in the trade unions. Chifley, they thought, was too 'soft' with the communists. He had allowed them to become too strong.

Figure 8.1
The work of Chifley's government

A new party and a new government

Chifley's government was defeated in 1949. The new prime minister was Robert Menzies, the leader of the Liberal Party, which he had formed in 1944. Menzies promised that the government would:

- not take over the banks
- end petrol rationing
- put an end to strikes and stop the growth of communism
- encourage private businesses.

These plans appealed to Australians. Menzies was to be prime minister for sixteen years, from 1949 to 1966. For most of this time things went well for Australia. The country was prosperous and many Australians were better off than they had ever been before.

Although Menzies was leader of the Liberal Party his government consisted of two political parties. The Country Party, which was supported mainly by people in the country areas, joined with the Liberal Party to form a **coalition**. In this coalition the Liberal Party, which had more seats in parliament, was known as the senior partner and the Country Party was the junior partner.

In 1974 the Country Party changed its name to the National Country Party, and later to simply the National Party.

Figure 8.2
'Mind if I squeeze the last drop out myself'?
Petrol was rationed during the Second World War. Chifley's government continued the rationing. In 1949, when this cartoon was published, Menzies promised to end petrol rationing. This appealed to many Australians.

The Menzies years

The communist problem

In October 1950 the government banned the Communist Party, as it had promised to do. The law was challenged as soon as it had been passed. The High Court decided that the government did not have the power to ban a political party. In September 1951, a referendum was held. Australians were asked if they thought that the government should be given the power to ban communism. There was a bitter campaign. By a very narrow margin the 'No' vote won. The Communist Party was not banned.

Although the Communist Party was not banned in Australia, many Australians were worried about the spread of communism in Asia. During the Menzies years, Australian troops were sent to fight against communists in Asia three times.

- In 1950 Australians were part of the United Nations force in Korea.
- In 1955 Australians helped British soldiers to fight communist guerillas in Malaya.
- In 1965 Australians were sent to Vietnam to support the USA in its fight against communists from North Vietnam.

In the first two of these conflicts only regular service personnel were sent to fight. In Vietnam, however, conscripted troops were sent overseas for the first time since the Second World War.

Spies

It was 13 April 1954. Parliament was sitting for the last time before an election was to be held. The Liberal Party had been losing support. Some people suggested that Menzies would have to 'pull a couple of rabbits out of a top hat' in order to win enough votes to be elected again.

Just a few hours before the close of parliament, the prime minister stood up and told parliament some startling news. Vladimir Petrov, a Russian diplomat in Canberra, had asked to become an Australian citizen. He had said that after seeing the way Australians lived, he no longer believed in communism. As well, Petrov had handed to Australian Security Intelligence Organisation (ASIO) officers some documents that proved there was a Soviet spy ring in Australia.

Petrov was allowed to remain in Australia but a week later, two Soviet officials took Mrs Petrov by car to Sydney airport and put her on a plane back to the USSR. A stewardess on the plane had been given the job of finding out whether Mrs Petrov really wanted to go back to the USSR or whether she was being forced to go against her will.

Mrs Petrov told the stewardess that the two Soviet officials who were with her were carrying guns. She also said that if she was sure her husband really wanted to remain in Australia, she would probably stay too.

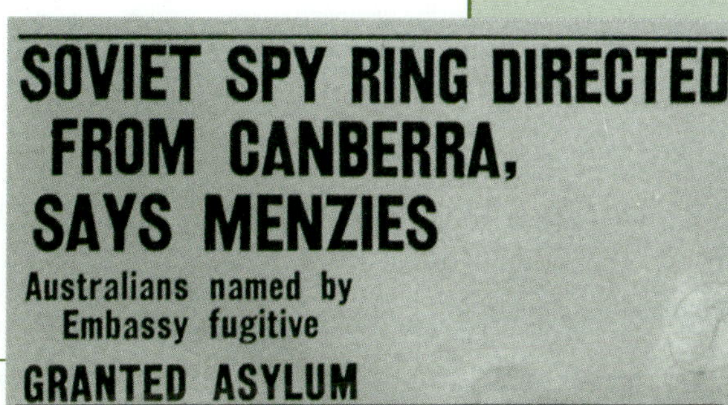
SOVIET SPY RING DIRECTED FROM CANBERRA, SAYS MENZIES

Australians named by Embassy fugitive

GRANTED ASYLUM

Figure 8.3
Who was the Embassy fugitive? What does 'granted asylum' mean? When was this headline published?

This information was radioed through to Darwin. When the plane stopped for fuel, Australian police arrested the two Soviet guards for carrying weapons in an aeroplane. Mrs Petrov spoke to her husband on the telephone and decided to remain in Australia.

Australians were stunned by the 'Petrov affair'. It seemed to show that everything the government had said about the power of communists in Australia was true. They were especially horrified by photographs in the paper that showed Mrs Petrov being dragged away by two burly Soviets. In the election a few weeks later, Menzies was once again voted into power.

Since 1954 there has been a lot of disagreement about the Petrov affair. Here are two points to think about:

1 Menzies knew that Petrov was going to ask to be allowed to remain in Australia for over a week before he made the announcement to parliament. He kept the news quiet until he could make the most of it. Why?
2 At the Royal Commission that followed the affair, Petrov said that he had been paid £5000 by ASIO to stay in Australia. Why would ASIO pay him to do this?

Figure 8.4
Two Soviet guards drag Mrs Petrov to the plane at Sydney airport. A crowd of 3000 people had gathered at the airport. Some of them tried to pull Mrs Petrov from her guards. How do you think this photograph helped Menzies to win the election later in 1954?

THE HISTORIAN AT WORK

The Communist Party referendum

The following is an extract from an editorial in the Melbourne *Herald*. It is about the Communist Party in Australia and was published on the day of the referendum.

> Have we any right to punish a person for his opinions? If we punish anyone for breaking the law of the land ... that is justice; but if we punish anyone for holding opinions with which we disagree, that is persecution ... The government is asking for ... the power to punish a man for his beliefs.

The following extract is from a pamphlet published in 1951 by the Australian Electoral Office. The pamphlet was entitled 'The Case For and Against'.

> Communist activity in Australia has become a grave menace to our industrial peace, to production, to national security and defence ... Australian communist leaders have worked their way into positions of leadership in key trade unions ... Communism is not just a local evil ... It is a national danger, and an international danger.

Figure 8.5
A cartoon published in an Australian magazine in 1950.

Figure 8.6
A leaflet produced for the 1951 referendum.

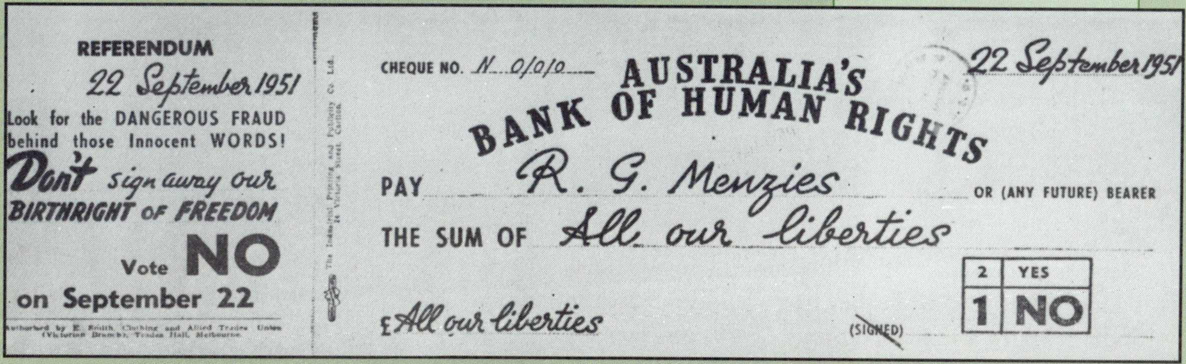

1 Whenever there is a referendum in Australia, the Australian Electoral Office publishes a pamphlet giving arguments for and against the question that is to be asked. Is the extract from the pamphlet arguing for or against the banning of the Communist Party? How would people who agreed with the arguments in this extract probably have voted in the referendum: YES or NO?

2 On what date was the editorial in the Melbourne *Herald* published? How do you think that people who agreed with this editorial would have voted in the referendum?

3 Explain what the words 'justice' and 'persecution' mean. Does the writer of the *Herald* editorial think that banning the Communist Party would be an example of **justice** or **persecution**? Why?

4 What does 'industrial peace' mean? Why did the writer of the second extract think that Communism in Australia had become 'a grave menace to our industrial peace'?

5 What overseas event in 1950 convinced many Australians that communism was 'an international danger'?

6 In two or three sentences of your own, sum up the arguments for the 'no' case that are being made in the leaflet in Figure 8.6.

7 Do you think that the people who designed and wrote this leaflet were necessarily members or supporters of the Communist Party? Discuss.

8 In the cartoon in Figure 8.5, what do the words 'Anti-Red Bill' refer to? What does the rat represent? How can you tell? What is the message of this cartoon? How would people who agreed with this message probably have voted in the referendum: YES or NO?

New settlers, new jobs

Between 1945 and 1965 more than 2 million migrants came to Australia. Some of these 'new Australians' were refugees who had lost their homes in the Second World War. Others were assisted migrants. The government paid most of their fare to Australia. In return, the migrants had to stay in Australia for at least two years. Some migrants had to work at whatever job the government gave them for those two years.

Figure 8.7
The Villawood migrant hostel, Sydney, in the 1950s. Why were hostels like this built in the 1950s? Why were many migrants disappointed when they found themselves living in places like this?

Many migrants spent their first months in Australia living in a drab hostel while they tried to find themselves a home. Many of them found work on factory production lines. Others took on hard, dirty and often dangerous labouring jobs. Skilled migrants sometimes found it difficult to find work to suit their qualifications and training. All migrants, and especially those who did not speak English well, had to put up with prejudice from a large number of Australians.

Thousands of migrants worked on the Snowy Mountains Hydroelectric Scheme, a project started by Ben Chifley's government in 1949. Dams, power stations and tunnels were built so that the water of the Snowy River could be used to provide power and irrigation. Many of the workers lived in camps. Others lived in newly built towns such as Cabramurra. Their work was hard and often dangerous.

Figure 8.8
Building a dam for the Snowy Mountains Scheme. Why did so many migrants work on jobs like this?

Great and powerful friends

Robert Menzies was a strong supporter of Britain and the Commonwealth of Nations. He wanted Australia to be very closely linked with Britain. He was less interested in what was happening in the Asian countries that were much closer to Australia.

But the Second World War had shown Australians that they needed the friendship of countries nearer to home. In 1951 Australia, New Zealand and the USA signed the ANZUS Treaty. In 1954 Australian became a member of SEATO, the South-East Asian Treaty Organisation. The other members of SEATO were the USA, France, Britain, New Zealand, Pakistan, the Philippines and Thailand. All these countries were concerned about the spread of communism in the Pacific area. SEATO was designed to defend the non-communist countries if they were attacked by a communist power.

Queen Elizabeth II visited Australia in 1954. It was the first time an English monarch had been here. Wherever she went, Australians gathered to watch, cheer and wave flags. Schoolchildren gathered in country showgrounds to cheer as the queen was driven around in an open car. There were receptions, balls, dinners, garden parties and many public appearances. Robert Menzies told the queen 'You may count on us. We are yours.'

Think *for yourself*

1. Why was the ANZUS Treaty signed? What did each of the members agree to do? (Clue: look back to the section 'Some regional organisations' in the last chapter.)
2. Use the evidence in the cartoon and newspaper report in figures 8.9 and 8.10 to write three or four sentences about the way Australians reacted to the queen's visit in 1954. You may also find information by asking older people who were in Australia in 1954 what they remember about the visit.

Figure 8.9
'She's passing now!' by Ian Gall

Figure 8.10
A newspaper article reporting on the arrival of Queen Elizabeth at a ball
Age, 6 February, 1954

CROWD DELAYS QUEEN'S PROGRESS

Minister Asks for Fair Play: Tired After Big Day

From "The Age" Staff Correspondent with the Royal party

SYDNEY, Friday. — Royal tour authorities are disturbed by the behavior of the Sydney crowds which mobbed the Queen's car this afternoon and have appealed for more consideration for Her Majesty.

Huge crowds, overcome with excitement, forced the Royal car to crawling pace. When the couple reached Government House after the daytime programme, they were one hour behind schedule.

Tonight the Minister in charge of the tour (Mr. E. J. Harrison) said: "The Royal couple have an arduous task before them. I urge the public to show towards them the sportsmanship and fair play for which Australians are renowned."

The Premier (Mr. Cahill) said: "Sydney crowds set a splendid example on landing day and yesterday. Please let us maintain that standard and make the Queen's task as easy as possible."

The Queen appeared hot and tired when she reached Macquarie Place at six o'clock for her last afternoon engagement after a strenuous seven hour day.

At the Royal ball tonight crowds outside the town hall were again difficult to handle. More than 2000 of the 150,000, collapsed in the crush.

Sydney experienced a hot, humid day. The maximum temperature was 87 degrees. The forecast for tomorrow is for warm and humid conditions.

... of the Royal couple's day —probably the most exhausting since the tour began.

The Queen and the Duke of Edinburgh left Government House just after 11 o'clock this morning for a gathering of ex-service men and women in Hyde Park.

Then they visited Sydney cricket ground, the showground and Centennial Park, to see 120,000 children.

In the afternoon there was a 23-mile drive from Government House to Concord Repatriation Hospital, and the planting of two trees in Macquarie Street.

At night they attended the lord mayor's ball.

... an hour late, after the afternoon engagements, they arrived at the town hall only a few minutes after the scheduled time of 9.30 p.m.

The morning programme ran to plan. The Queen began her day looking rested and at ease.

As the sun's heat increased, however, she used a parasol. After driving through cheering lanes of children in an open Land Rover, she looked hot and strained.

The Duke, too, seemed to be noticing the heat. He mopped his head with a handkerchief and smiled ruefully at the ...

The Queen at the Lord Mayor's Ball

The Queen presented a glittering figure in a magnificent gown at the Lord Mayor's ball at Sydney town hall last night. Above, she is pictured with the Duke of Edinburgh.

Efforts to Salvage Big U.K. Airliner

LONDON, Feb. 5.

Attempts to salvage the giant turbo-propeller Britannia airliner from the mud flats of the River Severn, where she crash landed yesterday, failed today and salvage crews were waiting for high tide tonight before trying to drag the 70-ton ...

Illness of Pope Takes Turn for the Worse

ROME, Feb. 5 (A.A.P.).—The condition of the Pope who has been ill for the past 11 days has reteriorated. A long medical bulletin issued by the Vatican today said that the Pope's doctors were having difficulty in feeding him.

The bulletin—the first to be issued dur- ... which the Pope had suffered for nine days ended ... Holy Father, together with slight movements of ...

Fun and games

In the summer of 1956 it was not unusual to see groups of people sitting or standing on the footpath at night staring into a shop window. They were watching television. Television came to Australia in September 1956. At first, sets were expensive. Those who could afford to buy a television sometimes invited their friends in to watch and admire it.

Television caught on quickly. By 1959 half of the families in Sydney had a television set. Many of them were bought on hire-purchase. A lot of cinemas and theatres closed down because people preferred to stay at home and watch television.

Television showed its value just two months after it came to Australia. It broadcast the Olympic Games that were held in Melbourne in November 1956. This was the first time the Olympics had been held outside Europe and the USA. The Olympic torch was flown from Greece and carried by runners to Melbourne. People lined the streets to cheer it on its way. More than 100 000 people watched as Ron Clarke, carrying the torch, ran into the Olympic stadium.

Australia did well at the Melbourne Olympics and Australians were proud of their swimmers and athletes who won thirty-five medals, including thirteen gold medals. Murray Rose, Dawn Fraser, Betty Cuthbert and Shirley Strickland became overnight heroes.

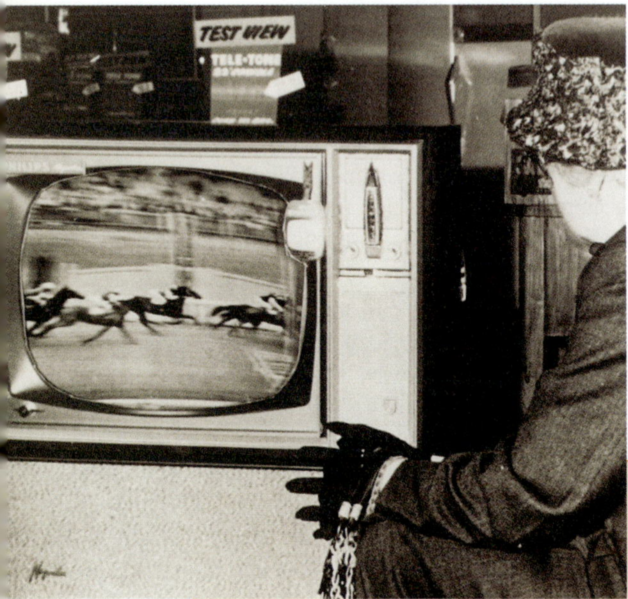

Figure 8.11
In 1960, for the first time, Australians could watch a live telecast of the Melbourne Cup. This woman was one of many who stopped to watch the race.

Figure 8.12
The cover for the official program for the 1956 Olympic Games. Can you identify the two symbols of the Olympic Games in this picture?

Think *for yourself*

These words were spoken in 1956:

> The introduction of television into Australia will have a marked influence on the life of the community … Television is capable of exercising a great influence for good.

1. Work out how much time you spend each day watching television. How many hours do you watch television each week?
2. What would you do with that time if there were no television to watch?
3. When television came to Australia in 1956, some people were concerned about its effects on Australian life. What sort of things do you think they might have been worried about?
4. Do you think television has been 'a great influence for good' in Australia?

Politics comes to the Games

A month before the Olympic Games began, troops from the USSR moved into Hungary to crush a rebellion. Hungarian athletes were not able to travel to Melbourne as a group. They came in ones and twos, often with no equipment, clothes or money.

The Hungarian water polo team was drawn to play against the Soviet team. Spectators, many of them Hungarian migrants, booed as the Soviet players entered the pool. The game became rougher and rougher. Punches were thrown and it seemed for a while that the spectators were going to join in. The police had to be called to restore order.

The Hungarian team won the match 4–0. They later won the gold medal for water polo.

Think *for yourself*

1 You have read in an earlier chapter of another time when politics disturbed the Olympic Games. What was it?

2 After the incident between Hungary and the USSR, an Olympic official said:

> We are dead against any country using the Games for political purposes … The Olympics are competitions between individuals and not nations.

Do you think it is possible for the Olympic Games to be separated from politics?

3 Can you think of any other occasions when sport and politics have become linked?

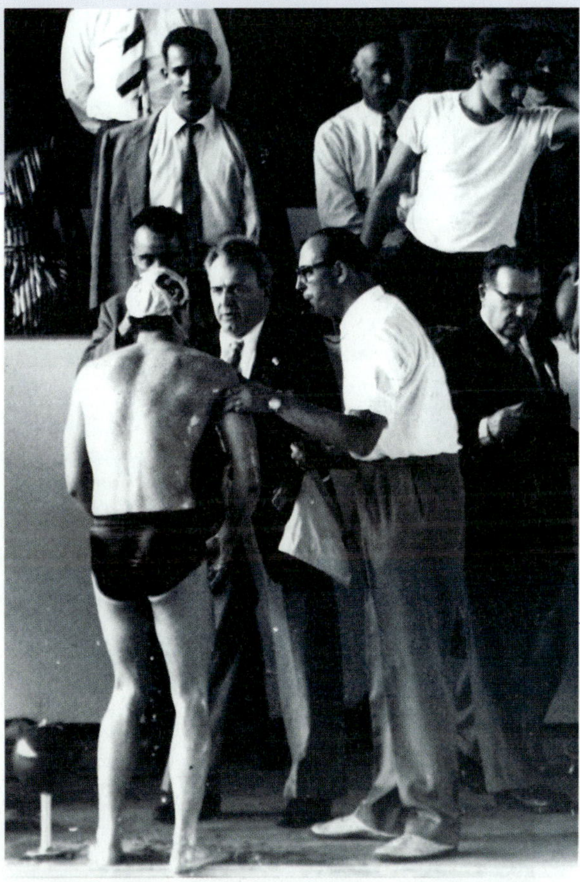

Figure 8.13
An injured Hungarian water polo player explains to officials how his eye was cut in the match against the USSR. Why were the USSR and Hungary enemies in 1956?

Teenagers

Teenagers discovered rock and roll in the 1950s. At first their parents were horrified by the new dance craze with its loud, wild music. Slowly, however, they learned to live with rock and roll and with the dance crazes that followed, such as the twist and the stomp.

By the end of the 1950s, teenagers were an important group. They had more money than ever before and were able to spend it on records, clothes and entertainment. Some teenagers joined groups such as the 'bodgies' and 'widgies', 'surfies' and 'rockers'. Each group had its own way of dressing and its own way of having fun. Most teenagers, however, were content with going to dances and the pictures, sitting in milk bars and, later, coffee shops, and occasionally going to a concert to see their favourite pop star.

Figure 8.14
Teenagers in 1960. What differences are there between this photograph and one of teenagers today?

The boom years

Most Australians did well in the Menzies years. Many families had their own house in the suburbs. They bought a new Holden every two or three years. The housewife's work was made easier by a variety of electrical appliances. Refrigerators and washing machines were in most homes by the end of the 1950s. There was often a radiogram and a television set as well.

The government encouraged overseas companies to invest in Australia. Many of Australia's largest industries were controlled by foreign companies.

Money from overseas companies was important in developing Australia's mineral resources. Uranium was found at Rum Jungle south of Darwin in 1949. Mining started there in 1953. A year later, another rich deposit of uranium was discovered near Mount Isa. It was called Mary Kathleen after the wife of one of the men who found it.

Australia's first oil strike was at Exmouth Gulf on the coast of Western Australia in 1953. There was great excitement but it was later found that the oil was not worth pumping. The first commercial discovery of oil was at Moonie in Queensland in 1961. Later in the 1960s, large amounts of oil were discovered under the waters of Bass Strait.

By the mid-1960s it seemed that the mineral boom would never end. Copper was discovered near Mount Isa. Bauxite was found at Weipa and in the Darling Range near Perth. Iron ore was found in the Hamersley Ranges in the Pilbara district of Western Australia.

Figure 8.15
Oil was discovered at Moonie in 1961. Since then, the search for oil has gone on in many parts of Australia and in the waters off the coast.

Killer diseases

One killer disease was deliberately brought to Australia in the 1950s. Two killer diseases were almost wiped out.

In 1859, twelve rabbits were freed from a property near Geelong in Victoria. Less than a hundred years later rabbits had spread over most parts of Australia. By 1950 there may have been 1000 million rabbits in Australia. They ate grass and crops. They also caused soil erosion by clearing all the grass from the land.

Figure 8.16
Before the 1950s, farmers tried many ways of getting rid of rabbits. They shot or trapped them and dug up their burrows. These two advertisements are for rabbit poisons. There were several kinds of poisons, but none of them worked very well.

Myxomatosis is a virus that kills rabbits. The CSIRO started testing myxomatosis in 1950 to see whether it would be successful in Australia. The results were staggering. Between 1953 and 1956, three-quarters of Australia's rabbits were killed by the disease. Later, rabbits became more resistant to the disease and stronger doses had to be developed.

In 1949 Chifley's government started a campaign to rid Australia of tuberculosis. All Australians over fourteen years of age had to have an X-ray each year. If the disease could be found early, it could be treated. New hospitals were built for TB patients. People suffering from TB were paid a pension so that they could afford to leave work to be treated. By the middle of the 1960s, TB was no longer a killer disease.

Polio was wiped out in a different way. In 1956 Australian schoolchildren lined up for their 'needles'. They were injected with a new Salk vaccine which had been developed by Dr Jonas Salk, an American scientist. By 1960 only 125 new cases of polio were reported in Australia.

The end of the Menzies years

Sir Robert Menzies retired in January 1966. Many Australian voters had never known another prime minister. He had formed the Liberal Party in 1944.

Figure 8.17
In 1965, the year before he retired, Robert Menzies was appointed as Lord Warden of the Cinque Ports. This was a traditional British honour. Menzies is shown here at Dover Castle in 1966 when he took over the position. Why did Menzies receive honours like this from Britain?

Figure 8.18
In 1963, Queen Elizabeth II made a second visit to Australia. This cover of a popular Australian magazine commemorates the visit. Who are the people shown on the cover? How did the queen honour the Australian prime minister during this visit?

While he was prime minister, the party was strong and united. The leaders who followed Menzies were not as strong as he had been. In the next few years, the Liberal Party lost much of the support that Menzies had been able to build for it.

CHECK the facts

Are the statements below true or false?

1. Ben Chifley died in July 1945.
2. The Liberal Party government successfully banned the Communist Party in 1951.
3. Australian troops were sent to fight communists in Indonesia in 1955.
4. Thousands of migrants were brought to Australia to work on the Snowy Mountains Hydroelectric Scheme in the 1950s.
5. Myxomatosis killed most of Australia's prickly pear in the early 1950s.
6. Coloured television came to Australia in 1956.
7. Salk vaccine helped to rid Australia of tuberculosis in 1956.
8. Overseas companies invested huge amounts of money in Australia during the Menzies years.

Three Liberal prime ministers

Harold Holt

Harold Holt was prime minister from January 1966 to December 1967. During this period Australia became more interested in Asia. Holt visited several Asian countries.

Australia's links with the USA became stronger. In March 1966 conscripts were sent to the war in Vietnam. But Holt was not a strong leader. He lived in the shadow of Robert Menzies.

In December 1967 Harold Holt disappeared while swimming in strong seas at Portsea in Victoria. After a frantic search, he was presumed drowned. His short career as prime minister was over. Another Liberal prime minister had to be found. There was a struggle in the Liberal Party. From it, a new leader emerged.

Figure 8.19
Prime Minister Holt disappeared while swimming

John Gorton

John Gorton was prime minister from January 1968 to March 1971. Gorton was a different kind of leader. He gave the impression of being 'a good bloke', an ordinary Australian.

Figure 8.20
Prime Minister John Gorton

But Gorton's style of leadership got him into trouble:

- He sometimes made rash decisions without discussing them with his cabinet ministers or the public service.
- His informal style annoyed some members of parliament and some supporters of the Liberal Party.
- He was unable to stop arguments, disagreements and rivalries among members of the Liberal Party.
- He believed that the Commonwealth government should become stronger. He wanted the Commonwealth government to control the minerals and oils found off Australia's coast. This angered the state governments.

In 1971 Gorton was attacked in parliament by his minister for defence, Malcolm Fraser. Fraser said: 'I do not believe he is fit to hold the great office of prime minister.' When it was clear that many other members of parliament no longer supported him, Gorton resigned.

William McMahon

Figure 8.21
Prime Minister McMahon

William McMahon was prime minister from March 1971 to December 1972. McMahon faced enormous problems.

- The Liberal Party was no longer a united party. Liberal members of parliament had different ideas about what the party should be doing and who its leader should be.
- McMahon was not a strong leader. He did not have the support of many party members.
- Many voters lost their enthusiasm for the Liberal Party because it did not seem to have worthwhile policies.
- Australia's economy was in a mess. Inflation was growing quickly. This meant that money was worth less. The unemployment rate was growing quickly.

These were world-wide problems. To solve them the government had to be prepared to take drastic action. McMahon was not prepared to take drastic action, so the problems remained and grew.

In the election of December 1972 the Liberal Party lost power. Australia had its first Australian Labor Party government for twenty-three years. The new prime minister was Gough Whitlam.

Figure 8.22
When was this cartoon published? Who is in the middle? What is meant by 'That's All Folks'?

Three years of Labor

Gough Whitlam was prime minister from December 1972 to November 1975.

Whitlam became the leader of the Labor Party in 1967. Since then he had worked hard to change the party. He made it more willing to change with the times. He gave it a new direction. By 1972 the Labor Party appealed to middle-class people as well as to workers, who usually supported it. As the Liberal Party became weaker and more divided, the Labor Party became stronger and more united. Many Australians accepted the ALP slogan of 'It's time' in 1972.

The three years of Labor Party government were busy ones. But Whitlam's government became more and more unpopular.

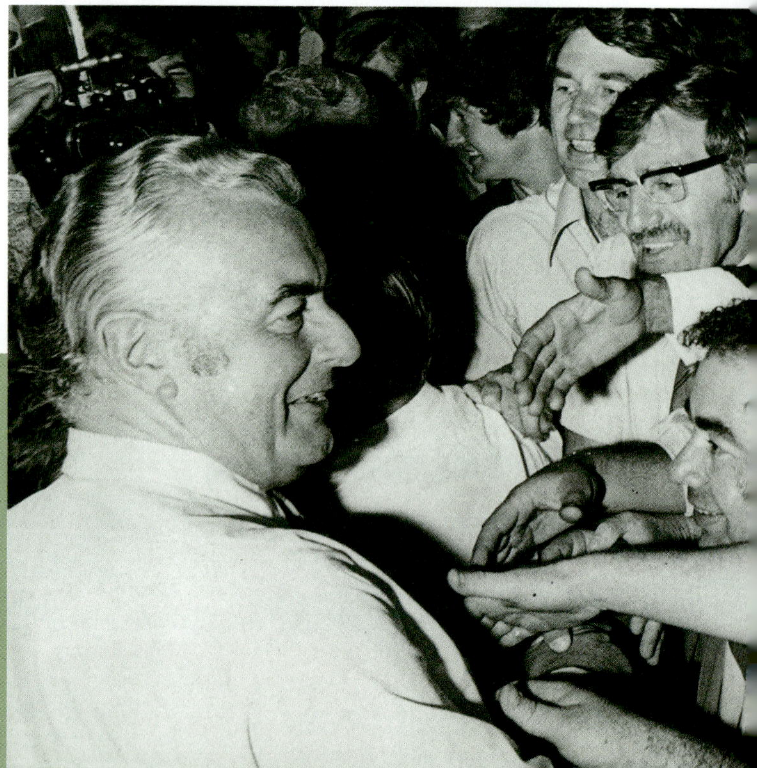

Figure 8.24
Crowds greet Gough Whitlam after the Labor Party victory in 1972. Why were people so excited about this event?

Figure 8.23
The slogan used by the Labor Party in the 1972 election campaign

The end of the Whitlam government

Although the Labor Party had a majority in the House of Representatives, or lower house, it did not have a majority in the Senate, or upper house. The Senate was controlled by the Liberal Party and the National Party. It was able to block many Labor Party bills and stop them from becoming laws.

In October 1975, Malcolm Fraser, the Liberal leader, said that the Senate would refuse to pass the money bills the government needed in order to rule. This was called 'blocking supply'. Whitlam tried to rule without the money, but government was becoming increasingly difficult as the two houses of parliament were in open conflict.

It was up to the governor general, Sir John Kerr, to try and solve the problem. He had the power to

- ask the Senate to pass the money bills
- call a new election of both houses of parliament
- discuss the problem with both leaders and try to find a solution that both would accept.

But Sir John chose another way. He dismissed Whitlam and appointed Malcolm Fraser as 'caretaker' prime minister until a new election could be held.

Figure 8.25
Gough Whitlam and John Kerr

Figure 8.26
Labor Party government 1972–75

Figure 8.27
Time's Up?

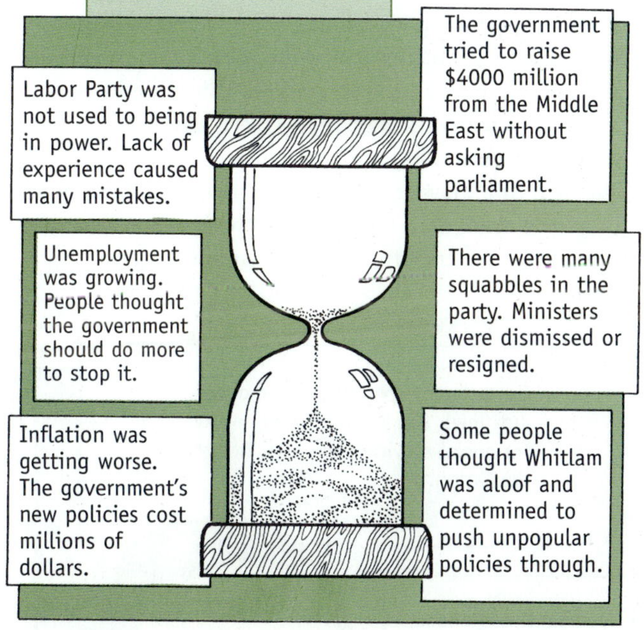

Before 11 November 1975, when Whitlam was dismissed, few people had realised that the governor general had the power to interfere in Australia's government to the extent of dismissing a government. This power had been written into Australia's constitution in 1901. It had never been used before. Many people believed that it should not have been used by Sir John Kerr. Others thought that he had done the right thing by dismissing a government which did not have the support of the Senate and which would not call an election to find out if it had the support of the people. What do you think?

Liberals again

At the elections of December 1975 the Liberal–National Party coalition under Malcolm Fraser won a big victory. Fraser remained prime minister until 1983. During his years as prime minister Australia went through some difficult times. Unemployment and inflation were constant problems and the government was never really successful in controlling them. The government tried to cut down the amount of money it was spending. Medibank, the free health scheme the Whitlam government had brought in, was ended and people had to pay for their health insurance.

Relations with the USA, which had not been so strong in the Whitlam years, once again became much more friendly. Some of the changes that Labor had made, however, were continued by the new government. The policy of giving land rights to Aborigines, for example, was carried on by the Liberals.

A record term for Labor

In March 1983 Malcolm Fraser announced a surprise early election. Many Australians did not think the Liberal government was doing a good job in handling the country's problems and at the same time, there were disputes in the Labor Party about who should be the leader. On the very day that Fraser announced there would be an election the Labor Party chose a new leader. This was Bob Hawke, who had only been in Parliament for a little more than two years but who was well known throughout the country as a trade union leader.

The Labor Party won the 1983 election. Under Hawke's leadership, it won another one in December 1984 and two more—in 1987 and 1990. The win in 1987 made the Hawke government the first Labor government in Australian history to win three elections in a row. After the 1990 election, which Labor won very narrowly, a bitter dispute grew between Bob Hawke and the treasurer in the Labor government, Paul Keating. Keating claimed that Hawke was no longer as popular as he had been earlier and should retire from the leadership of the Labor Party. Many members of the party agreed with Keating. In 1991 Keating challenged Hawke for the leadership. A majority of Labor members of parliament supported Keating, who was voted in as the new leader of the Labor Party, and therefore as the new prime minister. Hawke retired from politics soon afterwards. He was Labor's longest-serving prime minister.

In March 1993 the Labor Party, this time under Keating's leadership, won yet another election.

Figure 8.29
The prime minister, Bob Hawke (second from the right), at the economic summit in Parliament House in April 1983. At the right of the picture is the Australian treasurer, Paul Keating. When did Keating replace Hawke as prime minister?

Figure 8.28
Liberal Party government, 1975–83

Figure 8.30
Labor Party government 1983–96

The Labor government

When Labor won the 1983 election many people expected that, like the Whitlam government eleven years earlier, it would try to make a lot of changes very quickly. The new government, however, was very cautious. It tried to ensure that the community as a whole would agree to as many changes as possible.

One of the first things it did was to hold a special meeting, called an 'economic summit', in Canberra. Many of the country's top business people and prominent citizens were invited to the summit to express their ideas on how the nation's problems could be handled. The summit was held in Parliament House and was televised throughout the country.

Prime Minister Hawke claimed that he wanted his government to be one of 'consensus', which means agreement.

For some time the Hawke government seemed to be successful in pulling Australia out of some of its economic difficulties. Inflation began to come down and even though unemployment remained high, it did not seem to be getting worse.

Since 1985, however, there have been serious worries about Australia's situation. Some of the problems are that:

- Australia's industries are not efficient enough to compete with industries in other countries.
- Australia as a nation is spending much more than it is earning.
- Australia is importing from other countries much more than it is exporting to overseas countries.
- The Australian government has been borrowing too much from other countries to help pay for the running of the country.

A lot of Australians, including many Labor supporters, were very surprised when Labor won the election in 1993. What was even more surprising was that Labor won far more easily than it did in 1990. During the early 1990s the Australian economy had got worse and unemployment had risen to more than 10 per cent.

While he was prime minister, Paul Keating became identified with a number of important issues. One of these was the question of a reconciliation between Aborigines and non-Aboriginal Australians. You will read more about this in the next chapter. Another was the question of an Australian republic. Keating stated clearly that he thought it was time for Australia to cut its ties to the British monarchy. He wanted the queen (or king) of England to be replaced as Australia's head of state by a president, who would be an Australian citizen. The republic issue, as it became known, seemed likely to become one of the most widely discussed topics in Australia during the late 1990s.

Liberal leadership problems

When Malcolm Fraser was defeated in 1983 he resigned from politics. After that the Liberal Party had difficulty in choosing a successful leader. Andrew Peacock became leader after Fraser. Even though he did better than most people expected in the 1984 election, he was replaced in 1984 by John Howard. The Liberals, under Howard, lost the 1987 election, but Howard remained leader until May 1989, when once again Peacock became leader. When Labor won again in 1990, Peacock resigned and was replaced by John Hewson. Hewson was a former professor of economics. He devised a number of policies, known as 'Fightback', which were designed to win the 1993 election for the Liberal–National coalition. The main policy in Fightback was the introduction of a new tax, known as a Goods and Services Tax (GST). This meant that on almost all purchases, except food, Australians would have to pay a small percentage of the price in tax. Some other taxes were to be reduced to help compensate for this new tax. When the coalition lost the 1993 election, many people thought that this GST policy was to blame.

Hewson stayed on as leader for almost a year after the election and was then replaced by Alexander Downer. When Downer seemed to be unpopular with voters, John Howard was once again elected leader in early 1995.

Labor loses power

At the election that was held on 2 March 1996, the Liberal–National Party coalition came to power with a record majority. John Howard, as leader of the Liberal Party, became the new prime minister and Tim Fisher, as leader of the National Party, became the new deputy prime minister.

After the defeat of his party, Paul Keating resigned as the Labor leader. Soon after the election, Kim Beazley, who had been minister for finance in the Keating government, was elected as the new leader of the Labor Party, and so beame the leader of the opposition.

CHECK the facts

1 Which prime minster was in office from 1971 to 1972?

2 Which political party came to power in 1972?

3 Which prime minister ended the free Medibank scheme?

4 Who was the next Labor prime minister after Gough Whitlam?

5 Who became leader of the opposition after the 1990 election?

6 Which party won the 1993 election?

7 Who became prime minister of Australia in 1996?

Think *for yourself*

1 All the prime ministers in this chapter were men. Most of them were quite wealthy. Most of them went to university. Do you think rich, well-educated men make the best Australian prime ministers? What sort of person would you like to see as prime minister? Why?

2 Look at the policies of Gough Whitlam's government and compare them with those of Malcolm Fraser's government. Liberal Party government is sometimes called 'small government'. Labor Party government is sometimes called 'big government'. Can you work out what this means by studying the two sets of policies?

3 Some Labor supporters have complained that the Hawke government was more like the Fraser government than the Whitlam government. Can you find any evidence for this in the policies it followed?

KNOW the chapter

1 Figure 8.31 shows stamps that were issued to commemorate two important events in Australia in the 1950s. What were these events? Why were they important to Australians?

Figure 8.31
These stamps were issued in the 1950s

2 Study the newspaper headlines in Figure 8.32. Write a few sentences about each one. Explain when the headline was written and what it was about.

It's LABOR!

11-seat win likely after 23 years out

KERR SACKS GOUGH

AUSTRALIANS SAY NO TO GST

Figure 8.32
Newspaper headlines

3 Use the clues below to fill in the word puzzle. All the words are names of people. They are all in this chapter.

- **a** I was an Australian athlete. I carried the Olympic flame into the Melbourne stadium in 1956.
- **b** I was an Australian wartime prime minister. I died in July 1945.
- **c** I was a male swimmer. I won three gold medals in the Melbourne Olympic Games.
- **d** I was Australia's prime minister from January 1966 to December 1967.
- **e** I dismissed Gough Whitlam's government in November 1975.
- **f** I was in Parliament for less than three years before I became prime minister.
- **g** My government began the Snowy Mountains Scheme.
- **h** I formed the Liberal Party in 1944. I became prime minister in 1949.
- **i** In 1972 I became Australia's first Labor Party prime minister for twenty-three years.
- **j** I became prime minister in 1991. I replaced Australia's longest-serving Labor prime minister.
- **k** I was appointed as caretaker prime minister by John Kerr in November 1975.

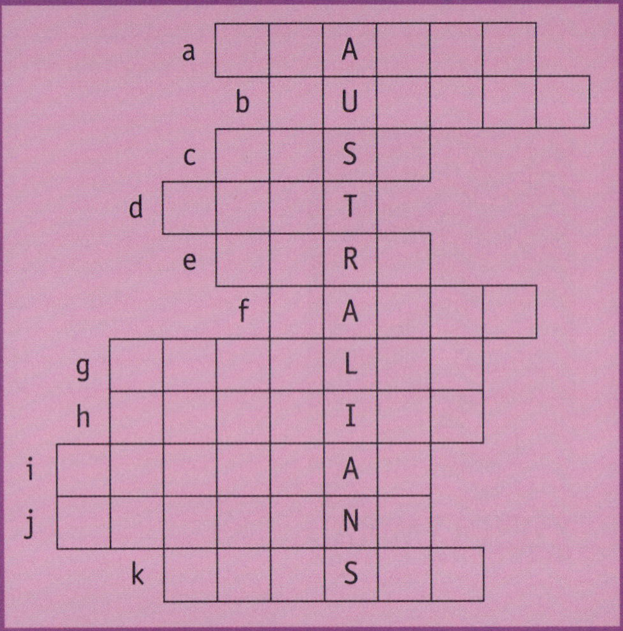
a A
b U
c S
d T
e R
f A
g L
h I
i A
j N
k S

Today *and* tomorrow

If you could get into a time machine and travel back fifty years to Australia in the period just after the Second World War, you would find yourself in a country that you would hardly recognise. In the late 1940s Australia's population was about 7 million. In 1995 it was almost 18 million. In 1945 the vast majority of Australians had British or Irish ancestors and almost all migrants to Australia came from the British Isles. In most places you would see only white faces and you would be very unlikely to hear anyone speaking a foreign language. Most people in the cities never saw or heard much about Aborigines. In those days Australia's Aboriginal people did not have the right to vote in elections and were not even counted when a census was taken. In the late 1940s unemployment was not a problem in Australia. Most women left their jobs when they got married. For them a career meant bringing up children and looking after the home.

In this chapter, we look at some of the great changes that have transformed Australia since the end of the Second World War.

Black and white Australians

Figure 9.1
Gippsland Aborigines in 1857

In 1991, 265 459 Australians were Aborigines or Torres Strait Islanders. Use an atlas to find out where the Torres Strait is. More than half of these people were under twenty years of age. Almost equal numbers of these people lived in New South Wales and Queensland (just over 70 000 in each state). Almost 42 000 lived in Western Australia and just under 40 000 lived in the Northern Territory.

We cannot be certain how many Aboriginal people were in Australia when Europeans first settled here in 1788. Estimates range from 300 000 to about 750 000. Their ancestors had lived in Australia for at least 40 000 years and had worked out their own ways of living. Aborigines had enough food to eat. They had rich traditions and a close family life. But they did not live in houses and did not gather many possessions. European settlers thought that the Aborigines were savages. They did not understand their society.

Europeans have treated Aborigines badly. They took Aboriginal land. This destroyed tribal life. They brought new diseases such as smallpox, measles and alcoholism. The Aborigines were once a proud, independent race. European Australians made Aborigines dependent on European ways. In the last thirty or so years, however, Aborigines have begun to fight back.

Figure 9.2
Aborigines are renovating this house at the Alice Springs town camp

Think *for yourself*

1 Can you think of some reasons why European settlers thought that the Aborigines were 'savages'?

2 Read the extract below. It was spoken by a nurse who works with Aborigines and tells what happens when Aboriginal children go to hospital.

> Really sick kids ... would come into Katherine Hospital and the people who had never been out to the camps would send them out with medicine and tell them to take it three times a day at certain times. [The parents] didn't have a watch anyway, so time didn't mean anything to them ... Really, half the time they were so nervous that they weren't really listening to what you were saying.

a Where is Katherine?

b What were 'the camps'? Why do many Aborigines live in camps rather than in houses?

c Why do you think Aboriginal parents were nervous when their children were in hospital?

d How does this extract show that even today European Australians do not understand Aborigines?

From assimilation to self-determination

In the 1950s the Australian government decided on a new policy towards Aborigines. It was called **assimilation**. The government believed that if Aborigines had better health, better houses, more schooling and better jobs, they could be **assimilated**, or absorbed, into non-Aboriginal society. They would be no different from other Australians.

A lot was done to help Aborigines in the 1950s and 1960s. The lives of many Aborigines were improved. But a lot of Aborigines did not want to become just like the white people. They wanted to keep their own culture and their own identity. They wanted to be able to choose the way they would live.

In the 1970s a new Aboriginal policy was worked out. It was called **self-determination**. Aborigines can now decide how they want to live. Some may choose to live in the traditional tribal way. Others may choose to live in towns and cities. The aim of the new policy is to help all Aborigines to live in the way they want to.

Kevin Gilbert, an Aborigine, explained the difference between the two policies in these words:

> Aborigines want to be Aborigines in their own right, to be people in their own right, rather than imitation white men.

ATSIC

An important step towards Aboriginal self-determination occurred in 1990, when the Australian government set up the Aboriginal and Torres Strait Islander Commission (ATSIC). ATSIC is now responsible for most decisions concerning Aboriginal people and runs most of the programs designed to help Aboriginal people. It consists of a board of commissioners and a number of regional councils that represent the interests of Aborigines in all parts of the country. All the commissioners are Aboriginal people and the regional councils are elected by Aboriginal people in different areas.

ATSIC has taken over most of the responsibilities of the Department of Aboriginal Affairs. In 1992–93 ATSIC spent about $800 million on Aboriginal welfare programs.

Problems of today's Aborigines

After 200 years of neglect, today's Aborigines have to face many difficulties. There are four serious problems that still need to be solved: housing, health, education and work.

Housing

Aborigines in cities often live in crowded slums in the inner suburbs. On the outskirts of country towns live the 'fringe dwellers'.

Figure 9.3
An Aboriginal shack at Wilcannia, NSW. How would homes like this cause poor health?

Figure 9.4
This house in Tingha NSW was bought for an Aboriginal family with a grant from the Department of Aboriginal Affairs

These Aborigines camp in huts and shacks made of iron, wood, sacks or old cars. Shacks are found on government reserves as well. They have no proper water supply, no power and no sewerage.

ATSIC spends a large amount of its budget on housing. It builds houses that can be rented or bought by Aborigines. It helps Aborigines who form groups to build their own homes. Aborigines can also buy or rent houses from state housing commissions. But there are never enough of these houses for all the people who apply for them. Often, too, non-Aboriginals are angry when an Aboriginal family moves into their street. Poor non-Aboriginal people often resent the money spent on Aborigines.

Before I got my Housing Commission home, both my neighbours were asked whether they would like an Aboriginal person living next to them. On the other hand, I wasn't asked whether I would prefer to live next door to a white or a black family.

Ruby Hammond, Aboriginal woman

Health

In 1990, 22 out of every 1000 Aboriginal babies in Australia died before they were one year old. Only about 8 out of every 1000 non-Aboriginal babies died.

The top graph in Figure 9.6 shows the percentage of Aboriginal people who were in different age groups in 1991. The lower graph gives the same information about the non-Aboriginal Australian population. You can work out, by adding both sides of the graph together, that more than half of the Aboriginal population was under twenty. This compares with less than three out of ten for the non-Aboriginal population. You will also see that a much smaller proportion of the Aboriginal population lives to be very old.

Aborigines as a group have a shorter **life expectancy** than other Australians. Most Australians now live for between seventy-five and eighty years. Most Aborigines do not live for more than sixty years.

Figure 9.5
This poster was produced in 1989. What message is it sending to Aboriginal people?

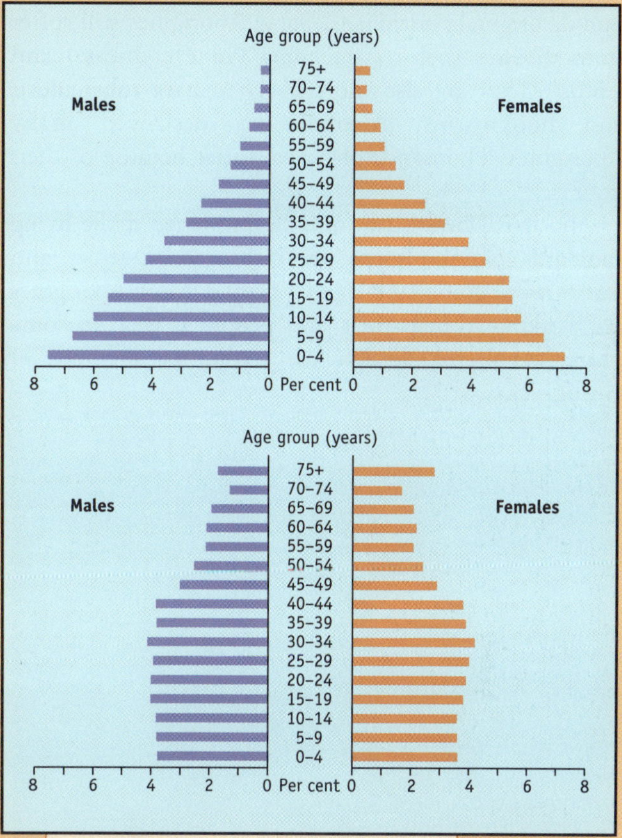

Figure 9.6
The top graph shows the percentage of Aboriginal Australians in different age groups. The bottom graph gives the same information for non-Aboriginal Australians.

Figure 9.7
This health service truck makes weekly visits to Aboriginal camps in the Alice Springs area

This is not very surprising when we consider that Aborigines suffer from many diseases that are rare among non-Aboriginal Australians. Some Aborigines still suffer from diseases such as trachoma (an eye disease) and leprosy. They are also more likely to have tuberculosis and hookworms. Alcohol has destroyed many Aborigines. Thousands of others suffer because of their poor diet.

Aboriginal health can only be improved if the living standards of Aborigines are improved. Doctors and nurses work among Aboriginal people. More Aborigines are working to help their own people as well. In some places, Aboriginal healers use traditional methods of curing sickness.

Think *for yourself*

1 Why are Aborigines more likely than other Australians to suffer from diseases such as trachoma and tuberculosis?

2 What is meant by the term 'life expectancy'?

3 Read the extracts below and answer the questions that follow.

> Malcolm Reid, thirty, had been at it since Tuesday night, when he had fallen over in the street, too drunk to find his way home unaided.
>
> As a four-year-old, Malcolm had found a bottle of liquor left on the Bourke reserve …
>
> Malcolm and his sister decided to try it, and to avoid being caught by their mother, climbed into a freshly dug latrine pit with the bottle. Had rain fallen heavily, they may have drowned, but someone found them.
>
> Twenty-six years later, drinking for Malcolm Reid was a way of life, a way of tolerating the seeming futility of his existence.
>
> *Sydney Morning Herald*, 5 November, 1981

> A lawyer in a country town told me, 'When I get drunk, the police drive me home in my Mercedes, or else get a taxi for me, but when an Aborigine gets drunk, he is put in the back of the van.'
>
> Dorothy Parker, anthropologist

a What does 'had been at it' mean?
b Where is Bourke? Use an atlas to find out.
c What is a latrine pit? Why were there latrine pits on the Bourke reserve?
d What is meant by 'a way of tolerating the seeming futility of his existence'? Does this explain why Malcolm became an alcoholic?
e Is the lawyer in the second extract an Aboriginal or a non-Aboriginal person?
f What is an anthropologist? Why would anthropologists study Aboriginal people?
g Using these two extracts as evidence, would you say that Aborigines and non-Aborigines are treated equally?

Education

In 1971 one-quarter of Australia's Aborigines had never been to school. Even today it is very hard for an Aborigine to go right through high school. Many Aborigines think school is a waste of time because they know that they will probably not get a job at the end of it.

In 1970 a scheme was started to help Aborigines at school. The government helped to pay for their fees, clothes, books and extra teaching. Another scheme helped Aborigines who wanted to study at TAFE colleges and universities. Some Aboriginal groups have set up their own schools. Pupils in these schools learn about traditional Aboriginal ways as well as about the things they need to know to get on in the non-Aboriginal world. In many of these schools pupils have lessons in their own traditional language as well as in English.

Figure 9.8
This Aboriginal woman teaches the Gidabal language to school children at Woodenbong in northern NSW. Teachers and pupils at the school have made up their own books in the Aboriginal language.

Work

The unemployment rate of Aboriginal Australians is much higher than that of other Australians. About one-third of Aborigines over fifteen years of age are unable to find work. Two reasons for this are, first, that most Aborigines are poorly educated and, second, that many Aborigines live a long way from where work is available. Can you think of any other reasons why Aborigines find it hard to get work?

Like other Australians who are unemployed, Aborigines become depressed and bored. Because they feel that there is nothing worthwhile they can do for themselves, they rely on government pensions and welfare payments.

One government scheme that has helped many unemployed Aborigines is the Community Development Employment Projects (CDEP) scheme. It was begun in 1977 but expanded greatly in the late 1980s and 1990s. Under this scheme, unemployed Aborigines are paid to work on building and other projects in Aboriginal communities. In 1992–93 more than 22 000 Aborigines were working in 219 Aboriginal communities under the CDEP scheme.

Think *for yourself*

Look at Figure 9.9 and read the opinion below. Use them and what you have read in this section to write a few sentences about the difficulties faced by Aboriginal people today. In your paragraph, explain how these difficulties are linked together.

> Housing is part of a circle, housing is a base to work from, and if you do not have a base to work from, children cannot go to school, men and women cannot go to work. If you have not got accommodation, you have got nowhere to come back to prepare to go out to work next day, to be able to get meals. You have got to have a house and that is it.
>
> Ruby Hammond

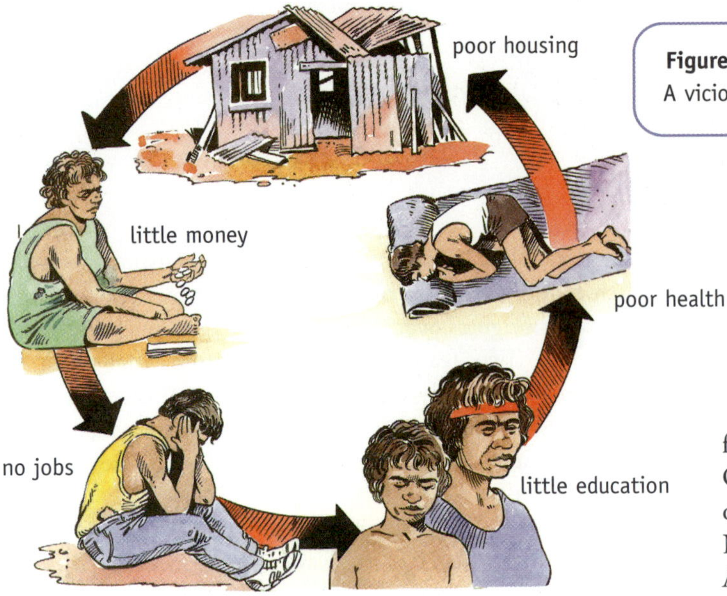

Figure 9.9
A vicious circle

Are these the answers?

Land rights

> We don't want the land to build a big motel or hotel. We want it to be there without it being touched ... so that our children can go there and see the places the old men are talking about in the 'Dreamtime'.
>
> Harry Djagamara

Aborigines have always been closely linked to their land. But after 1788 white settlers took land away from the Aborigines. It was then owned by the government or by white Australians. Aborigines could no longer wander over it.

In the 1960s Aborigines in the Northern Territory began demanding that their land should be returned to them. They wanted to set up cattle stations that would give work to Aboriginal people. At first the Australian government gave only small parcels of land to a few tribes. In 1977, however, about a quarter of the Northern Territory was returned to Aborigines. By 1984 Aborigines owned almost one-third of the Northern Territory. In 1981 the South Australian government returned 10 per cent of South Australia to the Pitjantjatjara tribe. In 1985 the Australian government transferred the Uluru National Park, which included the famous tourist attractions of Ayers Rock (Uluru) and the Olgas (Kata Tjuta), to their traditional Aboriginal owners. The new owners leased the park back to the National Parks and Wildlife Service. A board of Aboriginal people now manages the park, which is visited by hundreds of thousands of visitors each year.

Figure 9.10
Aboriginal people march through city streets to demand land rights. What answer would you give to the question on the placard?

Returning land to Aborigines has been made more difficult because governments want to control the minerals that may lie underneath the land. If the government or a company wants to mine on Aboriginal land, it must get permission from the Aboriginal people who own the land. It must also pay royalties to the Aboriginal owners. But, if the government decides that mining in an Aboriginal area is necessary, it can go ahead even if the Aboriginal people there decide that they do not want their land to be mined.

Figure 9.11
In October 1995, There were celebrations to mark the tenth anniversary of the handing over of Uluru to its traditional Aboriginal owners. Here, standing in front of the famous rock, is Mr Yami Lester, the chairman of the Uluru National Park board of management.

Outstations

Some Aborigines have chosen to live a more traditional way of life away from reserves, towns and cattle stations. They have moved to 'outstations'. Here they have combined their old ways with some of the benefits of the modern world. Aborigines on outstations live in small groups. They elect their own leaders.

Thousand of Aborigines live on outstations. Their work depends on where they live. Some groups hunt buffaloes, others catch fish, grow fruit trees, raise poultry, cattle, horses or camels. Aborigines on outstations do not want to turn the clock back. They use cars, trucks, radios and aeroplanes to make their work easier. But they believe that many of the old ways are worth keeping as well.

Figure 9.12
Collum Collum Station in northern NSW. This cattle station is run by the Baryulgil community of Aborigines.

Figure 9.13
Planes are used to deliver supplies to this outstation in Arnhem Land in the Northern Territory.

City life

In 1971 more than half of Australia's Aboriginal people (56 per cent) lived in remote country areas. Twenty years later the situation was completely turned around. By 1991 almost seven out of ten Aborigines lived in large cities or towns.

Aborigines from the country move to the city because they believe that it will be easier to find work there. But, as we have seen, Aborigines often find it hard to get work. They are forced to live in slums. City Aborigines are among the poorest people in Australia.

Figure 9.14
Aboriginal children listen to a story at the Murawina preschool in Redfern

Self-help

City Aborigines have sometimes been able to work together to improve their living standards and to make other Australians more aware of their problems. Aboriginal groups can support each other and fight together for better conditions. In Sydney, for example, the Aboriginal Medical Service and Aboriginal Legal Service have helped thousands of Aborigines. Murawina, an Aboriginal preschool, has been built in Redfern where most of Sydney's Aborigines live. This project began when a group of Aborigines started giving free breakfasts to Aboriginal children in a local park.

Aborigines in the country are also forming groups to improve their way of life. Housing groups can apply to the government for money to build homes for Aboriginal people. Other groups, such as those on the outstations, have set up many different projects. Instead of working for non-Aboriginals, groups such as these work for their own community.

The Mabo case

In June 1992 the High Court of Australia made an important judgment about the land rights of Aboriginal and Torres Strait Island people. Almost ten years earlier, in 1982, Eddie Mabo and four other people from Murray Island in the Torres Strait took a case to the High Court. They claimed that the Meriam people, as the people of Murray Island are known, were the rightful owners to Murray Island and the surrounding reefs. They argued that the Meriam people had lived and worked on Murray Island since before the time of European settlement. European settlers had never taken possession of the island or used it for farming or industry. They claimed that nothing had happened to change the original Aboriginal ownership of the island.

The judges of the High Court found in favour of the Meriam people and declared them to be the legal owners of Murray Island. If the judgment had only been about one tiny island, it would not have been particularly important. But the judges went further. They pointed out that if the Meriam people were the legal owners of Murray Island, some other Aboriginal groups may also be the legal owners of other areas. The judgment was important because it recognised for the first time in Australian law that Aboriginal people were the owners of Australia before European settlement. If, in some places, nothing had happened to take that ownership away, then those places could be claimed by their Aboriginal owners. The Mabo judgment, as it became known, established the **principle** of native title, or legal ownership of land. It contradicted the idea, which many people had believed, that nobody owned Australia when the Europeans took it over. This idea was called by the Latin name: 'terra nullius', meaning nobody's land.

In December 1993 the Australian parliament passed the Native Title Act, which was based on the Mabo decision. According to this act, Aboriginal groups could make a claim to native title over areas of land if they could prove that they were traditionally linked to this land and if they could also prove that they had occupied and used this land during the whole period since European settlement. They could not claim any land that was now owned by non-Aboriginal people.

Figure 9.15
Eddie Mabo never knew that his case before the High Court was successful. He died in 1992, about a month before the Court made its decision. On 26 January 1993 he was named as the *Australian* newspaper's Australian of the Year. Do you think he deserved this honour? Why

CHECK the facts

1 Find an expression from this section on 'Black and white Australians' that means the same as each of the definitions below.

- **a** A policy of absorbing Aborigines into the dominant society and making them as much like non-Aboriginal Australians as possible.
- **b** A policy of allowing Aborigines to choose how they want to live.
- **c** Aborigines who live in shanty towns on the outskirts of country towns.
- **d** An eye disease that is common among Aborigines, but rare among other Australians.
- **e** Areas in which groups of Aborigines live by combining some of the old ways with some of the benefits of modern life.
- **f** The right of Aboriginal people to claim ownership of some land.

2 Is each of the following sentences true or false?

- **a** There are half a million Aboriginal and Torres Strait Island people in Australia.
- **b** The Australian government wants all Aborigines to be assimilated into Australian society.
- **c** Aborigines suffer from some diseases that are rare among other Australians.
- **d** All Torres Strait Islanders are known as Meriam people.
- **e** Most Aborigines live in the Northern Territory.

THE HISTORIAN AT WORK

Henry Reynolds is one of Australia's leading historians. He has written a number of books about Aborigines and the relations between Aboriginal and other Australians. The following is part of an article he wrote about the Mabo case. Read it carefully and then answer the questions that follow.

Background

In the 1970s when Eddie Mabo was working as a gardener at the James Cook University in Townsville, he and I would talk about many things over lunch—traditional culture or political issues relating to Aboriginal and Islander questions. We had been involved in various civil rights organisations in the 1960s and, during the 1970s, he had set up the first Indigenous school in Australia—an enterprise with which I, too, was very much associated.

He would tell me a great deal about growing up in the Murray Islands in what were fairly traditional surroundings. Eddie had a great interest in traditional culture. While at the university he read the anthropological literature associated with the Torres Strait ... He also mentioned that on his island he and his family owned land. Although he had not been back home for ten years, he had no concerns about this land; everyone on the island knew it was Mabo land and the people there would care for it.

On one of these occasions I said to him, 'Look, you do appreciate, don't you, that although in your view this is your land, it's actually all Crown land. According to white Australian law, you don't own any land on Murray Island'.

I still remember the look that came over his face—it was a look of incredulity; how could anyone be so mistaken about the land not belonging to his family? He was horrified that what I had said might indeed be the case.

Now, I had an idea at that stage, that in the United States there had been an important case in which traditional rights to land had been established. I vaguely remember saying to Eddie, 'Because you are gardeners you might be able to establish your rights to your land in law.'

Further developments

Between 1977 and 1982, I secured a research grant to gather black oral history and Eddie agreed to be a research assistant to the project. Although he had no qualifications, the university agreed to send him to Murray Island to visit the old people there and record their history about the Torres Strait. He tried to get official permission, first to go to his own islands—and then to visit every island in the Strait. In those days the islands were still every much under the control of the Queensland government. But he was refused permission and was therefore unable to return home.

It was the cruel realisation that he was an exile that began the momentum towards taking the issue to Court.

In 1981, students at the university called a conference on land rights in Australia. They invited major interested parties, particularly legal experts with considerable experience in land rights legislation as well as significant experience working with Torres Strait Islanders. It was decided at the conference that the issue of a land claim by the Murray Islanders to traditional title would be taken to the High Court. The aim would be to establish in European law what the Islanders always felt to be the case—that they owned the land.

Legal process

... Finally, in June 1992, after Eddie Mabo's death, the High Court reached the historic decision. By a six to one majority, it decided that Eddie Mabo had been right, that he did own his land, not because he held a title from the Crown but because ... he owned the land according to traditional custom which still ran in the Torres Strait. So, the Meriam people of Torres Strait had the right to the full enjoyment of the Murray Islands ...

The Mabo case overturned the doctrine of Terra Nullius ... That [means that] when the British arrived, either the land was unoccupied or ... no one owned the land. It had not become the property of anyone, no one was in possession. The Crown became the sole owner of all Australian property.

Mabo has overturned the doctrine totally ...

1 Do some research to find out what each of the following terms mean: Crown land, anthropological literature, traditional rights to land, black oral history, land rights legislation.

2 Using the evidence in this article, write two or three sentences about Eddie Mabo's life and background before he took his case to the High Court.

3 Why did Eddie Mabo believe he owned land on Murray Island? Explain the difference between **traditional rights** to land and **legal rights** to land. Did Eddie Mabo have legal right to land on Murray Island before 1992?

4 What role did Henry Reynolds play in Eddie Mabo's decision to go to the High Court?

5 From the evidence of this article, what would you say were the main reasons that Eddie Mabo took his case to the High Court? Apart from Henry Reynolds, who supported and encouraged Eddie Mabo in his decision to go to the High Court?

6 Why do you think Henry Reynolds said to Eddie Mabo: '*Because you are gardeners*, you might be able to establish your rights to your land in law?'

7 Which government prevented Eddie Mabo from visiting the Torres Strait islands between 1977 and 1982? Can you suggest any reasons why this government did not want him to go there?

8 In a few sentences of your own, explain what 'terra nullius' means. Why do you think the early European settlers considered Australia to be 'terra nullius'? (Clue: think about the ways the Aborigines lived and how Europeans would have thought of this.)

9 From reading this article what do you learn about some of the ways professional historians gather their evidence?

Old and new Australians

> Australia wants, and will welcome, new healthy citizens who are determined to become good Australians.

With these words in August 1945 Australia's minister for immigration, Arthur Calwell, introduced a new migration policy.

The government agreed to pay most of the fares of suitable migrants who were chosen to come to Australia. At first only migrants from Britain were assisted. Later, migrants came from Holland, Italy and Germany. Since then, migrants have come from many countries in Europe, Asia and South America.

Refugees are people who leave their own country to escape from war or hardship. Since the Second World War, many refugees have come to Australia. The first refugees came from countries in Europe which had been taken over by the USSR after the Second World War. Later, refugees came to Australia from countries such as Czechoslovakia, Hungary, Greece and Chile, when violence broke out in their own countries. During the early 1990s large numbers of refugees came to Australia from Vietnam, Cambodia , Iraq and the republics that were once part of Yugoslavia and the USSR—regions that have been shaken by war and revolution.

Why did Australia want migrants after 1945?

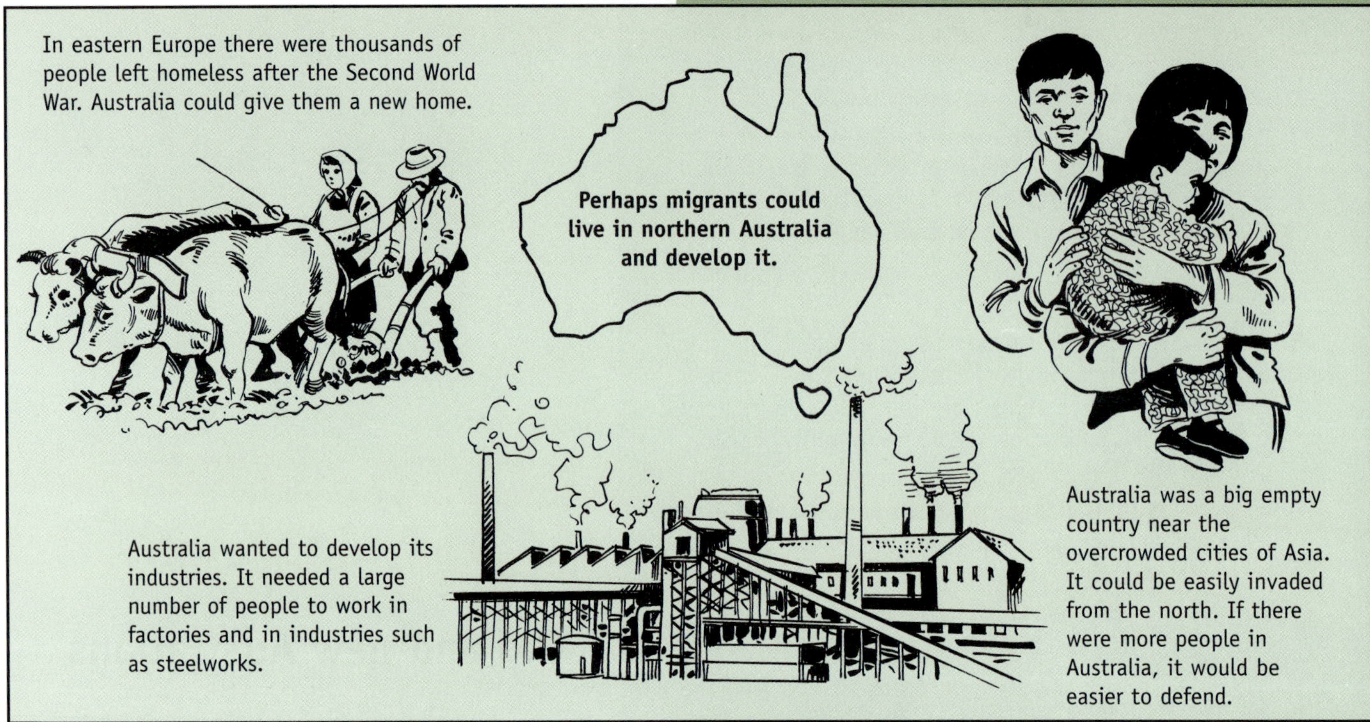

Figure 9.16
Four reasons why Australia wanted migrants in 1945

Where have Australia's migrants come from?

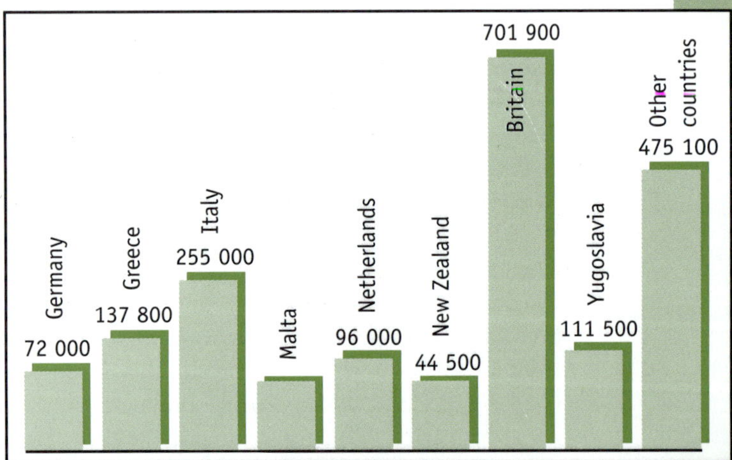

Figure 9.17
Where Australia's migrants came from, 1947–70

Between 1945 and 1970 most migrants came from Europe.

In the 1970s the policy was changed. People from other countries found it easier to come to Australia. Migrants have come from Asia, the Middle East and South America as well as Europe.

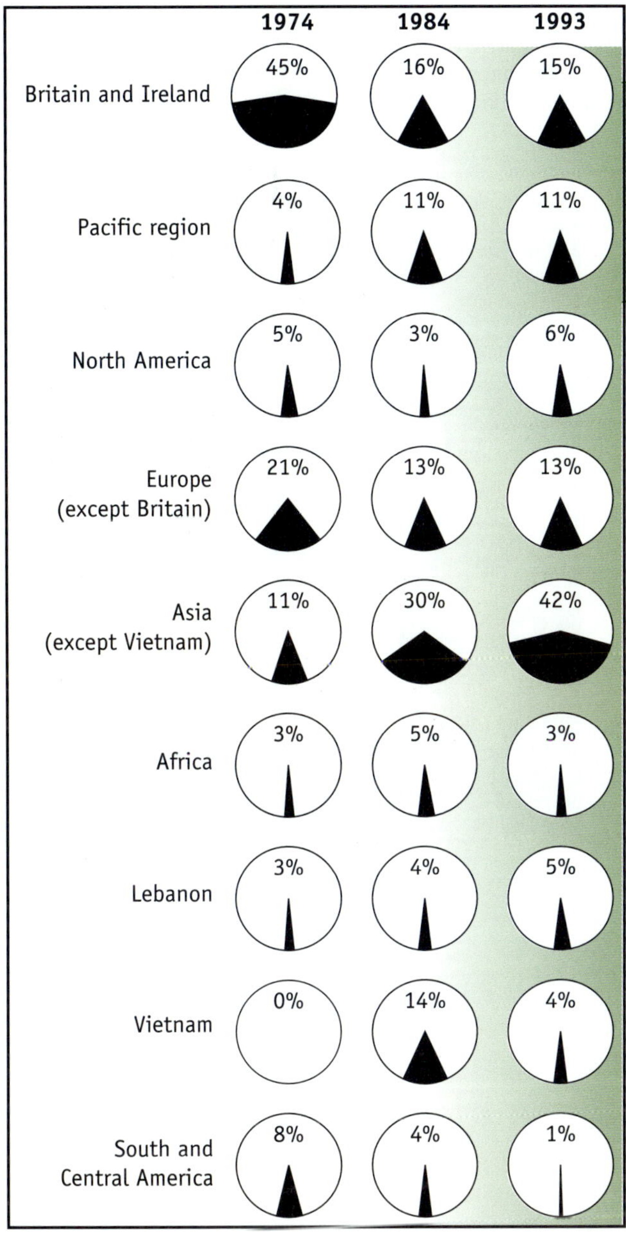

Figure 9.18
Where Australia's migrants came from, 1974, 1984 and 1993

Think *for yourself*

1 Name two or three countries in the Pacific region, in Europe, in Asia, in South and Central America.

2 In what part of the world is:
- **a** Vietnam
- **b** Lebanon.

3 Write out these sentences. Use information from Figure 9.18 to finish them.
- **a** In 1974 most migrants came from ____
- **b** In 1984 most migrants came from ____
- **c** In 1993 most migrants came from ____
- **d** The number of migrants from Britain ____ by ____ per cent between 1974 and 1993.
- **e** In 1993, 46 per cent of migrants to Australia came from ____
- **f** The percentage of migrants from ____ and ____ and the other countries of ____ fell by 32 per cent between 1974 and 1984, but was at about the same level in 1993.

4 Can you suggest some reasons why the percentage of migrants from Vietnam rose between 1974 and 1984 but then dropped away in the next nine years?

5 The total number of migrants to Australia in 1993 was just under 158 000. Work out approximately how many people came to Australia in 1993 from:
- **a** the whole of Asia
- **b** Britain and Ireland
- **c** the Pacific region.

6 Figure 9.19 gives some reasons why people came to Australia. Can you think of any other reasons?

7 How many people do you know who have migrated to Australia? Find out why they came. Are their reasons like the ones given in Figure 9.19?

Figure 9.19
Why migrants have come to Australia

Figure 9.20
These two Russians came to Australia as refugees after the Second World War. What problems do you think they would have faced in their new home?

Refugees: a special case

Unlike other migrants who choose to leave their own country and move to another country, refugees flee from their homeland because they are afraid to stay there.

Refugees are allowed to come to Australia because Australia has signed a United Nations agreement about refugees. Australia wants to help people in Asia and other parts of the world who have been made homeless by wars, revolutions or hostile governments.

Figure 9.21
Vietnamese refugees struggle ashore as their boat sinks. These people were among the lucky ones. Why?

In the late 1970s, after the communist government had gained control of Vietnam, thousands of people who were afraid of that government left Vietnam in small boats. In 1978 the first boatload of refugees to reach Australia sailed into Darwin harbour. Suddenly Australians were made aware of the problems of refugees.

By the end of 1979, 2011 'boat people' from Vietnam had survived the dangerous boat journey to Australia. Many more had died trying to make the voyage. Other refugees had reached other parts of Asia, where they were put into special refugee camps.

In 1979, most refugees (about 20 000) were selected by immigration officers in camps in Thailand, Indonesia and Malaysia. Those with relatives in Australia or with useful skills and a knowledge of English were chosen to come to Australia. A small number of students and diplomats (about 1000) were also allowed to stay.

By the middle of 1983, 70 000 refugees from South-East Asia, most of them from Vietnam, had arrived to settle in Australia. In 1982 the Vietnamese government agreed to allow refugees to leave the country. Many Vietnamese people were then able to come to Australia to be reunited with members of their families who had come earlier as boat people or from refugee camps.

Throughout the 1980s and until 1992 more refugees came to Australia from Vietnam than from any other country. In 1992–93 almost 11 000 refugees came to settle in Australia. Of these, more than 3000 came from the war-torn countries that used to be part of Yugoslavia. More than 1500 came from countries that were formerly part of the USSR. Just under 2000 came from Vietnam.

By 1995, fifty years after the end of the Second World War, almost 500 000 refugees from more than forty countries had settled in Australia.

Figure 9.22
Two opinions about refugees. Which one do you agree with? Why?

How migrants are chosen

Migrants who want to come to Australia must pass two 'tests'. First, all those who apply are given 'points'. They may gain points if they have a skill or training that Australia needs. They may gain more points if they have relatives in Australia who will be able to help them settle down here. Second, people who want to come to Australia are interviewed by immigration officers. They try to find out how well they will adapt to living in a new country. What sort of questions would you ask if you were choosing migrants for Australia?

How migrants have changed Australia

In 1984 a newspaper article about a Sydney suburb began this way:

> **'Chao' replaces 'G'day' in the ethnic capital**
>
> Two dark-haired Asian women in jeans stroll through the shopping centre, chatting in their musical tongue. Around Ashfield, that's no novelty. The typical Australian greeting of 'G'day' is often replaced by the Vietnamese 'Chao', the Greek 'Yassu' the Spanish 'Ola' or its equivalent in many other tongues.
>
> Ashfield has a strong ethnic mix. About 40 per cent of residents were born overseas.

Sydney Morning Herald, 26 March 1984

Australia today is a **multicultural** society. This means that it is made up of people from many different cultures. In 1990 almost one person out of every four in Australia was born overseas. About 100 different languages are spoken in Australia. Australians are learning about the way people from other countries live and about their customs and traditions. Some people have become more open-minded because of the number of migrants in Australia. Others have not.

> I am very much against turning Australia into a multi-racial country. I believe people have been given their own countries, their own language, foods, habits, dress, way of living, dances, entertainment and even body odour.

Sydney woman, 1970s

Figure 9.23
Many migrants, like these two women from Yugoslavia, have maintained the way of life and the style of dress of countries they came from. Many too, continue to speak the language of their former country.

Figure 9.24
Migrants brought new ideas about food

Espresso coffee, pizza, chop suey, souvlaki, falafel and salami. Migrants have brought with them new ideas about food and restaurants. These sorts of things have helped to make Australia into a more varied and interesting country.

Today one worker in every four is a migrant. Migrants have helped to develop Australian industries. Over 60 per cent of the workers on the Snowy Mountains Scheme were migrants. Factories often depend on migrant workers—especially migrant women. The steelworks at Port Kembla and Newcastle employ thousands of migrant labourers. Many other migrants work as builders or miners.

Migrants work in all kinds of jobs, just as other Australians do. There are migrant teachers, doctors, nurses and farmers. There are migrant mechanics, actors, dancers and sports stars.

Did you know?

- More than 4 million Australians—almost one in four—were born outside Australia. They came from more than 100 countries.
- More than half of these people came from countries where English is not the main language.
- More than 3 million people who were born in Australia have at least one parent who was born overseas.
- In the 1990s almost half of Australia's new migrants have been Asian.
- Australia has a higher proportion of foreign-born people than any other English-speaking country.
- Australia has the second largest foreign-born workforce in the world.
- Melbourne is the third largest Greek-speaking city in the world.
- One-third of schoolchildren in NSW have migrant parents.
- Almost one person out of every six in Australia speaks a language other than English at home.

Migrants and their problems

It isn't easy leaving your home and making a life in a new and different country. Imagine leaving Australia and trying to settle in a foreign country far away from your relatives, your friends and the things you know and understand. What problems do you think you would face?

These are some of the problems that many of our migrants have to tackle. How do you think you would manage?

Some Australians fear that migrants will take jobs and work for less money than other Australians. Others do not want non-European migrants to come to Australia because they think they will cause racial problems. Migrants often have to cope with prejudice from other Australians.

> On the playground it was always 'Hi oily' or 'Come on oily'. In school, I remember one kid explaining to the teacher, 'Oily has to help his dad in the fish shop, so he can't do his homework'. It was always 'oily' and … at nine I thought I had oil in my veins instead of blood like the other kids.
>
> Migrant schoolboy, 1970s.

> There will always be someone who reminds us that we are foreigners or, to put it exactly as it is often said, bloody foreigners, dings, nungs, dagoes, krauts, and many more.
>
> Migrant from Austria
> who came to Australia in 1954

Figure 9.25
Migrant women working in a factory. What sort of work are they doing? Why is this work often done by migrant women?

Migrants from countries that do not use the English language have to learn to speak English. There are special classes for children and adults, but it is often hard to learn well enough to be accepted by other Australians and to cope at school and work. Older migrants, especially women, find learning English a very difficult task.

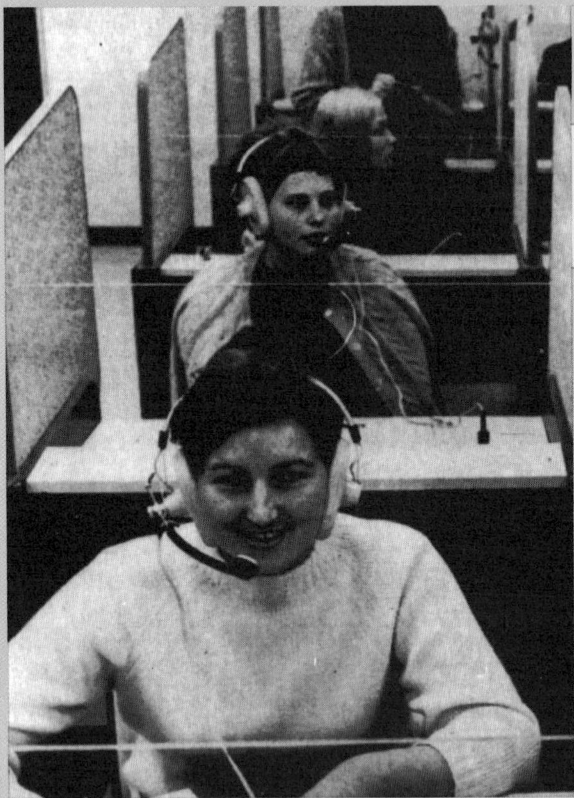

Figure 9.26
Adult migrants learning English

Migrants often find it hard to get work in Australia. Migrants with good qualifications and skills frequently have to work in unskilled jobs because their qualifications are not recognised in Australia. Many of the migrants who come to Australia lived in small villages in their home country. They find it hard to get used to working in noisy, dirty factories in Australia's cities. Migrants often find it difficult to understand what their rights are at work. They may not understand what trade unions are for. These problems, of course, are worse for migrants who do not speak or understand English.

> I don't like it when people scream at us Yugoslav women as if we were pigs … timing us in the toilet must be stopped … the boss shouldn't call us by numbers, we are human beings and we have names … here they work us like horses without compassion.
>
> Yugoslav factory worker

> They would put a Turkish woman in a pit underneath a car along with a man (to work on the under-section of that car) and the woman would collapse out of anxiety two days later. No one understood that she had done so because she had violated [broken] an essential Turkish family taboo: Turkish women aren't allowed to be alone with a man unaccompanied by their husbands.
>
> Social worker involved with migrants on car assembly plant

Think *for yourself*

1 Who is Australia's minister for immigration?

2 Imagine that you are one of the people in Figure 9.19. Explain what you thought Australia would be like. Was it the way you expected?

3 Make a survey of your class. Find out:

a How many students in the class were born outside Australia.

b How many of the students who were born in Australia have a parent who was born outside Australia.

c How many students whose parents were born in Australia have a grandparent who was born outside Australia.

d How many students do not fit into groups a, b or c.

e Work out what percentage of the class falls into each of the groups a, b, c and d.

f Try to find out some of the reasons why people in each of the groups a, b and c came to Australia.

g Try to find out what were the main problems the migrants met when they arrived in Australia.

4 Think about your town or suburb. Make a list of the way migrants have changed it. You might think about questions such as:

- Are there any Chinese restaurants or other restaurants selling foreign food?
- Does the newsagent sell newspapers in foreign languages?
- Do shops sell foods from other countries? What sort of foods are they?
- Are there any migrant clubs or organisations in your town or suburb?
- Are there any public signs or notices in languages other than English?
- Do you often hear other languages being spoken in the street or in the shops?
- Does the newspaper description of Ashfield on page 227 also apply to your suburb? In what ways?
- How typical of Australian communities do you think Ashfield is? Why do you think this?
- What does the expression 'a strong ethnic mix' mean?

Figure 9.27
How have migrants changed *your* town or suburb?

Figure 9.28
As this early twentieth century illustration shows, feminism is not a new idea

Figure 9.29
Women at home—three different views

Men and women

Who do you think is a 'typical Australian'? Is there more than one type of Australian?

Is there any chance that your typical Australian is a woman? Probably not. Australia has, for a long time, been considered a man's country.

But there have always been women in Australia who have wanted to improve their lives. Many of these women have wanted to do things that only men were allowed to do. At first, women fought to gain the right to vote. Then they struggled for the right to work. They also wanted to be able to work in reasonable conditions. More recently women have struggled for equal wages and for the right to choose what part they want to play in society. For example, women want to be able to choose whether to stay at home and bring up children or go out and work.

These women have been given different names at different times. Three of these names are 'suffragette', 'feminist' and 'women's liberationist'.

During the 1960s and 1970s many Australians (both women and men) were influenced by the Women's Liberation Movement. This movement convinced a lot of people that women should have equal rights and opportunities no matter what they choose to do. In 1975 the United Nations International Women's year did a lot to make people aware of the problems many women faced.

One result of the campaigns for women's rights has been that women have been accepted into occupations that had previously been thought to be unsuitable for them.

Women and home

Until the First World War most Australians believed that 'a woman's place is in the home'. Women worked hard for long hours doing boring, routine jobs in the home. They also cared for their children—and they usually had larger families than most Australians today.

From the 1920s on, women were able to buy and use more and more appliances and gadgets to help do the household chores. Today most families are small. Usually there are just two or three children. Many women now feel that there is not enough to do at home to fill up the whole day. When their children are old enough to be cared for by other people, they take up work again.

Other women prefer to stay at home. Do you think they are lazy? Or do they have an important part to play in the way society works?

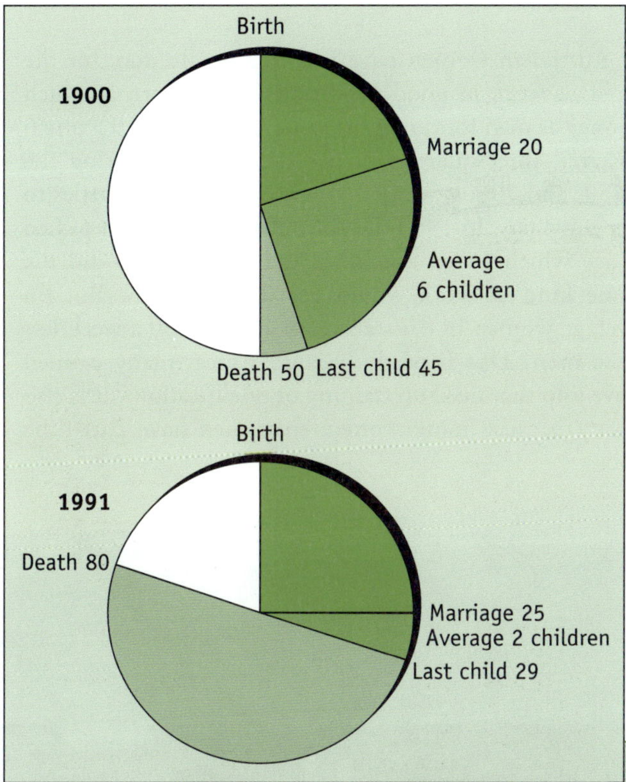

Figure 9.30
How women's lives have changed since 1900. The shaded area shows how much more time today's women have after the birth of their last child. How should they use that time?

Women at work

There have been times in Australia's history when women have been encouraged to go out to work. In the First World War women did a lot of unpaid work providing services to the troops. During the Depression, women were sometimes allowed to keep their jobs because they were paid less than men. In the Second World War women worked in factories and on the land. They did a lot to keep Australia going during the war.

But when the war finished and the soldiers came home, women were no longer needed or wanted in the workforce. A lot of women lost their jobs, even though they needed money to support themselves and their children.

Think *for yourself*

1 Is housework a full-time job? Make a list of the electrical appliances in your home. Have they really made a difference to running a house?

2 Look at Figure 9.31 and answer the questions below.
   a What attitude does Hagar have to his wife?
   b Do men still have this attitude?
   c People often do not consider housework as 'real' work? Why?
   d Do you think women should be paid to stay at home and care for children? Give reasons.

Figure 9.31

Figure 9.32
Are there any reasons why a woman could not be a good carpenter?

Australian women have had to struggle, too, for the right to work in good conditions and to earn as much money as men for doing the same work. In 1949 women received three-quarters of the men's wage. During the 1950s and 1960s, women fought several court battles to get equal pay. In 1969 the Australian government passed a law which stated that men and women who did the same kind of work would get the same pay. But on average women in Australia earn about $200 a week less than men. This is partly because a great many women have jobs that need no training or qualifications. It is also partly because more women than men have part-time jobs.

Women had a long fight to gain the right to work in whatever job they chose. The fight is still going on. In some Australian states it is now against the law to refuse to employ a woman for a job if she has the right qualifications and experience. But a lot of people still think that there are some jobs that only men should do.

Think *for yourself*

1. What is unusual about Figure 9.32?
2. Why do some women take up jobs like this one?
3. Architect, nurse, doctor, typist, plumber, truck driver. Which of these jobs are usually men's jobs? Which ones are usually women's jobs? Is there any job in this list that could only be done by either a man or a woman? Explain your answer.
4. Are there any jobs that women couldn't do? Why?

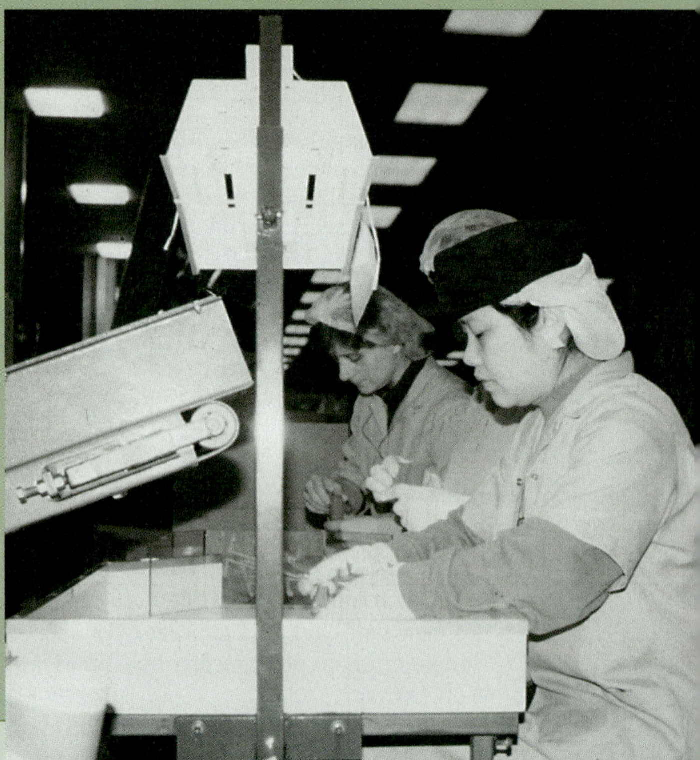

Figure 9.33
Women factory workers. What are they doing? Do they have a hard job? Is it a boring job?

Think *for yourself*

1. There are more women than men working in Australia's factories. Suggest some reasons for this.
2. Many of the women who work in factories are migrants. Why?
3. There are more men than women in Australia's trade unions. Suggest some reasons for this.
4. Six out of every ten working women in Australia are married. Does this cause any problems?
5. In 1993, 47 out of every 100 women over the age of 15 did paid work. The graph (Figure 9.34) shows the kind of work they did.
   - **a** Into which of the groups would these jobs fit:
     bus driver
     cook
     electrician
     store manager
     typist
     dentist
     car factory worker
     supermarket checkout assistant?
   - **b** Why are so many women clerical workers?
   - **c** Why are there so few managers?
   - **d** What does 'para-professional' mean? Can you name two occupations that would be called para-professional?

Figure 9.35
A government leaflet encouraging girls to learn a trade. Today, many girls are finding that an apprenticeship in a skilled trade is the path to a whole range of interesting and well-paid jobs.

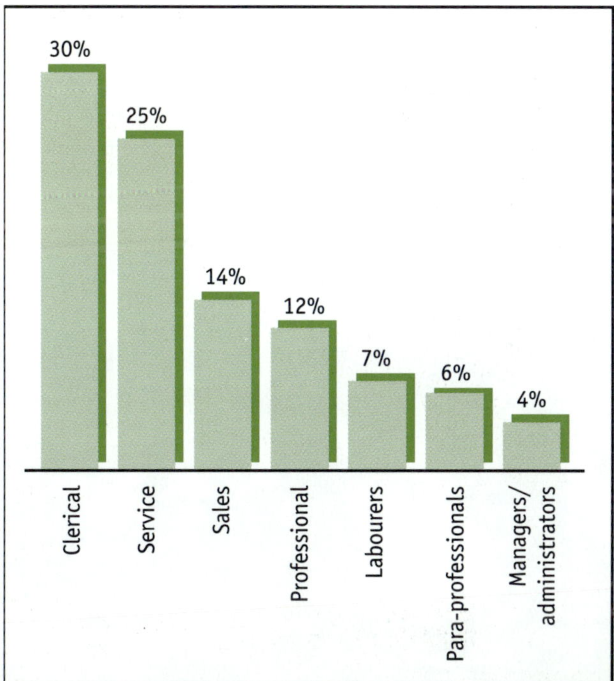

Figure 9.34
Types of paid work done by Australian women, 1993

- **e** Government departments are trying to get more girls and women to learn a trade. Why? Do you think that a girl who knows a trade is better off than a shop assistant?
- **f** Think of the women you know. Do any of them have unusual jobs? Why did they take them up?

6 Figures 9.36 and 9.37 give different versions of two nursery rhymes. Think about nursery rhymes, fairy stories and children's books. What parts do boys play? What parts do girls play? Are the girls as important as the boys?

Figure 9.36
What is Miss Muffet doing?

Figure 9.37
'Jack and Jill went up the hill to get a pail of water. Jack fell down and broke his crown—and Jill bandaged it up and later became a famous doctor.'

Workers and bosses

We hear a lot today about unemployment. In July 1993, 871 300 Australians who were looking for work did not have a job. But most Australians go to work. Some of them work for themselves. Most of them, however, work for other people. They may be employed by a company or by a government department. They may be one of many thousands of people working in a huge factory. Or they may work closely with only one or two other people. Although the kinds of jobs they do may be very different, most work for wages or a salary. They are employed for fixed hours each week or, perhaps, have certain jobs that must be done each week. Today, workers in Australia have better wages than ever before. They work fewer hours each week than ever before. Conditions of work are improving all the time. Workers now have paid holidays, sick leave, reasonably safe workplaces and a pension or superannuation at the end of their working lives.

Figure 9.38
Some shearers who were on strike in the 1890s. They have set up a camp in the bush.

Trade unions

Improvements such as these did not happen by accident. Workers have had to fight very hard to get most of them. Usually this fighting has been done by trade unions. Trade unions are associations of workers that have been formed to improve working conditions and wages.

There have been trade unions in Australia since the 1850s, but they did not become important until the 1890s when they organised a number of big strikes. After 1901, trade unions became linked with the Australian Labor Party. They were both trying to help improve the lives of workers.

Trade unions became stronger after 1927 when the Australian Council of Trade Unions (ACTU) was formed. The ACTU is an Australia-wide association of trade unions. Most trade unions belong to it. Today the ACTU is a very powerful body. It speaks for all workers on matters such as wages, leave and working hours. It also speaks out on many other issues that are not directly related to work. The ACTU has, for example, strongly opposed Australia's involvement in the Vietnam war, the testing of nuclear bombs in and near Australia, and uranium mining. When a trade union and an employer group are in conflict, the trade union may ask the ACTU to act for it.

Think *for yourself*

1 Do you know any people who work for themselves? What kind of work do they do? What do you think the advantages of working for yourself would be? Would there be any disadvantages?

2 Do you think the ACTU should speak out about social and political issues? Or should it be concerned just with wages and working conditions?

3 Do you think that all workers should have to belong to a union? Or should they be able to decide for themselves whether they want to belong or not?

4 Who is the president of the ACTU?

Solving disputes

Let us imagine that a group of workers in a factory feel that they should get extra pay for some of the dangerous and dirty jobs that they have to do. How can they go about getting what they want?

Direct bargaining

Perhaps the workers' union will arrange a meeting with the employers. Union officials will tell the bosses what they want and explain why. The employers may agree to all the workers' demands. They may agree to some of them. Or they may refuse to consider them at all.

Arbitration

Since 1940 there have been laws in Australia about how disputes between workers and bosses should be solved. If the workers in our imaginary factory do not get anywhere by talking directly with their employers, they might use this **arbitration** system. Use a dictionary to find out what arbitration means.

In the arbitration system, workers and employers both present their case before an arbitration commission. It is rather like a trial in court. Each side gives evidence and presents witnesses to back up its case. The factory workers might show how the health of some of the workers has been badly affected by the jobs they have to do. They might use the opinions of experts to show that other workers doing similar jobs are getting more pay. The employers might claim that they are already paying their workers extra to do these jobs and that they cannot afford to pay them any more.

The judge, or **arbitrator**, listens to both sides and questions the witnesses. Then he or she makes a decision. Usually, neither side gets exactly what it asks for. The result is a compromise.

The arbitration system has solved a lot of disputes between workers and bosses. But it does not always work well. Very often there are long delays before a case is heard. Some cases drag on for many months or even years. Workers may become tired of waiting. Sometimes, too, workers may disagree with the judge's decision about their case. They may feel that they have been unfairly treated, or the judge is biased against them.

A strike

If our factory workers' union was not satisfied with the results of arbitration, it might decide to call a strike. Union members will refuse to work in the factory unless their demands are met. They will not get any pay from their employer while they are on strike. But their union may be able to pay them 'strike pay' from union funds instead. If other workers believe in what the factory workers are striking for, they may also go on strike to support them. When strikes have involved workers from many industries they are called 'general strikes'.

Strikes are common in Australia. Many workers believe that strikes are the best way of getting what they want because they make it hard for employers to keep their businesses going. Once, strikes were used only by unskilled and semi-skilled workers. Today we read about strikes by all kinds of workers, including nurses, teachers, pilots, truck drivers, firefighters and bank officers.

Some strikes affect only the workers on strike and their bosses. Some, however, affect many other people. Strikes by workers in the electricity and petrol industries are two examples of this. These industries affect so many people that they are called 'key industries'. When the workers in key industries go on strike, the government often becomes involved. It tries to find a solution to the problem that caused the strike.

Figure 9.39
Garbage piles up on a street because collectors are on strike. How would a strike like this affect ordinary people?

Think *for yourself*

1 Think about these two opinions of a strike by petrol-tanker drivers in Figure 9.40.
   a What is meant by 'holding the country to ransom'? Why can petrol-tanker drivers hold the country to ransom when they go on strike?
   b What does the driver mean by saying that he would be no better than a slave if he were not allowed to go on strike?
   c Do you think that either of these people is completely right?

2 When trade unions put a case to employers or to the arbitration commission, they usually ask for far more than they are likely to receive. Why do you think they do this?

3 Be a strike-watcher. Follow the next important strike that is reported in the news. Try to find out:

Figure 9.40
Two points of view on a strike

a who is on strike
b which union the strikers belong to
c who the employers are
d why the employees are striking
e how the strike began
f whether the strikers tried the arbitration system
g what is being done to end the strike
h whether other workers are striking in support of the strikers
i the views of both sides in the strike —whether you agree with either side, or think that both sides are partly right
j how the strike is affecting ordinary people
k how the strike is affecting businesses
l whether the government is involved in the strike and if so, how
m how the strike ended
n what the workers got from the strike
o which of their demands they did not gain.

Changing work

Do you know anyone whose name is Fletcher or Thatcher or Marshall? Their names came from jobs that people did many hundreds of years ago. A fletcher made arrows. A thatcher made roofs from grasses and saplings. A marshall looked after the horses of a nobleman. These jobs no longer exist. Inventions have made them unnecessary. We no longer hunt or fight with bows and arrows. We have roofs of tiles or iron. We use cars, planes, trains or buses instead of horses.

Jobs are changing all the time. Only about a hundred years ago in Australia there were bullockies and whalers. These jobs are very rare today. Often, too, the name of a job remains the same but the job now is very different from what it was a hundred years ago. Modern drovers use helicopters, trucks and motorbikes as well as horses. Shearers use electric shears instead of hand shears.

Think about how much office work has changed since photocopying became common. Think of the changes that television and films have brought to teaching.

Today, there are some jobs that were not even heard of ten or twenty years ago. Look at job advertisements in the paper. You will find advertisements for 'data processors', 'word processors', 'computer operators' and 'nuclear medicine specialists'. Jobs such as these have been created by new knowledge and new machines.

Figure 9.41
All kinds of workers can strike as these headlines show

Garbagemen refuse to empty household bins

Free parking for cars as city workers strike

Train chaos threatened over $20 pay penalty

Compromise ends 25-day ballet strike

City trains may stop: tradesmen meet today

Hospitals hit hard by strike

This strike stinks

Figure 9.42
Jobs such as these did not exist fifty years ago

Computer Operator/Receptionist: This position calls for excellent telephone skills, PABX experience (NEC) and word processing skills (Windows Word 6). Good opportunity for advancement. $25 000.

Computer Technician: Assistant—computer enthusiast aged 16, 17 or 18 years required to assemble and assess IBM compatible microcomputers. $375 per week with bonus payable after three months. City.

Word Processor Operator: Wang experience essential, Will cross train. $30 000 plus benefits.

In many ways this knowledge and these machines have improved people's working life. But some groups of workers are concerned about the effect of this technology on their own jobs. They feel that, like the thatchers and fletchers, their work will soon no longer exist. In the next twenty years, perhaps one-third of the jobs that exist today will not be needed or will have changed so much that we would not recognise them.

Bank employees are one of many groups of workers who are worried about the effect of technology on their jobs. Computers now do many of the jobs that were once done by clerks and tellers. Look around your bank. How many jobs are now being done by machines that were once done by people? Remember that even the typewriter is only about 120 years old!

Figure 9.43
Banks now have machines which work by computer. What sort of jobs do they take over? What sort of jobs do they create?

Think *for yourself*

1 Make a list of jobs that no longer exist today. Why are they no longer needed?
2 Make a list of jobs that might exist in the future. What sort of qualifications would people need to do these jobs?
3 Can you think of any jobs that have not changed in the last hundred years? Why have they not changed while so many other jobs have changed?
4 Do you think there is any point in bank workers and others going on strike because their jobs are being taken over by machines? Is there anything that they or their employers can do about it, or is this just one of the ways in which society changes?

POSITION VACANT

Space ship attendant

We need a flight attendant for weekly trip from Earth to Mars. Good education and an interest in travel essential. Previous experience in inter-planetary travel an advantage. We want somebody with a sense of adventure. Apply in writing to:

Interplan Travel
GPO Box 1234
Melbourne
Vic. 3001

Figure 9.44

No work

In Australia and in many other countries there are a lot of people who do not have jobs. This is not because these people prefer not to work. It is because there simply are not enough jobs for all the people who want to work.

As we saw in chapter 4, Australia had a very high rate of unemployment during the Depression years of the 1930s. But from the end of the Second World War in 1945 until the early 1970s, Australia had almost full employment. During this long period, ninety-eight out of every one hundred people who wanted to work were able to find jobs.

But in the early 1970s, the number of unemployed people rose quickly. There were several reasons for this. Many people think that new machines such as computers are to blame. Others think that when wages went up, companies could not afford to employ as many people. Australia, as we have seen, has trading and financial links with many other countries. What happens in Australia, including the unemployment rate, depends partly on what is happening in these other countries.

Today unemployment is still one of Australia's most serious problems. In the middle of 1995 Australia's official unemployment rate was between 8 and 9 per cent, although two years earlier it had climbed to over 11 per cent. In other words, during 1995, out of every 100 people who were able and wanted to work, only about 91 were able to find jobs.

During the 1980s and 1990s the Australian government has introduced a number of different schemes to try to reduce the rate of unemployment, especially among young people. During 1994, for example, the government published a paper called *Working Nation*. It described a series of programs that were designed to help unemployed people find work. Some of these involved training schemes that would help young people to learn the skills they needed to obtain work.

Many of today's unemployed have never had a job. They are young people who have left school and cannot find work. Many others are older people in their fifties who have lost the jobs they had and now cannot find new ones because employers think they are too old.

Think *for yourself*

1. Do some research in your school or community library to find out:
   - **a** what training schemes are available to help young people find jobs.
   - **b** what financial help the government gives to people who are looking for work but cannot find a job.
2. Unemployment is greatest among these groups:
   - **a** young people between 15 and 19
   - **b** newly arrived migrants
   - **c** women.

   Can you suggest why it is hard for these people to find work?
3. Do you think that the number of people who are officially stated as being unemployed is a true indication of the number of people who cannot find jobs? Why?
4. Many people think that schools should do more to train their students in work skills. Do you agree with this? What do you think your school could do to make it easier for you to find a job when you leave?

Index